The German *Novelle*

The German *Novelle*

by Martin Swales

Princeton University Press

Princeton, New Jersey

Copyright © 1977 by Princeton University Press
Published by Princeton University Press,
Princeton, New Jersey
In the United Kingdom: Princeton University Press,
Guildford, Surrey

Library of Congress Cataloging in Publication Data will
be found on the last printed page of this book

Publication of this book has been aided by a grant from
the Paul Mellon Fund of Princeton University Press

This book has been composed in VIP Baskerville
Printed in the United States of America
by Princeton University Press, Princeton, New Jersey

For Erika

"Holborn straight ahead of you," says the policeman. Ah, but where are you going if instead of brushing past the old man with the white beard, the silver medal, and the cheap violin, you let him go on with his story, which ends in an invitation to step somewhere, to his room, presumably, off Queen's Square, and there he shows you a collection of birds' eggs and a letter from the Prince of Wales's secretary, and this (skipping the intermediate stages) brings you one winter's day to the Essex coast, where the little boat makes off to the ship, and the ship sails and you behold on the skyline the Azores; and the flamingoes rise; and there you sit on the verge of the marsh drinking rum-punch, an outcast from civilization, for you have committed a crime, are infected with yellow fever likely as not, and—fill in the sketch as you like.

As frequent as street corners in Holborn are these chasms in the continuity of our ways. Yet we keep straight on.

Virginia Woolf,
Jacob's Room

Contents

Preface

The nineteenth-century German *Novelle* is very much part of the staple teaching diet within university German departments. Certainly, I have had the great good fortune to be able to discuss much of the subject matter of this study with a variety of student audiences, and I am particularly grateful to my "guinea pigs" in Birmingham, Toronto, and London for their enthusiasm, patience, and healthy skepticism. I am also aware of the great debt I owe to many colleagues and friends. I think particularly here of Walter Herrmann, Roy Pascal, and Peter Stern, and of Norma Rinsler of the French Department at King's College, London, who was kind enough to discuss with me aspects of the shorter prose form in nineteenth-century French literature. I am also especially grateful to my fellow Germanists at King's College who patiently allowed me to exploit a whole afternoon of their time with a recital of my problems and uncertainties concerning the writing of this book. On that occasion—as on many others—I have profited from their sympathy, encouragement, and criticism.

My indebtedness to published research on the novelle is, I hope, made clear by the acknowledgments in the text. I feel, however, that I should record an especial debt to Josef Kunz and to Karl Konrad Polheim. Both have published anthologies of novelle theory and criticism, and without these volumes the theoretical section of this study could not have been written. Their compilations have enabled me to read and reread the theoretical pronouncements on the novelle as I would a series of literary texts. Without this opportunity (and without the sensitive and probing analytical commentary of Polheim's *Forschungsbericht*) I would have certainly lost my way in the maze of novelle theory even more thoroughly than is at present the case. I am also particularly indebted to the work done by Fritz Martini and J.

P. Stern on nineteenth-century Germany's literature, on the resonance and limitations of its prose literature.

I should like to thank the editors of *Forum for Modern Language Studies*, *Germanic Review*, *German Life and Letters*, and the *Publications of the English Goethe Society* for allowing me to draw on material that first appeared in the pages of their journals. I am also grateful to the Literary Estate of Virginia Woolf, to the Hogarth Press, and to Harcourt Brace Jovanovich, Inc., for giving me permission to cite the passage from Virginia Woolf's *Jacob's Room* (London, 1960, pp. 94–95) that appears as the prefatory quotation to my study.

I am aware of a great debt of gratitude to Princeton University Press for agreeing to publish my work, and to their advisers whose comments and criticisms helped me to see more clearly what I was trying to say. My especial thanks go to R. Miriam Brokaw, Associate Director and Editor at Princeton University Press, for the kindness, patience, and efficiency with which she piloted my typescript through the process of consideration. My study has also benefited enormously from the care and good sense of Virginia W. Morgan, the copyeditor.

Finally, I wish to thank the two people who read and criticized the whole typescript for me: Dr. John J. White of Westfield College, London, and my wife. Their interest, enthusiasm, and critical acumen have helped me more than I can say.

The translations throughout are my own.

Martin Swales
February, 1976

Abbreviations

DVjS	Deutsche Vierteljahrsschrift für Literaturwissenschaft und Geistesgeschichte
FMLS	Forum for Modern Language Studies
GLL	German Life and Letters
GR	Germanic Review
GQ	German Quarterly
GRM	Germanisch-Romanische Monatsschrift
MLN	Modern Language Notes
PEGS	Publications of the English Goethe Society
PMLA	Publications of the Modern Language Association of America
RLV	Revue des Langues Vivantes
VASILO	Vierteljahrsschrift des Adalbert-Stifter-Instituts des Landes Oberösterreich
WW	Wirkendes Wort
ZfdP	Zeitschrift für deutsche Philologie

The German *Novelle*

Introduction

Within German literary scholarship of the last 150 years or so, the *Novelle* as a genre has attracted particular critical attention. Perhaps more than any other single form, the novelle has been subjected to a process of ceaseless definition and redefinition to the point where any possible consensus threatens to disappear in the welter of strenuously advocated thematic and formal prerequisites. Furthermore, the unabating volume of recent secondary literature concerned with the German novelle would appear to have exacerbated rather than relieved this state of affairs. It therefore seems appropriate that anyone rash enough to add to that large critical corpus should begin by clarifying some of the methodological presuppositions behind his undertaking.

In this study I propose to examine the theory and practice of short prose writing within nineteenth-century German literature. Any concern with this field of study inevitably confronts one with the highly loaded term *novelle*. For good or ill, many practitioners and theoreticians of the shorter prose form in nineteenth-century Germany—and many of the subsequent commentators in the twentieth century—persistently speak of the *novelle*. It seems to me, therefore, that little good is done by abandoning the term, or by pretending it does not exist. In this study I use the label *novelle* as a general term for the "medium-length story,"[1] as practiced by nineteenth-century German prose writers and as analyzed by nineteenth- and twentieth-century writers and critics. The texts with which I shall concern myself fall into two distinct (but, of course, interrelated) categories: first, a number of theoretical pronouncements about the genre; and second, a broad, and I hope fairly representative, selection of individual works

[1] Emil Staiger's term, quoted in Bernhard von Arx, *Novellistisches Dasein*, p. 8.

3

traditionally held to be novellen. The criterion that guided my choice of stories was twofold. The first consideration was artistic quality. I have chosen a group of stories that would, I believe, be ranked among the major achievements of nineteenth-century German literature. The second consideration was their susceptibility to a certain kind of close textual reading. In all cases, I have tried to offer detailed analyses of narrative perspective, of the way the events in the story are recounted and interpreted by the narrative voice. Of course, there could be many other approaches to these stories, approaches that yield valuable and significant insights. However, I find that the analysis of the narrative point of view allows one fruitful access to the stories selected, and I have found that such an approach pays particularly rich dividends when applied to the novelle—for reasons that, I hope, become clear in my discussion of the theory. Of course, the stories I have chosen do not in any way reflect all the varieties of the shorter prose form in nineteenth-century German literature. There are many omissions (Kleist, E.T.A. Hoffmann, Mörike, Droste-Hülshoff, Gotthelf, Storm) and these I greatly regret. However, stringent selectivity was necessary if the study were to be of manageable proportions. Furthermore, in the section devoted to the theory of the novelle I have endeavored to refer to those authors who do not figure in the chapters of specific analysis. I have hoped thereby to suggest that many of the features of the novelle that I highlight do also appear in those texts not selected for detailed discussion.

There is one aspect of my chosen area of study that needs further clarification here: the limitation to a single historical period. Here I am attempting to work within the consensus of established opinion that suggests that the novelle comes to its greatest prominence in the nineteenth century, a prominence it gradually loses in the twentieth. Whatever lineage one chooses to attribute to the novelle, whether one traces it back to Boccaccio, Marguerite de Navarre, or Cervantes, or back to the biographies of the troubadours, to the *Arabian Nights*, or to the very origin of oral narrative, the fact remains that, as Rolf Schröder has shown in his admirable book,[2] the short prose narrative achieves overwhelming dominance of the literary scene in Germany from the 1820s on. Also at this time there emerges a coherent and sustained attempt to arrive at a theoretical understanding of the genre. To concentrate on the nineteenth century, then, does not imply that there are no historical antecedents nor subsequent heirs, but simply that there is a coherent body of important work, produced within a relatively short time span, which has urgent claims to make on our capacities for textual and literary-theoretical analyses.

While, therefore, I shall be dealing with a specific, historically defined period of prose writing, I do not primarily intend to document a linear progression through the nineteenth century. Of course, one could argue that there is such a sequence at work (in the sense, for example, that Paul Heyse—both as theoretician and practitioner—manifestly belongs to the late nineteenth century).[3] However, my concern is to argue that the novelle as it emerges in the early years of the nineteenth century, both in theory and in practice, comes to a mature realization of many of its possibilities; moreover, the later prose writers of the century carried out a series of important variations on and explorations of that narrative constellation they inherited.

This study will examine two different kinds of texts: on the one hand, works of imaginative fiction, and, on the other, aesthetic theorizations about the genre to which these works are felt to belong. I shall attempt to look at the theory as I would examine any literary text, in the sense

[2] *Novelle und Novellentheorie in der frühen Biedermeierzeit.* Cf. Friedrich Sengle's remark: "Der Aufschwung der deutschen Novelle datiert nicht von Goethes *Unterhaltungen deutscher Ausgewanderten*, sondern von den zwanziger Jahren, in denen Tieck mit seinen Altersnovellen hervortrat" (*Biedermeierzeit*, vol. 2, p. 807).

[3] See Jost Hermand's suggestive analysis of Heyse's links with the ideology of the *Gründerzeit* (*Gründerzeit*, Munich, 1971, pp. 50ff.), and Hans Norbert Fügen, *Dichtung in der bürgerlichen Gesellschaft*, pp. 45ff.

that I am interested not simply in overt statement, in the laws that the various theories propound, but also in the implicit meanings, in, as it were, the spirit behind the letter of the theory. Moreover, in my view, the interaction between the theory and the practice of the nineteenth-century German novelle has many insights to contribute to our understanding of the literary imagination of the time. A brief survey of secondary literature on the novelle leaves little doubt that the last twenty years or so have shown a resurgence of interest in it. Even though the practice of novelle writing would appear to have declined in the twentieth century, the critical and theoretical interest has not. This fact suggests that this specific segment of nineteenth-century German literature has something important to tell modern readers.

There is a final point that deserves mention here, and it also concerns the limitation of my field of interest. It might at first sight seem a little odd to restrict the discussion of the novelle to German literature alone. By so limiting the discussion I do not wish to imply that this particular form of prose narrative is unique to Germany. On the other hand, the intellectual and literary scene in nineteenth-century Germany is, as far as I am aware, uniquely rich in the amount of significant novellen—and novelle theories—that it produces. Friedrich Sengle makes the point that German prose literature—unlike that of the rest of Western Europe in the nineteenth century—found its center of gravity in the novelle.[4] Also, Roy Pascal argues: "It is a curious and interesting phenomenon that in the short story, the 'Novelle' . . . German writers, including Romantics, could achieve masterpieces; in the novel there is failure after failure."[5] In other words, nineteenth-century German literature is impressive for the sheer bulk of recognized achievement within the novelle form and for the sheer bulk of theory concerned with that fictional mode. I would argue that this material constitutes enough

---

[4] *Biedermeierzeit*, vol. 2, p. 807.
[5] *The German Novel*, p. 32.

text to justify a monograph. I suspect that some of the general problems raised by the study of the German novelle are indeed relevant to other national literatures. Indeed, it is my belief that this material is not simply a significant achievement in its own right but is profoundly important for any understanding of the European nineteenth century. For this reason it is especially to be regretted that so little is known of the German novelle outside specialist circles. It is doubly to be regretted because in my view much of what I shall be discussing here constitutes proof of the remarkable—and precocious—modernity of German literature, a modernity that we are only gradually beginning to recognize.

I. The Novelle as Historical Genre

Three publications within the last twenty years or so have performed the immensely valuable service of compiling a summary of the principal arguments advanced by theoreticians of the German novelle.[1] Of these three, the most useful in an interpretative sense is the *Forschungsbericht* by Karl Konrad Polheim. Polheim draws a most valuable distinction when he points out that there are two basic schools within novelle theory: the normative and the historical. The normative theoreticians (represented most obviously by Arx, Grolman, Hirsch, Klein, Lockemann, and Pongs)[2] attempt to establish certain structural and thematic features that constitute the norm of what a true novelle should be. They seek to combine these features, as Hirsch puts it, "into a logically complete ideal type."[3] For them, the genre is an ideal construct that can serve as a yardstick for measuring the extent to which any given story is or is not a novelle. Two problems immediately occur. First, one wonders how important it is to know whether a specific work

---

[1] Walter Pabst, "Die Theorie der Novelle in Deutschland (1920–1940)" (see also *WB*, pp. 243ff.); Heinz Otto Burger, "Theorie und Wissenschaft von der deutschen Novelle," *Der Deutschunterricht* 3 (1951), no. 2, pp. 82ff. (see also *WB*, pp. 288ff.); Karl Konrad Polheim, *Novellentheorie und Novellenforschung: Ein Forschungsbericht 1945–1964*. (Because of the ready availability of Josef Kunz's compilation of Novelle theory—*Novelle* [*Wege der Forschung*] Wissenschaftliche Buchgesellschaft, Darmstadt, 1968—I have, wherever appropriate, given this volume as the source of the quotation. Such page references are preceded by the letters *WB*.)

[2] Bernhard von Arx, *Novellistisches Dasein*; Adolf von Grolman, "Die strenge Novellenform und die Problematik ihrer Zertrümmerung," *Zeitschrift für den deutschen Unterricht* 43 (1929): 609ff. (see also *WB*, pp. 154ff.); A. Hirsch, *Der Gattungsbegriff "Novelle"* (see also *WB*, pp. 116ff.); Johannes Klein, *Geschichte der deutschen Novelle*; Fritz Lockemann, *Gestalt und Wandlung der deutschen Novelle*; Hermann Pongs, *Das Bild in der Dichtung*, vol. 2, pp. 109ff. (see also *WB*, pp. 139ff.).

[3] Hirsch, *Gattungsbegriff "Novelle,"* p. 84.

8

belongs within some abstract definition of the "pure" novelle form. Second, it can very easily happen that the process of defining some ideal (i.e. abstract) norm becomes value-laden; the critic can make the implicit assumption that the strict form is good, and that deviations from the norm are at the very least to be labeled as such, if not actually regretted.

The other school of theorizing is described by Polheim as "historical" and is represented by such critics as Bennett/ Waidson, Ellis, Himmel, Kunz, and Silz.[4] Within this approach, the normative inquiry is either explicitly rejected or is at any rate not pursued, and the novelle is seen as something that varies from one historical context to the next. The quest for the novelle as such is seen as illusory. There can, we are told, be no abiding norm; there are only individual novellen. The term *novelle* simply functions as a convenient label for prose narratives that are longer than the short story but shorter than the novel. Obviously such an approach has a great deal to commend it; common sense tells one that varying historical (and psychological) situations must produce differing novellen. Yet one wonders if the rejection of any normative thinking is not just a little too easy; after all, many of the writers of actual novellen were aware of the presence of some kind of established norm with reference to which they shaped their individual creations. Furthermore, any formal construct of a genre must allow room for experimentation and variation, or it becomes a dead thing; but this is not to deny the relevance of the construct. The conceptual presence of traditional novelle expectation can and did exert a potent influence on the way individual authors wrote.

For this reason, the best studies of the German novelle to date have tended to combine these two approaches. What

[4] E. K. Bennett and H. M. Waidson, *A History of the German "Novelle"*; John M. Ellis, *Narration in the German Novelle*; Hellmuth Himmel, *Geschichte der deutschen Novelle*, Bern, 1963; Josef Kunz, *Die deutsche Novelle zwischen Klassik und Romantik*, and *Die deutsche Novelle im 19. Jahrhundert*; Walter Silz, *Realism and Reality*.

makes Benno von Wiese's and Fritz Martini's[5] arguments so suggestive is the fact that both of them recognize that the historical process that acts upon each individual writer of novellen has an important normative component; the transmission and reshaping of the norm is part of the historical self-understanding of the writers themselves. It is this combinational approach that I hope to adopt in the present discussion.

On several occasions recently, distinguished commentators on the German novelle have demonstrated that the origins of certain seemingly normative theories are in fact specific to certain historical situations. Schunicht and Negus have both shown that Tieck's "theory of the turning point" (*Wendepunkttheorie*) is linked with contemporary aesthetic theory, specifically with Solger's notion of "punctualism" (*Punktualität*).[6] Moreover, they have both perceived that Paul Heyse's equally famous "theory of the falcon" (*Falkentheorie*) does not amount to the establishment of symbolic intention as a normative presence in novelle writing, but rather is to be understood as the expression of the extreme individualism of late nineteenth-century bourgeois society. Quite clearly Schunicht and Negus are right: the theories as originally propounded were the expressions of specific, historically determined self-understanding, and it is only in the hands of later critics and theoreticians that they acquire normative dimensions. Hence, the subsequent critics were wrong in that they misunderstood their original sources. Yet, with respect to the valuable insights that we owe to both Schunicht and Negus, it seems to me that the conclusions they draw

---

[5] Wiese, *Die deutsche Novelle von Goethe bis Kafka*; Martini, "Die deutsche Novelle im 'bürgerlichen Realismus' " (see also *WB*, pp. 346ff.).

[6] Manfred Schunicht, "Der 'Falke' am 'Wendepunkt.' Zu den Novellentheorien Tiecks und Heyses" (see also *WB*, pp. 433ff.). Similar issues are raised by Richard Hamann and Jost Hermand in *Gründerzeit*, Munich, 1971, and by Hermand in his article "Hauke Haien: Kritik oder Ideal des gründerzeitlichen Übermenschen?" in Jost Hermand, *Von Mainz nach Weimar*, Stuttgart, 1969, pp. 250ff.); Kenneth Negus, "Paul Heyse's 'Novellentheorie': A Revaluation."

are a little too simple. At a general level, it must be stressed that misunderstanding and misinterpretation can be just as significant as fundamentalist accuracy. Even though generations of critics were wrong to elevate Tieck's and Heyse's observations to normative utterances, it seems to me not enough simply to point this out. One has to ask why they were impelled to misinterpret their original sources, why they looked so eagerly for normative statements when in reality they had only highly relative, historically circumscribed observations. The kind of norm they create is part of their historical self-understanding, and, as such, it is as much a legitimate object of interest as is the original meaning of Tieck's and Heyse's theories. Indeed, the fact that these original statements allowed themselves to be interpreted, reinterpreted (and misinterpreted) is the source of their importance. Hence, their significance for modern readers resides both in their specific historical meaning and in the subsequent quasi-normative function they acquired within the history of nineteenth- and twentieth-century theorizing about the nature of the novelle. In other words, while Heyse's theory is not a theory of symbolic focus (which is what Pongs, for example, makes of it), it does lend itself to this interpretation. Pongs has engaged in the fruitful misunderstanding of unconscious reinterpretation; he has not simply done willful violence to Heyse's arguments. Indeed, one is tempted to say that this kind of—largely unconscious—reinterpretation of given statements is the process by which normative thinking is a significant part of the historical unfolding of novelle theory in Germany.

One could say that the whole existence of a genre as normative presence partakes of that intellectual process known as the hermeneutic circle. The genre is made up of those specific works that at one time or another were felt by writers and critics to constitute (and help toward the definition of) the genre. Moreover, the specific works were made in all their specificity with reference to (and thereby extending the scope of) the construct that was felt to be the traditional normative presence of the genre expectation. Such a model is anything but an exercise in willful complexity. E. D. Hirsch in his *Validity in Interpretation* persuasively argues that "all understanding of verbal meaning is necessarily genre-bound."[7] This vindication of the genre concept involves a dialectic of extrinsic and intrinsic in the sense that we can only define the intrinsic genre—"that sense of the whole by means of which an interpreter can correctly understand any part in its determinacy"[8]—with reference to the extrinsic genres that are literary modes and conventions. Reference to the extrinsic genre concept is also part of the historicity (and individuality) of any given work of literature. Hirsch rightly reminds us that "the reality of these larger genre concepts exists entirely in the function that they actually served in history," for such genre concepts "have actually been used by writers and hence are not arbitrary classifications set up by the interpreter."[9] We must, in other words, beware of subscribing to a false notion of originality in our understanding of specific artistic creations. As Adorno cogently puts it, an artist's reputation for creativity wrongly relegates his work "to the level of capricious inventiveness."[10] The historicity of any work of art is to be found in its relationship to those norms, to those modes of artistic expectation with reference to which the specific creation is shaped. By that act of individual creation the genre concept is stretched, extended, modified. Todorov illuminates this point in a particularly helpful way when he draws the distinction between the notion of *species* within the natural sciences and that of *genre* within the humanities. He stresses that, whereas in the former case "the appearance of a new example does not necessarily modify the characteristics of the species . . . the birth of a tiger does not modify the

---

[7] *Validity in Interpretation*, p. 76.

[8] Ibid., p. 86 (see also Robert Scholes, "Towards a Poetics of Fiction: An Approach through Genre," *Novel* 2 [1969] 101ff.)

[9] Ibid., pp. 108f.

[10] T. W. Adorno, *Ästhetische Theorie*, p. 298.

species in its definition," in the latter *"every* work modifies the sum of possible works, each new example alters the species."[11] Hans Robert Jauss advances similar arguments when he refers to that "horizon of expectation" within which any given work is made. The process of historical change is enacted precisely in the dialectic of general and specific, of genre expectation and its concrete exploration and modification:

> A literary work, even when it appears for the first time, does not present itself as an absolute novelty within an informational vacuum; rather, by means of various kinds of announcement, by manifest and concealed signals, by familiar characteristics or implicit hints, it predisposes its public toward a quite specific mode of reception. It awakens memories of former reading experiences, it induces in the reader a specific emotional attitude, and its very beginning raises expectations concerning both "middle and end," expectations that in the ongoing process of reading can be strengthened or modified, reshaped or even ironically dissolved—all according to definite rules of the genre or of the kind of text involved.[12]

In other words, it seems to me a falsity to reject any notion of genre as an arbitrary straitjacket, to assume that there is an infinite variety of discrete works that are created—and that exist—in a void. This is the principal error committed by John M. Ellis in his recent study *Narration in the German Novelle*. He insists that the term *novelle*— like all definitions—"has *prescriptive* force and is a matter of the rules of language; it is therefore an error to go searching purely *descriptively* for common properties of a group of things to try to discover a definition."[13] Ellis contends that, like the terms *weed, bush*, or *tree* in botany, a category such as the *novelle* owes its existence to the "need it an-

---

[11] T. Todorov, *The Fantastic: A Structural Approach to a Literary Genre*, pp. 5f.

[12] *Literaturgeschichte als Provokation*, p. 175.

[13] *Narration in the German Novelle*, p. 14.

swers in the community which uses it."[14] He goes on to define that need in the following terms: "In Germany in the nineteenth century there were few important writers of novels, but very many talented writers who wrote neither novels nor short stories but something of intermediate length. The thing which distinguishes German fiction in the nineteenth century from that of other countries is precisely this. An important need arose for a way of grouping together those literary productions which were most characteristic of that age in that community. The word 'Novelle' thus answered an important need, and that need in a sense created it."[15] Up to a point, of course, this is true. Yet Ellis raises here a fascinating issue without pursuing it. One wonders why the medium-length prose form should have achieved such dominance in the literature of nineteenth-century Germany—why, in other words, there should have been such a need. Moreover, the analogy with such botanical categories as *tree* or *bush* is highly questionable. It should be noted that when we examine the applicability of literary genre concepts to specific works of imaginative literature, we find that both the category and the objects designated have a common medium: language. Works of literature exist exclusively within the framework of human discourse in a way that is not true of botanical organisms. It follows from this that literature owes its very existence—like language itself—to the human need to structure and give meaning to experience, and the notion of genre, of a generality of expectation, is vital to this process.

Yet Ellis's arguments offer many salutary warnings. It is not the aim of this study to set up a new definition of the novelle. Rather, I am endeavoring to examine the dialectical interrelationship of theory and practice in the nineteenth-century novelle, in the belief that this process is the expression of certain vital issues in the artistic imagination of the time. The inherent dialectic is all-important if one is to avoid the temptation to divorce theory from prac-

[14] Ibid., p. 19.
[15] Ibid.

tice. Jürgen Jacobs, in his study *Wilhelm Meister und seine Brüder*, speaks of the German *Bildungsroman* as *"eine unerfüllte Gattung"* ("an unfulfilled genre").[16] Thereby he abstracts the notion of genre from its realization in specific literary works and operates with a genre concept that is somehow extraliterary. However, if one allows the genre to function as a component of expectation to which individual texts refer, then the degree to which this expectation is or is not fulfilled ceases to be the criterion for participation in the genre construct. As long as the model of the genre is intimated as a sustained presence in the work in question, then the genre retains its validity as a structuring principle within the palpable stuff of a given literary creation. In other words, the notion of a genre must operate as a function of the imaginative literature written with reference to that concept; it cannot be a petrified, extraliterary thing. Even the nonfulfillment of consistently intimated expectation can then, paradoxically, represent a validation of the genre by means of its controlled critique.

Any genre concept has validity insofar as it is allowed to function as a reservoir of potentiality, as a structuring principle that generates specific phenomena and that by that act of generation is then modified for its subsequent practitioners. In my analysis of novelle theory I hope to suggest what this underlying potentiality might be—and that it functions as a structuring force rather than as an aggregate of observable features. Klaus W. Hempfer argues for precisely this presence of the genre as structuring principle when he criticizes the "taxonomic" approach that seeks to isolate a number of specific features or characteristics. Hempfer pleads for a "structuring" approach that concerns itself with the relations that obtain between the various features or elements: "To the taxonomic-classificatory approach, which ascribes texts to a particular genre on the grounds of the presence or absence of particular qualities (elements) one should prefer a—in the es-

---

[16] *Wilhelm Meister und seine Brüder*, Munich, 1972, p. 271.

15

sential sense—'structuring' approach, which reveals specific relations between these elements, relations that are more characteristic of the type of text in question than is the simple accumulation of isolated elements."[17] It is with this notion of novelle potentiality that I shall be concerned in the following pages. However, this potentiality cannot be understood independently of the dialectical process by which it realizes itself in the stories that we actually possess.

Much of Ellis's impatience with the novelle genre derives from its nebulousness. Paradoxically, this very nebulousness—this serviceability—accounts for the historical viability of the term in nineteenth-century Germany, for its unceasing usage. A glance at theoretical statements made during the nineteenth century confirms a certain continuity of concerns (and even of formulations). The category of the *Begebenheit*—of the "central event"—occurs in Goethe, Laube, Hebbel, Marggraff, Feuchtersleben, and Ernst. The notion of the *Wendepunkt*—the "turning point"—appears in A. W. Schlegel, Mundt, Tieck, Wilhelm Meyer, and Heyse. The dialectic of exceptional and everyday experience in the novelle is asserted by A. W. Schlegel, Schleiermacher, Ast, Solger, Spielhagen, and Lorm. Such theoretical statements are made at the same time as—and with reference to—an absolute glut of creative writing within the shorter prose form. Quite clearly, the unity and consistency of opinion that is suggested by the above list of theoretical observations is largely deceptive. Indeed, the continuity is maintained precisely because the important concepts allow so much room for an associative, almost intuitive stretching of the concept—for the writer's seizing his chance to work within the genre construct by adapting it to his own concerns.

If one looks, then, at the role of the shorter prose form in nineteenth-century German literature, one notes two

[17] *Gattungstheorie*, p. 190. For a discussion of Hempfer's study (and of other recent contributions to genre theory) see R. Fellinger's review article in *GRM*, n.f.24 (1974): 365ff.

things. First, the practice of writing stories designated—or felt to be—*novellen* and of offering theoretical remarks on the genre was so widespread that no writer or theoretician could possibly be unaware of the ongoing debate. Second, the term *novelle* was a vast umbrella covering a wide variety of differing positions and viewpoints. The novelle was hailed as supremely Romantic and as unmistakably post-Romantic (very often depending on whether the writer in question approved of the early or of the late Tieck!). The novelle was celebrated as a discursive, conversational form—and also as essentially events with no narrative reflection. The novelle was seen as akin to the novel—and as diametrically opposed to it. Theoreticians tirelessly referred both to other theoreticians—and to actual writers. Also, writers themselves referred to other writers and to theoreticians, and sometimes claimed that their stories *were* their theory. All this debate was made possible by the term *novelle*; the debate existed because the term supplied the vital focus. How did this state of affairs come about? One answer is sociological: certain forms of publication came into being on a massive scale—periodicals, almanacs, pocket books. There was, in other words, a market for the shorter prose form. Yet, clearly the market did not simply create public demand; it was also a response to a specific need, which was embedded in the bourgeois literacy of the period.

Hence, Ellis's strictures on the vagueness of the genre construct in my view miss the point. The vagueness allows this term to capture so many voices within the literary-historical debate of nineteenth-century Germany; and that same vagueness provokes the truly creative interest of so many talented—and different—writers. From this it follows that any attempt nowadays to produce a new definition of the novelle is nonsensical. Rather, we must concern ourselves with the debate itself. What kinds of reader expectation were felt to be appropriate to the novelle? What artistic possibilities were the theoreticians suggesting when

II. The Theory of the Novelle

Within the overall framework outlined in the previous chapter, the theory of the novelle can, I believe, prove a significant and rewarding field of study. If one approaches the various theoretical statements and asks what kind of imaginative constellation they advocate and what this tells us about the intellectual life of Germany in the nineteenth century, then the theory of the novelle can yield genuine and helpful insights, insights that sharpen our understanding both of the age as a whole and of the literary works it produced. Indeed, it is interesting to note that those critics who are concerned with short forms of prose narrative and who are unaware of the nineteenth-century German novelle—and of the theorizing to which it has given rise— are very much impoverished in their understanding of the expressive potential inherent in the shorter prose narrative. (One thinks, for example, of the studies by H. E. Bates, Sean O'Faolain, and Frank O'Connor.)[1]

What is particularly remarkable about German novelle theory is that some of the earliest arguments (for example those advanced by Friedrich and August Wilhelm Schlegel) are as subtle and probing as is anything that follows them. They indicate interpretative tensions within the genre— the tension between the social and the nonsocial, between the real and the unreal—that in one form or another claim the attention of subsequent commentators for almost a century. Such insights are an important—and an auspicious—beginning. The debate I hope to document in discussing novelle theory is not one that yields a new normative definition of the novelle. Rather, it makes possible a broader and more differentiated awareness of the context

---

[1] Bates, *The Modern Short Story*, London, 1942; O'Faolain, *The Short Story*, New York, 1964; O'Connor, *The Lonely Voice: A Study of the Short Story*, Cleveland and New York, 1962.

within which the individual writers and their works are to be understood. Analysis of genre theory can help in this way, and one should beware of asking it to do any more than this. As Helmut Prang puts it in the conclusion to his *Formgeschichte der Dichtkunst*: "A concern with the historical development of literary forms does not aim at distilling pure, intact models nor at maintaining the validity of existing definitions; rather, it seeks to complement analyses based on historical, biographical, or *geistesgeschichtlich* principles. Thereby it endeavors to enrich the frequent studies of content, theme, or literary indebtedness, of the history of style, subject, or motif."[2]

In the following discussion of the main preoccupations of novelle theory, I have attempted to organize the material under various headings, of which five represent, broadly speaking, thematic considerations and two represent structural features. Of course, I am well aware that one cannot treat theme and structure as separate entities—because, by definition, they constantly interlock. I have adopted this division purely for the sake of convenience; certain critics have tended to comment on the thematic possibilities of the novelle, and others on its structural characteristics. In the course of my argument I hope to suggest that there is considerable overlap between the various novelle theories—not in the simple sense that they are all saying the same thing, but rather in that certain conceptual patterns recur within the interpretative relationship to the world that is felt to characterize the novelle.

I have attempted to illustrate the various headings by a brief selection of quotation and reference. I have tended to choose examples that span the whole period of novelle theory from the early nineteenth century to the present day. I have done this because in my view the specific theories of the novelle are to be seen not so much as once-and-for-all promulgations, but rather as recurring varia-

---

[2] *Formgeschichte der Dichtkunst*, Stuttgart, 1968, pp. 216ff.

tions on a number of basic concepts that are at the heart of nineteenth-century novelle production.

THE CENTRAL EVENT

One thematic feature that is almost invariably associated with the novelle is its concern with one central event or sequence of events. In a recent study, H. H. Malmede, having rejected all the insights of specific novelle theories, finds himself left with the only irreducible sine qua non of the genre, the "event that causes one to take notice."[3] In other words, as has been frequently suggested by critics of the novelle, the genre derives both its being and its name from man's inexhaustible interest in new and surprising events. The short prose form of the novelle is, as it were, the answer to the familiar question "what's new?" Yet this by itself tells us very little, because most examples of the novelle in nineteenth-century German literature are more complex and more substantial than the newspaper headline (which presumably always reports an event that causes one to take notice). If one follows this notion of the central event through theoretical statements of nineteenth- and twentieth-century novelle criticism, it becomes apparent that there is more to the event than its simple novelty. One thinks, for example, of the famous comment made by Goethe to Eckermann: "What is a novelle but an unprecedented happening that has actually occurred" (*"was ist eine Novelle anders als eine sich ereignete unerhörte Begebenheit"*)?[4] Once again, the event is seen as of central importance; indeed, the event is equated with the novelle itself. Goethe, however, adds two comments about this event—*"sich ereignet"* and *"unerhört"*—and in so doing, he indicates an interpretative tension within the genre, a tension that in one form or another asserts itself in countless theoretical dis-

[3] *Wege zur Novelle*, p. 154.
[4] Goethe to Eckermann, 29 January 1827.

cussions of the novelle. What, then, does Goethe mean by *"sich ereignet"* and *"unerhört?"* The second term causes less trouble than the first. *"Unerhört"* presumably expresses the sense of newness, the sense that the event is surprising, unprecedented, is "unheard of" in that it is not part of the common discourse about human affairs. It does not, in other words, partake of the average generality of man's experience. Yet, although it is an exceptional event, a unique and unfamiliar experience, it is also "real"; it has happened (*"sich ereignet"*). It is inextricably and undeniably embedded in our world, and, by implication, therefore, it must stand in some sort of relationship to the human world as commonly interpreted and lived in. Hence, for Goethe, the mainspring of the novelle experience is an interpretative dualism: an event is at one and the same time part of the common human universe and yet at variance with the interpretative structure that normally sustains that universe.

In one form or another, this dualism recurs over and over again in those theories that lay great weight on the function of the central event in the novelle. The crucial presence of an event means that the novelle is concerned with concrete happenings, and yet that event is also an implicit challenge to accepted definitions of reality. This tension is at the heart of Tieck's remarks on the *Wendepunkt* or "turning point." However much his observations may have been indebted to contemporary aesthetic theories, and however regrettable may be the frantic pursuit of "turning points" in which subsequent critics have indulged,[5] one must not, in my view, be too eager to jettison Tieck's comments altogether. Obviously, as with so many other novelle theories, one must beware of attributing too much importance to the specific feature they highlight (in the sense of allowing the presence of that feature to become a norma-

[5] Even Fritz Lockemann's suggestive contributions to novelle theory seem to me to suffer from excessive schematism when he insists on the presence of two "turning points" which express the transition from order to chaos and from chaos back to order.

tive determinant of what constitutes the "true" novelle). On the other hand, one often finds that implicit in the specific argument is a set of general observations about the kind of narrative intention that produces the novelle. It is at this level, in my view, that Tieck's discussion of the *Wendepunkt* is still important. He writes: "The novelle . . . should . . . distinguish itself by the way it focuses intensely one great or modest occurrence, which, however easily it can happen, is yet wonderful, perhaps unique. This turning point in the plot—at which the story so unexpectedly changes direction, while yet developing the consequences with a certain naturalness, according to character and circumstances—will imprint itself the more strongly on the reader's imagination because the central concern, for all its wonderfulness, could, in other circumstances, equally well be everyday."[6]

It will be remembered that Goethe's definition insists on the dominant function within the novelle of an "unprecedented happening that has actually occurred"—in the sense that the novelle consists of little else but this ("What is a novelle but . . ."). Similarly, Tieck's *Wendepunkt* clearly is an event of paramount importance in the story; it largely determines the interpretative direction that the material takes. Furthermore, the nature of that event—and in empirical terms it can be a "great or modest occurrence"—is such that it yields an unmistakable interpretative dualism: we feel that "it can easily happen" and yet that it is "wonderful, perhaps even unique." The development that follows from this event is as paradoxical as the event itself, for it is both "unexpected" and "natural, appropriate to both character and circumstances." The whole experience, then, of reading such a novelle is that one's imagination is engaged by an event that, for all its strangeness, could yet under other circumstances seem everyday and utterly acceptable.

There are two obvious points that must be made here.

[6] Ludwig Tieck, *WB*, p. 53.

First, at a conceptual level Goethe and Tieck express much the same perception of the essential nature of the novelle genre. This does not mean to say that what Tieck intended to describe as a *Wendepunkt* was what Goethe had in mind when he thought of the "unprecedented happening that has actually occurred." Yet while the phenomenon they seek to describe may not be the same in both cases, their descriptions overlap extensively, and the overlapping takes place at the level of narrative interpretation of event within the novelle.[7] Second, common to both remarks is a significant awareness that the event itself involves conflicting interpretative contexts, in the sense that on the one hand it seems to stand outside the normal human context, while on the other it is undeniably part of the facticity of ordinary reality. Indeed, Tieck's argument implicitly pushes the question of interpretative ambiguity a stage further in that he suggests that the novelle reader is confronted not simply with a dualism, but also with the consequence of this dualism: interpretative uncertainty. Ultimately, according to Tieck's argument, we are faced not simply with a recognizable world within which improbable things happen, but with the whole question of what is interpretation itself. Interpretation presupposes contextualization, presupposes understanding a new event within the context of an already established preunderstanding. Hence, if one changes the circumstances within which one places (contextualizes) an event, then the improbable can become—for all its strangeness—just as probable as the commonly interpretable events ("the central concern, for all its wonderfulness, could, *in other circumstances*, equally well be everyday." [my italics]).

The implications of both Goethe's and Tieck's comments are, in my view, as challenging as anything that has subsequently been written on the importance of a central event or sequence of events for the novelle. (Indeed, in one

[7] That Tieck's theory implies a particular narrative constellation is stressed by Ralf Stamm in his study *Ludwig Tiecks späte Novellen*.

form or another, most recent statements tend to be variations on the notion of interpretative ambiguity I have tried to outline above.) For Goethe, the novelle is *nothing but* an ambiguous event; the form has its raison d'être in hermeneutic conflict and uncertainty. Tieck stresses the intensity of interpretative focus by which the novelle throws into relief the inherent possibilities of the central event. This notion of brilliant interpretative focus is an important one. At the most obvious level, it is something that derives from the concision of the novelle. While any attempt to give definite guidelines for the maximum and minimum lengths of a novelle is clearly absurd, the fact remains that the novelle is, vis-à-vis the novel, a short form.[8] Furthermore, this crucial brevity informs the narrative tone. The novelle is not a leisurely form in an interpretative sense; it does not have the breadth to allow for detailed and expansive exposition. It works by intense concentration: by focusing on one event or cluster of events, and by suggesting that its intense selectivity is justified by one overriding interpretative issue. The exposition of many novellen is, then, interpretative rather than descriptive; we begin with the immediate posing of a problem rather than with the spacious documentation of a given world. The implications of this will be discussed more fully later. At this stage I merely wish to stress that it is part and parcel of the whole concept of the event in the novelle that that event shall be mediated through a particularly insistent process of narrative argument. One of the most obvious examples of this technique at work is Annette von Droste-Hülshoff's *Die Judenbuche* (*The Jew's Beech Tree*, 1842). Her story is concerned not so much with the overall sequence of Friedrich Mergel's biography; rather, she concentrates on the interpretative problem that Mergel's life poses—the nature of human guilt and of the retribution appropriate to that guilt. The narrator announces the theme, the center of interpretative interest, in

[8] See Friedrich Sengle, "Der Umfang als ein Problem der Dichtungswissenschaft," in *Gestaltprobleme der Dichtung*, ed. R. Alewyn, Bonn, 1957, p. 302.

the short poem that opens the story. Only then does he describe the world that yields the interpretative issue. Furthermore, it is because of that carefully explained interpretative relationship to the facts he describes that the narrator is able to pass over some twenty-four years of the hero's life with the briefest of summaries. We do not need to know details of that time because they would contribute nothing to the main thread of narrative argument. Similarly, Eduard Mörike in his *Mozart auf der Reise nach Prag* (*Mozart on his Way to Prague*, 1855) contents himself with portraying a few outwardly trivial hours in the life of the great composer. Yet by his intense narrative illumination of this brief time span Mörike is able to explore the relationship between artist and society, between intense, self-consuming creativity on the one hand and that social reality within which the creativity functions (and to which it relates) on the other. Such narrative concentration is a recurring feature not only of novellen themselves but is also a central preoccupation within the theory of the genre.

The Role of Chance and Fate

At the simplest level of thematic summary, many critics have been at pains to suggest how important the role of chance and fate is in novelle plots. Rolf Schröder in his study of the early *Biedermeier* period stresses that often novellen of the time take natural catastrophes that had actually happened as their central event, and the fictitious story that is built around such occurrences seeks to show the necessity of the seemingly random happening.[9] Furthermore, he insists that providence is one of the great themes of the *Biedermeier* novelle.[10] Similarly, Johannes Klein argues that the German novelle is born in an age that has just known the upheaval of the French Revolution, and that from this experience the whole nature of the genre derives: "The history of the German novelle necessarily

[9] *Novelle und Novellentheorie in der frühen Biedermeierzeit*, p. 182.
[10] Ibid., p. 231.

26

became a sequence of artistic expressions of fate-ful confrontations, for the unusual event and the power of fate had become everyday experiences."[11] Paul Ernst argues: "Novellen are stories of remarkable occurrences that are never fully accessible to human reason and that leave much room for the workings of inscrutable powers—whether we describe them as chance, as divine guidance, or as an inner compulsion."[12] Paul Ernst here suggests more than a simple spectrum of thematic possibilities ranging from chance to fate. Rather, he sees that the interpretative complexity of the novelle is produced by experiences that are marginal in the sense that they are not completely accessible to rational, ordering elucidation. The process of coming to terms interpretatively with these experiences involves the question of their definition; in what context are they to be set—chance, divine will, pathologically dictated behavior patterns? Once again, we are confronted by a hermeneutic problem implanted at the very heart of the genre. This problem is discussed at length by Georg Lukács in his *Theorie des Romans*. Lukács argues that the lyrical subjectivity (i.e. intense selectivity) of novelle subject matter means that the form concerns itself with an isolated event or sequence of events.[13] The event is isolated not simply in terms of stringent artistic selectivity but also in the sense that the kind of event that intrinsically recommends itself to such selectivity is the isolated event, the sudden, chance happening. It would, therefore, seem that the novelle ought to be a simple celebration of the freak happening. There is, however, more to it than this. Lukács insists that the way the novelle treats its subject matter is strikingly at variance with the nature of that subject matter. It brings the maximum of artistic control to bear on the experience of which it speaks; and artistic control implies hermeneutic control. In other words, without the narrator having to give an overt commentary on the process in which he is

[11] *WB*, p. 196.
[12] *Der Weg zur Form*, Munich, 1928, p. 288.
[13] *WB*, pp. 9off.

engaged, he is able, by the implicit formal—and interpretative—control with which he encompasses the
freak event, to compensate for (and hence to come to terms
with) the seemingly meaningless *donnée* of his art.
Meaninglessness acquires meaning by the formal control
with which it is faced and articulated. The random workings of chance, as expressed in the novelle acquire a curious and paradoxical necessity; that which is inimical to
order is implicitly ordered.

Many of the specific points which Lukács makes may be
highly debatable. Yet the kind of interpretative tension
that he highlights is central, not only to a great many novellen, but also to much novelle theory. I would argue that the
mainspring of much novelle writing is the contact between
an ordered and reliably interpreted human universe on
the one hand and an experience or set of experiences that
would appear to conflict utterly with any notion of order or
manageable interpretation on the other. Hence, the
novelle derives its peculiar and insistent energy from what
one can best describe as a hermeneutic gamble, as a shock
confrontation with marginal events. Implicitly, the attempt
to make an ordered statement of that which by definition
resists the ordering intention is one of the central under-
takings within the narrative universe of the novelle. Furthermore, as I hope to show in my analysis of individual
stories, this hermeneutic challenge expresses itself in the
kind of interpretative relationship that the narrator has to
his subject matter. The theme of chance is, in other words,
part of a much larger problem. The crucial issue is not how
often the concept of chance is mentioned, nor even
whether the novelle hero is essentially passive (more acted
upon than acting). Rather, the question whether given
events are attributed to chance or to necessity (be it divine,
social, or personal) is essentially a question of their inter-
pretability. When does a seemingly fortuitous sequence become a coherent order? This problem affects not only the
characters' understanding of themselves and their circumstances but also the narrator's perspective on what he re-

counts. Once a story yields interpretative cohesion, then chance becomes part of a significant (even if unpleasant) order; chance becomes the *necessary* expression of the functioning of the particular world with which we are concerned. This is one of the central themes of Kleist's novellen. Ellis has persuasively shown that the human act of interpreting one's experience is the crucial thematic issue of *Das Erdbeben in Chili* (*The Earthquake in Chile*, 1810)—and that the narrator is as much part of this problematic undertaking as are the characters.[14] If the world order is faulty, if it is founded simply in the creaky mechanics of randomness, then chance constitutes the ruling power in men's lives. It is the only agency at work. Because the Kleistian hero (or heroine) is so often the kind of person who adheres to a more grandiose interpretative structure (most usually one that is founded in some kind of absolute value scale), who always demands more from life than random experience, then the chanciness of the world will contradict him at every turn, and will, ultimately, break his cherished value structure. His inability to accept chance means that he attempts unremittingly to order (that is, to do violence to) the world around him. At every turn the world proves stronger, and chance thereby becomes his fate, becomes the necessary power acting upon and shaping his life. Kleist is, of course, sufficiently honest to admit that not every such confrontation issues in explicit tragedy. There is always the possibility of accommodation to "the faulty arrangement of the world." However, such accommodation involves the abandonment of a particular interpretative relationship to human experience, of a relationship that operates with such total values as absolute right and absolute wrong, as "angel" and "devil" (in *The Marquise of O.*, 1810). Such an accommodation is not without consolation; it is workable. However, its workableness is the measure of its bleakness; judged by the standards that Kleist's narration so precisely intimates, it is cold comfort, but comfort nonetheless.

[14] John M. Ellis, *Narration in the German Novelle*, pp. 46ff.

29

The Novelle and Literary Realism

As has been implicit in much of the foregoing discussion, one of the most contentious aspects of the various theories of the novelle is the whole question of the relationship of the genre to reality, or, more accurately, to what is commonly understood as literary realism. Many critics have stressed that the novelle has to have a close relationship to empirical reality. It is, furthermore, interesting to note the historical connotations of the term *novelle*: Rolf Schröder points out that in the 1820s in Germany the element of "newness" inherent in the term *novelle* was understood to mean "real" or "true to life."[15] Indeed, at the time the term came into favor largely as part of the contemporary reaction against Romanticism, for Romanticism was linked—pejoratively—with *romanhaft*, *novelesque*, whereas the novelle was exempt from such unfortunate connotations. Quite apart from this specifically localized historical understanding of the genre, however, a great variety of critics and theoreticians have insisted that the novelle must maintain a closeness to observable reality. One of the earliest commentaries on the genre insists on its realistic intention. In Wieland's *Rosenhain Hexameron* (1805) one of the narrator figures is made to say: "With a novelle one presupposes that the story takes place . . . not in any ideal or utopian land, but in our real world, where everything occurs naturally and comprehensibly, where the events—while they are not everyday—could yet, in the same circumstances, have occurred anywhere at any time."[16] Once again, we are back on familiar ground; the novelle takes place in the real world, yet its central event is not intrinsically ordinary. It is *potentially* everyday in the sense that a slight shifting of interpretative context could make it ordinary. All this, of course, is very close to Tieck's comments on the *Wendepunkt*, and once again the same interpretative tension is involved, a tension that allows the central experience to

---

[15] *Novelle und Novellentheorie*, ch. 8.
[16] C. M. Wieland, *WB*, p. 28.

emerge as both everyday and remarkable, as both real and strange.

Within the constellation of this theoretical discussion the most significant and challenging contribution is made by Friedrich and August Wilhelm Schlegel. In their remarks one finds a remarkable precociousness and many of the insights of later theoreticians are clearly implicit in the Schlegels' arguments. Friedrich Schlegel insists on an inherent irony in the novelle, and in his view, this irony springs from the intrinsic discrepancy between what is being narrated and the way in which it is narrated. He stresses that the implicit narrative tone is social, is "the way one would tell a story in society."[17] The narrative attitude is informed by an awareness of a societally defined universe within which and to which one tells one's story. Yet the subject matter—the event or sequence of events—does not partake of the societal presuppositions of the narrative voice; it is a special event, intrinsically unusual in that it could arouse interest without having to be rendered generally acceptable or relevant. Yet the form in which it is encompassed sets out to do just this: to mediate between the uniqueness of the event and the generality of the audience to which it is being recounted. Several of these points will be discussed in greater detail later. At this stage it is necessary to insist on one general feature of the narrative constellation that Friedrich Schlegel indicates: the tension between the societal expectation of reader (and narrator) and the fact that the material stands outside that expectation and has to be interpreted, mediated via the narrative voice, before it can have meaning for that societal universe. It is the measure of the discrepancy this undertaking seeks to overcome that the form itself, for Friedrich Schlegel, is by definition ironic.

These and similar implications are reinforced and explored further by August Wilhelm Schlegel. He insists very strongly on the realistic direction of the novelle, much of which is embodied in the narrative tone: "the essential

[17] *WB*, p. 41.

model for novelle narration is the educated, sociable narrator."[18] Yet for A. W. Schlegel, as for so many theoreticians of the novelle, there is more to the realism of the genre than this. Once again, paradox is all-important:

> To tell a novelle well, one has to deal as briefly as possible with the everyday things that the story contains; one must not try to strengthen them in any special way. One must concentrate on the extraordinary and the unique—without going in for analytical motivation. One must simply assert it positively and require that it be believed. Even the greatest improbabilities should not be omitted—rather, these things may be the deepest truth, in context, absolutely right. The narrator must bind himself to the material possibility, i.e. to the reality conditioning an event. Here his purpose will demand the greatest accuracy.[19]

One notices immediately the complexity of interpretative relationship that A. W. Schlegel sees as central to the novelle. Having previously stressed that the form must display a closeness to ordinary reality, a respect for the laws of common experience, Schlegel now insists that the narrator must deal with this reality as briefly as possible; he must not painstakingly document it in order to insist on its reliability of specification. A brief concession to empirical social experience is, apparently, all that is necessary. Rather, the narrator must spend time on the extraordinary and unique aspects of his material, and in his interpretative handling of these aspects he must be quite uncompromising. He must not attempt to reduce their improbability, to suggest that they are more readily explicable (capable of being motivated) than might at first appear. He must simply insist that they have to be accepted for what they are. A. W. Schlegel goes on to recommend a particular radicalism in this context: the narrator must seize on even the most improbable things—because, apparently, they

[18] Ibid., p. 49.
[19] Ibid., pp. 48f.

represent the deepest truth of what he has to say. At this point in the argument, it would appear that any notion of realism has been left far behind. Only the manifestly improbable can be true; the probable and ordinary has been devalued in favor of the improbable and extraordinary. Yet, almost as though Schlegel realized that he was getting too far away from his opening premise, he suddenly concedes the claims of reality by asserting that the narrator must observe and describe the real context within which the unreal takes place; he must stress that the laws of concrete reality surround, and thereby impinge on, the improbabilities with which he is crucially concerned.

This, then, is a very paradoxical commentary on a paradoxical phenomenon, and the reader may be forgiven for wondering whether A. W. Schlegel was quite clear in his own mind as to what he wished to say. Yet in its oscillation, this passage is a probing commentary on the interpretative ambiguity that informs so much nineteenth-century novelle writing. Implicit in the argument is a most important point: that, however fantastic or improbable the central event of the novelle may be, it must never be allowed to become a dissociated fantasy, a willfully invented happening that is divorced from everyday realities. In fact, the oddity must be seen as part of social reality, as embedded in ordinary contingencies. It may be antisocial, but it is not intrinsically asocial. As A. W. Schlegel goes on to say: "The novelle recounts remarkable events that have, as it were, occurred behind the back of bourgeois conventions and regulations."[20] It follows, then, that the strange event does not transport us to another planet, but rather that it occurs on the edge of respectable bourgeois society. It is marginal to the broad generality of ordered social experience, but it is not located in a separate world. This confrontation between the marginal, unprecented event and the social universe (as represented by the narrative voice) is, for A. W. Schlegel, central to the realism of the novelle. The deepest

[20] Ibid., p. 50.

truths it conveys are to be found in the surprising, odd moments when the restraints of social order are challenged by new experiential dimensions. Once again, what I have called the hermeneutic gamble becomes all-important in the narrative constellation of the novelle.

THE TENSION BETWEEN POETIC AND PROSAIC

One of the strangest pairs of opposites that recurs in novelle theory is that between the "poetic" and the "prosaic," and it is an opposition that informs much of the aesthetic debate in nineteenth-century Germany about the nature of epic forms. The terms tend to be used evaluatively, and at times the criteria for the value judgments are, to say the least, idiosyncratic. On the whole, however, the novelle tends to find favor, because in its brevity and artistic concentration (what Lukács calls its "lyrical" quality) it lends itself to a poetic depiction of human affairs. Indeed, implicit in much novelle theory is the contention that the short prose form is able to isolate certain aspects of reality and to bring to them such an intense interpretative illumination that the real becomes transfigured, that the prosaic becomes poetic. It is important to remember that this whole tension between prosaic everyday reality and the demand for poetry as the true aesthetic mediation of that reality is something that recurs over and over again in nineteenth-century German novel theory. Fritz Martini has well shown that the aesthetics of German realism are dominated by ideas inherited from both Hegel and Schopenhauer, both of whom see modern bourgeois reality as something debased and prosaic, as something that militates against poetry.[21] It is in the context of such arguments that one has to understand Otto Ludwig's recipe for modern epic writing: "It must create realistic ideals."[22] The novelle is very much part of this undertaking because, as a genre, it is felt

---

[21] "Zur Theorie des Romans im deutschen 'Realismus,'" in *Deutsche Romantheorien*, ed. Reinhold Grimm, pp. 142ff.

[22] *Gesammelte Schriften*, vol. 5, Leipzig, 1891, p. 411.

to combine a high degree of closeness to reality (*Wirklichkeitsnähe*) with a maximum of artistic forming of that reality. Indeed, at times it seems as though the writer of novellen is bombarded with contradictory precepts, with the result that his work is bound to be too "realistic" for some readers, too "poetic" for others. It is, for example, highly interesting (and typical of the man) that Franz Grillparzer should be suspicious of the novelle form, seeing it as a kind of debased and prosaic currency: "Novellen—Who does not write them? Is it not the case that for some time now the poetic incapacity of modern Germany has made itself comfortable on this broad idler's couch?"[23] Hence, Grillparzer repudiates the term *novelle* for his own story *Der arme Spielmann* (*The Poor Musician*, 1848), although his reaction as artist to the genre is, of course, very much part of the story's meaning (in that it explores, in radical form, the dialectic of prosaic and poetic modes of being and creating). When Grillparzer turns to prose in this work, he faces the full weight of prosaic reality, of that reality that helps to account for what he understands as "the poetic incapacity" of the genre.

Despite Grillparzer's harsh denunciation, however, the novelle can at times be hailed as the form most able to mediate between the prosaic and the poetic. One should not, however, forget that, although this possibility of aesthetically achieved compromise exists, it does involve a considerable interpretative undertaking. The compromise has to be worked for, it has to be created in the specific work of art. In other words, poetry is no longer immanent in everyday reality. Ordinary human facticity is irredeemably prosaic; redemption is only possible by an artistic labor of love. At times the compromise, if achieved, is at best only a partial one. It works with regard to a specific, isolated segment of the human world; it works within the context of a specific interpretative relationship to that segment. It may be a compromise that is only subjectively real-

---

[23] Quoted by Schröder in *Novelle und Novellentheorie*, p. 63.

izable—more accurately, that is only realizable in the subjectivity of a specific narrative perspective.

THE TENSION BETWEEN SUBJECTIVE AND OBJECTIVE

This whole question of the subjectivity of the novelle is a recurring feature of theoretical discussion of the genre. Indeed, many commentators have seen the tension between subjective and objective as the hallmark of the novelle. Examples of this idea appear in the earliest beginnings of novelle theory and persist in contemporary criticism. Friedrich Schlegel, an early theoretician, sees the genre as "well suited to the indirect and, as it were, symbolic depiction of a subjective mood and intention—indeed of the deepest and most individual of such moods."[24] Manfred Schunicht, a recent critic, describes the "spectrum of this form" as follows: "On the one hand, strictest objectivity, the distance of the reporter, a perspective that, with every means at its disposal, objectifies; on the other, concealed behind the fiction, a structured reality informed by a subjective teleology, through whose artistic concealment the subjective reality is passed off as the seemingly given reality."[25] It is in this sense that the novelle seeks to mediate between sheer unredeemed facticity and the subjective interpretative perspective that can distill poetry from the prosaic. The novelle retains a seeming objectivity, in that it is concerned with facts, with events, with concrete experience. It seems to be reporting what is. Yet the relationship to reality inherent in the form is one of extreme selectivity. Given this basis, the attempt on the part of the narrative voice to sound objective, to play the role of dispassionate observer, can be only one strand within the story's overall import.

Up to a point, this is true of many actual stories. At one level, the tension between subjective and objective modes is

[24] *WB*, p. 40.
[25] Ibid., p. 459.

another way of conceptualizing the recurrent hermeneutic (interpretative) ambiguity of the novelle that I have endeavored to stress in the preceding pages. Yet one has, in my view, to be somewhat cautious with this large issue of subjectivity and objectivity. Obviously, every work of art—even a lengthy novel—is intensely selective in its approach to the generality of human affairs on which it seeks to comment. In this sense, there is no absolute distinction to be drawn between the nineteenth-century novelle and a work of realistic novel fiction such as *Anna Karenina*. The distinction can only be one of degree, not of kind. Furthermore, the realistic novel, as we understand it, is not usually concerned with average people. The protagonists of *Anna Karenina* and *Madame Bovary* are hardly obvious ciphers for the "man in the street" within their respective societies. Indeed, there is something intrinsically uncommon in the uncompromising way in which their lives express the interaction between their individual being and the corporate social pressures around them. Their experience has a radical intensity that makes them exceptional, but this radical confrontation with the social norms of their times allows them to act out the deepest moral issues inherent in the world to which they belong. Hence, both Flaubert and Tolstoy were being highly selective when they created their heroines, but the end product of this intense artistic selectivity tells us a great deal about the generality of their respective societies and times. Clearly, there is no reason why the nineteenth-century German novelle, as defined by its theoreticians, cannot do just this, even though most of the major novellen would not normally be seen as examples of literary realism—for reasons I wish to discuss later. If, then, the novelle does express some of the deepest spiritual and intellectual issues of its time, it achieves this because of—and not in spite of—the radically isolating nature of its interpretative focus. In this sense, the seemingly objective nature of its tone, the fact that it appears to retain some allegiance to concrete experience, to "facts," is not simply a

37

tention."[26] When he refers to the symbolic character of the novelle he raises what is a central issue in much subsequent criticism: the extent to which symbolism is a sine qua non within novelle writing. This latter notion has been asserted—either implicitly or explicitly—by a number of critics, most forcefully by Hermann Pongs and by Benno von Wiese.[27] Although this approach has been frequently attacked, in my view there is considerable validity to it. Once again, however, it is important not simply to use the symbol as one ingredient in one's checklist of what a valid novelle must have, but rather to ask what kind of narrative relationship to experience has to obtain in order that symbolic writing becomes a recurring feature of novelle texts. The novelle, by bringing an intense interpretative focus to bear on its very selectively constituted subject matter, tends by definition to attribute powerful interpretative significance to the experience or set of experiences with which it is concerned. It intimates to the reader a dual sense of concrete reality on the one hand and of newness of understanding on the other. This, of course, is an intrinsically symbolic constellation, although it does not by any means follow in all cases that the resultant work of art will be constructed around one central symbol. Yet the tendency is unmistakably present. To take obvious examples, the two horses in Kleist's *Michael Kohlhaas* (1810) have an important contribution to make to the overall meaning of the story. They are memorable because Kleist's novelle is the story of what these two animals mean in the context of the protagonist's life, and each time they appear they provide a commentary on that life. Similarly, the reader remembers the shadow from Adalbert von Chamisso's *Peter Schlemihl* (1814) not simply because it is associated with intrinsically unusual happenings (there are plenty of these in the story),

---

[26] Ibid., p. 40.

[27] Pongs, *WB*, pp. 139ff.; see especially Benno von Wiese's article "Bild-Symbole in der deutsche Novelle," *PEGS* 24 (1954–1955): 131ff.

but because it forms the interpretative center of the story Peter has to tell. All of which is not, of course, to say that the shadow or the horses are by definition symbols; but on the other hand, they are not simply little random details that happen, perversely, to remain in the reader's memory. They are related to the central thematic argument of the stories in which they appear. They are—in Paul Heyse's terms[28]—the specific things that intimate the particular concerns of a given story.

One has, of course, to be cautious with regard to this whole argument about symbols in the novelle. Obviously the genre can intrinsically lend itself to symbolic expression—but often this tendency toward the symbolic can prove problematic, because ultimately the whole complex question of interpretative relationship is involved. I have already described the constellation embodied in the novelle as a hermeneutic gamble, as a tension between an experience and the interpretations, the readings to which it gives rise. If the tension is at all severe, then there is always the possibility that the whole interpretative relationship will break down, that the event will stand in livid isolation, uninterpreted, not symbolic "of" anything (or symbolic at best of that which cannot be understood or known). If, in other words, the world with which the novelle concerns itself cannot be related to the generality of the human universe, then any symbolic energy generated by the interaction of narrative viewpoint and experiences described will point away from the knowable and discernible, and the symbol will cease to be "the artistic vindication of the reality of a lovable world."[29] As the novelle becomes more problematic, as the interpretative task confronting its narrator becomes increasingly difficult, then by definition the narrator is increasingly unable to relate the individual segment of described experience to any interpretative generality. If this happens, the symbol, if present at all, acquires diminished resonance in that it is not asserted with any total

[28] *WB*, p. 68.
[29] Erich Heller, *The Disinherited Mind*, p. 96.

and generalizing certainty by the narrator. Indeed, the symbol may work in the context of one character's experience, in the sense that a detail from the real world appears with significant recurrence in his affairs, that it thereby forms some kind of interpretative pattern in his life, but the narrative voice (and hence the story as a whole) may be excluded from any real understanding of what that symbol denotes. Perhaps the point can be made clear by citing individual cases. A story such as Jeremias Gotthelf's *Die schwarze Spinne* (*The Black Spider*, 1842), for example, operates with the central symbol of the wooden beam in which the spider is imprisoned. The two stories told about the devastation wrought by the black spider give meaning to the beam in that it is invested with sacramental (symbolic) quality. It becomes an outward and visible sign denoting an attitude toward human experience that is founded in the Christian faith. The beam has this symbolic function not simply for certain of the characters in the story but for the narrator himself and for the authorial voice too. The symbol is intimated as binding, as a truth within the story, and this truth encompasses not only certain individual people living at a specific time, but ultimately the unchanging law of a divinely ordained world. The symbol is anchored, then, in a totality of narrative assent. Less overtly, other nineteenth-century German novellen operate with similar symbolic insights that are unequivocally underwritten by the narrative voice. In Keller's *Die missbrauchten Liebesbriefe* (*The Misused Love Letters*, 1874), for example, the passage where Ännchen and Gritli put on their best clothes is informed with total narrative assent, and the details of their actions, the very things they handle become the "vindication of a lovable world," and serve to unmask the preposterous and phony "literariness" of Viggi Störteler. The moment when they dress, then, although it has none of the cosmic implications of Gotthelf's beam symbol, still vibrates with total narrative affirmation. Keller's story tells of that process by which the sacramental reality gains recognition from even the somewhat quirky world in which it is embedded. Conversely, it is from that same reality that Sali and Vrenchen, the protagonists of *Romeo und Julia auf dem Dorfe* (*A Village Romeo and Juliet*, 1856), feel themselves to be so utterly excluded.

In other novellen, however, the symbolic focus point is unmistakably more tentative, in that first, the symbolic resonance is not shown as generally apparent (i.e. few of the characters depicted are at all alive to the symbolic function of what confronts them) and second, the narrative voice is largely excluded from any total interpretative access to the symbol. One example is Chamisso's *Peter Schlemihl* where critics have desperately tried to interpret the shadow as a consistent and reliable symbol, but with little success. The reason for this is that the shadow is at best an unstable symbol; it means certain things to certain characters at certain times, but it does not consistently embody a coherent corpus of meaning. Furthermore, the shadow is an insubstantial thing, a trifle, a nothing, and hence it cannot intrinsically embody anything. The shadow acquires meaning only in the context of people's attitude to it, and even then, it scarcely acquires consistent meaning—it tells us something about the people rather than something about itself. Even the narrator himself, the older, wiser Schlemihl, is uncertain what to make of the shadow; he asserts, if anything, the curiously ambivalent relationship to it that has conditioned his life story. At the end, he admonishes the reader to honor his shadow before money. This may mean something in terms of the moral attitude implied on the part of the human being, but it does not serve to make the shadow any more substantial than it intrinsically is. Similarly, Ludwig Tieck's *Der blonde Eckbert* (*Blond Eckbert*, 1796) abounds in what ought to be symbolic incidents and figures—one thinks particularly of the magic bird and its song. Yet the bird and its whole function in the story remain ambiguous, like so many of the characters and experiences. Tieck's story never even remotely approaches the overall interpretative (and narrative) clarity of Gotthelf's *Black Spider*. Similarly, one wonders about the violin in

Grillparzer's *Poor Musician*. For the old man, the violin has sacramental significance, and after his death Barbara treasures that violin as some kind of sacred memento. Yet the narrator never gives unequivocal assent to this sacramental value. Ultimately, the violin is as ambiguous as the old musician himself, as ambiguous as the narrator's whole relationship to the main character. Hence, the violin itself becomes an interpretative problem for us: do we see it as symbolic of a last, desperate mediation between prosaic reality and the ideal world of pure, untainted intention, or is it simply the object of a monumental obsession that borders on the pathological, a kind of grisly relic that properly belongs in a chamber of horrors devoted to man's capacity for self-delusion? In other words, once that which potentially generates symbolic resonance only does so by virtue of a highly individual, indeed exceptional, viewpoint, a viewpoint, furthermore, in which the narrative voice cannot share, then we as readers are excluded from any general interpretative understanding—and creation—of that symbol.[30] That the event or fact in question may have symbolic meaning for that individual viewpoint is not in doubt here. However, if that viewpoint cannot be made part of an interpretative generality that includes us the readers, then it stands in special, dissociated isolation. One wonders, therefore, if one can talk of "symbolic value" in such cases, or whether one is not rather obliged to think in terms of pathological fixations. (One thinks, for example, of Grillparzer's fascinating note in his diary entries: "the novel psychological, the novelle psychopathic.")[31] To take a particularly radical example, Kafka's work embodies this problem as its central interpretative issue. His fiction is shot through with a multitude of seemingly symbolic interrela-

---

[30] My argument here (and on the subjective/objective issue) is particularly indebted to three studies of German narrative prose: Richard Brinkmann, *Wirklichkeit und Illusion*; Walther Killy, *Wirklichkeit und Kunstcharakter*; and Hubert Ohl, *Bild und Wirklichkeit*.

[31] Franz Grillparzer, *Sämtliche Werke*, vol. 3, ed. P. Frank and K. Pörnbacher, Munich, 1964, p. 292.

tionships; one thinks, for instance, of the friend in *Das Urteil* (*The Judgment*, 1912), the friend who never appears but yet exerts a curious pressure on the events described in the story. Narratively, however, we are never told anything reliable about the friend. Indeed, his very existence is left shadowy, even perhaps called into question. Yet the friend works within the story, he has an important part to play because Georg gives recognition to him, thereby assigning to him significance for his (Georg's) life. Similarly, in *The Trial* Josef K is on trial because he keeps on attempting to get to the court and to make it acquit him. Because he gives recognition to the court—instead of ignoring it—he carries his own trial with him wherever he goes. The friend in *The Judgment* and the court in *The Trial* are not symbolic focus points in the sense that we, the readers, know them to be symbols and participate in the creation of their symbolic reference. Clearly the actual court (or what Josef K and we see of it) is utterly questionable. The facts will not sustain symbolic meaning. Yet the characters create symbols for themselves, symbols that imprison and destroy them. These are, as it were, pathologically constituted meanings; they are not "our" symbols in the sense that Gotthelf's blackened beam is. All we know is the questionableness of these symbols—and the fact that they work; they can hurt and destroy. Yet we are excluded from meaning, and this exclusion from meaning is potentially inherent in that hermeneutic challenge that is at the heart of the nineteenth-century novelle. For once the unique event is not relatable to the narrator's (and our) generality of comprehension, then no symbolic clusterings are allowed to form. For all the symbolic predisposition of the genre, many nineteenth-century novellen evoke a world without commonly held symbols, a world with no lovable reality to vindicate. The symbolic potential may remain; but what to some is sacramental substance to others is prosaic facticity. The interpretative gamble at the heart of the novelle does not readily yield an image of an intact world.

44

The *Rahmen* or Narrative Frame

Most of the aspects of novelle theory I have discussed up to now have been principally concerned with theme or import rather than with structure. The last section, however, in which I attempted to comment on the presence of a symbolic intention in the novelle demonstrates that the two kinds of inquiry overlap. Because of a certain interpretative relationship to human affairs, because of a certain thematic purpose, the novelle may yield events or situations where a symbolic focus becomes apparent. I want to pass on now to one of the structural features of the novelle that has received repeated commentary in the past—the *Rahmen* or narrative frame. I hope to suggest that what is important for our purpose is not the question of historical transmission (of who inherited the *Rahmen* from whom), nor indeed the checklist function (that any valid novelle will have an implicit or explicit *Rahmen*). Rather, it seems to me that the importance of the frame as a structural feature derives from its embeddedness in a particular kind of narrative constellation, indeed from that specific kind of hermeneutic situation that has emerged as the implicit presence behind so many thematic features that have already been discussed.

Now, quite obviously, any discussion of the narrative implications of the frame technique has to concern itself with those works in which the presence of the *Rahmen* has real import for the meaning of the work as a whole. It is possible that the frame is used as a pointless piece of narrative sophistication—or simply as a chattily digressive lead-in to a specific story or group of stories. However, in the examples that concern us here, the *Rahmensituation*, the "frame situation," is an important and necessary component of the total narrative statement that is being made, and in this sense it can have profound implications for any understanding of the narrative technique of the novelle as such. Any significant use of the frame technique by definition means that the work as a whole operates with two kinds of narrative direction: there is a world of which the narrator tells, and also a world within which and to which he tells his story. The central interpretative issue is the relationship between these two aspects of narrative reference.

One should begin by stressing that the frame situation is one of the oldest features of narrative technique. One thinks immediately of the *Arabian Nights*, of the *Seven Wise Men*,[32] indeed of the extensive tradition within folktale collections of forms such as the "neck-riddle" or *Halslösungsrätsel*. The latter operates with the time-honored situation of a man under pain of imminent death who manages to postpone his execution, or even to annul it, by a narrative act.[33] Specifically, he poses a riddle—and if the riddle remains unsolved, then he is to be allowed to go free. This is an almost archetypal situation: narration under pressure, where our narrator is concerned not simply to amuse or intrigue his readers, but where he is ultimately using the process of narration for a purpose (to postpone a dreaded event, or to pass a dangerous deadline). If one asks what implications this frame situation has for our understanding of narrative possibilities, then one obvious answer is that it gives a kind of extrinsic excitement to the business of narrating. However cursorily, it creates a tension between the narrator and the world that receives his art. It contextualizes the meaning of what he narrates in a carefully defined social situation. In other words, we as readers respond not simply to the meaning of what is narrated, but we also ask ourselves what effect that narratively intimated meaning has on the immediate world to which it is directed. In a sense, then, the aim and function of narrating (and of listening) becomes part of the overall import.

[32] For a most illuminating documentation of the widespread use of the *Rahmen*—and of its particular significance within the various versions of the *Seven Wise Men* see Otto Löhmann, *Die Rahmenerzählung des Decameron, ihre Quellen und Nachwirkungen*, Halle (Saale), 1935, pp. 8ff.

[33] See Hansjörg Meyer, "Das Halslösungsrätsel," Phil. diss., Würzburg, 1967.

Sheherezade's narrative tour de force is perhaps the most famous example of this process. It is interesting to observe how often in one form or another this basic situation of narrative tension occurs. One of the clearest examples, of course, is Boccaccio's *Decameron*. The frame situation again involves the notion of threat; this time, it is a general rather than a specific process that exerts pressure on the narrator figures. The plague has broken out in Florence, bringing with it not only physical suffering and death, but also social and moral chaos. The laws that sustain the societal framework have crumbled, all cohesion has been lost: "In this extremity of our city's suffering and tribulation the venerable authority of laws, human and divine, was abused and all but totally dissolved. . . . Every man was free to do what was right in his own eyes."[34] The infection at work in Florence is, then, not simply medical in nature; there is also the whole process of inward, moral disintegration. In order to overcome this threatening situation, a group of seven ladies and three gentlemen retire to a country estate, and they set about restoring and strengthening the social order in microcosm—by telling "stories, in which the invention of one may afford solace to all the company of his hearers."[35] The exercise of storytelling is the process whereby harmony is restored because it involves a synthesizing of two forces that can potentially be (and in the context of Florence at this time are) in conflict: individualism and submission to societally dictated restraints. On the one hand, the stories will be products of an individual imagination ("the invention of one"); they will allow for a personal (indeed, even idiosyncratic) treatment of a given theme. Yet, on the other hand, storytelling is a supremely social art because it brings together the individual and his hearers into one or-

[34] Boccaccio, *Decameron*, trans. J. M. Rigg, London, 1930, p. 7.

[35] Ibid., p. 19. See Erich Auerbach's interesting observation that the telling of stories involves a reinstatement of "die Kraft der gesellschaftlichen Form"—of the power of social form (*Zur Technik der Frührenaissancenovelle in Italien und Frankreich*, p. 7).

dered group. In order to strengthen this cohesive quality, it is agreed that the stories shall not simply be random inventions, but rather that there shall be a theme for the day, with the day's storytelling under the direction of a master or mistress of ceremonies (who wears a wreath of bay leaves as a special insignia). The emphasis—as befits the troubled situation to which they are trying to find an answer—is to be on the communal, ordered pleasure of storytelling. Although individualism (in the form of individual fantasy and invention) will be encouraged, basically the framework is to be as orderly as possible. Indeed, the actual process of telling (and listening to) stories does help to establish cohesion within the group. The formal control of the stories means that the audience readily hears each story through to its conclusion—and comments favorably on the skill of each narrator.

Despite this extensively ordering quality, however, it should be noted that the interaction between *Rahmen* and *Binnenerzählung*, between frame and enclosed narration, between the world within which and to which the stories are told and the world of which the stories tell sets up a tension within the work as a whole. For all the urbanity of the narrative tone, the stories are frequently concerned with odd events, with individual aberrations, with human quirkiness, with destructive passions. The hermeneutic challenge is still there; the stories recognize both the continued existence of all those human failings that have so undermined the social order of Florence, and the interpretative problem inherent in any attempt to come to terms with them narratively. Indeed, Hans-Jörg Neuschäfer has recently shown that the stories are not by any means exemplary or unambiguous.[36] They pose an interpretative problem, they generate an ambivalence. Furthermore, Neuschäfer insists that nothing is solved in any final or total way by the end of the *Decameron*. No answer has been given to the fact that under pressure a serene, harmonious

---

[36] *Boccaccio und der Beginn der Novelle.*

social world can turn into a jungle. The citizens of Florence are not intrinsically depraved; the unprecedented happening can make devastating inroads into the ordered, societal presuppositions of any civilized man. The stories themselves express this in the overall ambivalence of their import. By the fact that such stories are told in the specific frame context that Boccaccio creates, the *Decameron*, while attempting to exorcise a threat to the ordered world of social man, constantly reminds us that freak external catastrophes (such as the plague) are not the only forces that can undermine civilized man.

In his *Unterhaltungen deutscher Ausgewanderten (The Conversations of German Emigrants*, 1795) Goethe adopts a frame situation that has much in common with that of the *Decameron*. The threat in this case is the French Revolution, a threat that is not safely confined to the territory across the Rhine because some of the ideas and aspirations of the revolutionary movement are present in the actual group of people who make up the frame situation—and particularly, of course, in Karl. The tension in the frame is not simply left as an implicit presence; rather, it is an overt factor in the conversations that take place, and indeed at one point flares into open conflict as an argument develops between Karl and the Geheimrat.[37] It is, then, within this context that the stories are narrated. The stories help to restore order in the social world of the *Rahmen* in a variety of ways: first, there is the simple fact that the brief, formally controlled stories impose some measure of cohesion on the audience in that they command silent and respectful attention.[38] Furthermore, there is much discussion among the figures in the *Rahmen* about the thematic implications of certain stories. All the stories center upon the juxtaposition of a rational, socio-moral world order and an irrational, strange universe that conflicts with it. Some of the stories

[37] On the importance of this confrontation see Joachim Müller, "Zur Entstehung der deutschen Novelle."

[38] On the narratively generated tension in the stories see M. R. Jessen, "Spannungsgefüge und Stilisierung in den Goetheschen Novellen."

are ghost stories (and the strange happenings even invade the frame when a table suddenly and mysteriously shatters). There is, however, a gradual upward progression from stories of inexplicable oddities to stories that can yield a clear moral interpretation.[39] In other words, we progress from a concern with the inscrutable and uninterpretable to stories that are interpretatively fruitful in that the events depicted can teach an important lesson. The stories known as *Der Prokurator* and *Ferdinand und Ottilie* are important precisely because they are susceptible of interpretation within the moral order of human society. They are relevant to the turbulent times of the French Revolution and hence to the frame situation. The earliest stories are not interpretable within this framework; hence, they are largely irrelevant to the present needs of the society in which they are told.[40]

Goethe, then, shows the learning process at work in the *Unterhaltungen deutscher Ausgewanderten*. For this reason, a great deal of time is spent on the frame situation, and Goethe constantly reminds us that the stories are narrated within a quite specific context by devoting much space to the conversations that follow in the frame after each story has finished. By discussing the stories, the characters of the frame situation participate in a pedagogic process.[41] Ultimately the morally ordering import of the later stories triumphs and helps to bring cohesion into the microcosm

---

[39] See Ilse Jürgens, "Die Stufen der sittlichen Entwicklung in Goethes *Unterhaltungen deutscher Ausgewanderten*"; August Raabe, "Der Begriff des Ungeheuren in den *Unterhaltungen deutscher Ausgwanderten*," *Goethe* 4 (1939): 23ff.; H. Popper, "Goethe's *Unterhaltungen deutscher Ausgewanderten*."

[40] I have in this discussion made little reference to the *Märchen* that concludes the *Unterhaltungen*. This is because the *Märchen* clearly transcends the frame situation. On the relationship of the *Märchen* to the work as a whole see G.-L. Fink, *Das Märchen*.

[41] For a persuasive analysis of the nature—and importance—of this pedagogic process see Theodore Ziolkowski, "Goethe's *Unterhaltungen deutscher Ausgewanderten*," and Gerhard Fricke, "Zu Sinn und Form von Goethes *Unterhaltungen deutscher Ausgewanderten*."

of a threatened society that is evoked in the frame. One of the principal themes of the *Unterhaltungen deutscher Ausgewanderten* is the hermeneutic process itself; the work asks what it means when one interprets a story, what happens in the crucial process of interaction between narrator and audience. It is necessary to stress at this point the variety of different meanings that can emerge from this structural constellation. In the *Unterhaltungen deutscher Ausgewanderten* the process of telling and listening to stories is morally educative—just as it is morally and erotically educative for Reinhard and Lucie in Keller's *Das Sinngedicht* (*The Epigram*, 1881). However, for a writer such as C. F. Meyer in *Das Leiden eines Knaben* (*The Sufferings of a Boy*, 1883), this same process can fail utterly (the hearer in question, Louis XIV, enjoys the story, but he does not learn from it the lesson that the narrator, Fagon, had hoped to impart by telling the life story of Julian Boufflers).

The crucial importance, then, of the *Unterhaltungen deutscher Ausgewanderten* resides not so much in its literary-historical implications (in that Goethe establishes by this work a link with a great tradition that goes back at least as far as Boccaccio and that thereby he asserts an unshakable claim to be the father of all subsequent novellen). Rather, the importance of the *Unterhaltungen* lies in the fact that it explores with real insight the full thematic implications of a particular kind of narrative constellation: one in which narrative interpretation of experience and the reader's (or hearer's) understanding of that narrative interpretation comes to function as a central component in the overall meaning of the work in question. If one understands the significance of the *Unterhaltungen* (and of the frame) in this way, one can avoid the temptation to absolutize the *Unterhaltungen* into some norm of what novelle narration should be.

The kind of frame technique that I have been discussing up to now is often referred to as the "cyclical" or "closed" frame (in that it embraces a sequence of stories recounted by one narrator or by a series of narrators to a specifically defined audience). There is a further possibility that deserves comment here: the individual frame, which encloses one specific story, and which is open in that we, the readers, implicitly constitute the audience. Once again, it is difficult to lay down hard and fast rules as to the import generated by the individual frame. Basically, however, we are concerned with a structural constellation that creates a specific context within which (and to which) the individual story is told. Frequently this involves some kind of image of human society (however it may be constituted). Often this society is meant to operate as a model of recognizable, known reality, to which the story told will stand in some kind of interpretative relationship. The possibilities of this relationship are manifold (as are the possible constitutions of that social grouping that contextualizes the inset story). Many Romantic writers, for example, use the frame in order to establish some kind of familiar point of reference, but only in order to undermine that familiarity. For Stifter, the frame situation can evoke the abiding, unchanging law of the natural world, for Storm it pinpoints the temporal (and psychological) context of the narrative undertaking. Whatever the thematic possibilities, the structural intimation remains the same: within one world a story is told of another world. The interpretative question, then, is what kind of relationship obtains between these two worlds, and what is the meaning of that relationship. The process and context of narration becomes part of the theme of the work as a whole.

In a recent study Harald Weinrich has concerned himself with the phenomenon of narrative frames.[42] He stresses particularly that within Eastern cultures there exists the notion that man comes to insight and understanding not so much by a thought process as by telling and listening to stories. The presence of a threat in the *Rahmen* suggests that the telling of stories can be very much embedded in the real world of power politics and absolute despots and

[42] *Tempus.*

that (as in the *Seven Wise Men*) this real world can be challenged by the exemplary moral force of what is narrated. This didactic quality, whose effect is documented in the frame, makes the link between the fiction narrated and the real world that hears and interprets it. Weinrich makes the interesting suggestion that with the development of the realistic novel in the nineteenth century, the function of the frame (its mediation between a specific story and world) is taken over by the broad description of the socio-economic background against which the individual story is acted out. Weinrich's argument cogently draws attention to the crucial interpretative function of the *Rahmen*. He suggests that, in so far as the novelle recognizes the claims of social reality, it does so not by realistic documentation of that reality, but by embodying the values of human society in a particular set of narratively intimated assumptions. In the novelle the common reality of social experience is expressed not as a group of binding facts but rather as a possible interpretative attitude. By contrast, the story actually told tends to center upon experiences that are somehow unusual, unique, isolated from the common run of human affairs. The frame establishes a context around the particular inset story. That context can serve to mediate interpretatively between the isolated experience or set of experiences and the generality of the social universe, or it can serve to isolate the experiences still more—by failing to come to terms with them. In its special, sharply illuminated subject matter, the novelle can generate an exemplary— and didactic—import, or it can achieve the effect of increasing estrangement and isolation. The interpretative difficulty, then, is given in the structure, because there is always the possibility that the mediation can break down. The *Rahmen* can create a bridge or help to define a gulf. Indeed, even in cases where the novelle functions with all its exemplary rigor, there is always the risk that the example will go unheeded, that the real world will reject rather than accept. This is the excitement of the frame situation in the *Seven Wise Men*. It is the same excitement, in my view, that

some ironic counterpoint to what is being told. While the argument may be overstated, Schlegel's contention does serve to draw our attention to what is a recurring feature of many significant nineteenth-century German novellen: their interpretative complexity. Frequently one notices how subtle, how oblique the narrative perspective is, how often it chooses to imply more than it says, how often it employs irony to suggest registers within its perspective that it will not make explicit. In part, this sophistication derives from the fact that the process of interpretation is itself embodied in the theme of the story. Implicitly the question is raised of how one mediates between the remarkable and unusual experiences described and the presupposed human generality the narrative voice evokes. Often the only possible mediation is irony, in that the narrator stands for one thing, but tells a story in such a way that his own stance is questioned by the implicit intimation of other possible perspectives which the story as a whole makes. In other words, the novelle frequently centers upon a hermeneutic tension that makes for ironic intimations rather than explicit statements. This is perhaps the deepest reason why the nineteenth-century novelle offers such a challenging interpretative experience. It confronts that which is marginal to the reliably understood universe, and from that confrontation there seldom results either an unequivocal vindication of the marginal experience or an unequivocal vindication of the societal universe. Rather, we are made aware of what it means to attempt the interpretation of something that resists the act of interpretation. We are acquainted with the fact that, when we understand something, we do so by virtue of already existing expectations within us. We bring a preunderstanding to bear on the new experience. If that new experience does not lend itself easily to our interpretation, then, as we attempt to understand it, we have to become conscious of our preunderstanding—and we have to be prepared to relativize it. Such a process must involve primarily our relationship to the narrative voice in the story.

For this reason it seems to me crucially important, when analyzing nineteenth-century German novellen, to pay particular attention to the narrative perspective they establish. In a particularly concentrated sense, the *process* of telling and interpreting events is made thematic in the novelle. Furthermore, in my discussion of the various theoretical pronouncements about the genre I have tried to look behind the specific features they advocate in order to establish some kind of primary process of imaginative structuring that allows all these features to arise and develop. Frequently I have attempted to define this structuring process as a narrative constellation, as an expression of narratively intimated relationship to experience. From this narrative relationship everything else (whether it be the symbol, the "turning point," the *Rahmen*) follows. Here I must acknowledge Benno von Wiese's term *"novellistisches Erzählen"* ("novelle-typical narration").[46] Von Wiese in effect suggests that, rather than try to define the novelle by concretely observable features, we ask what kind of narrative predisposition has to exist in order for such features to manifest themselves. This is very much the line of questioning that I have sought to follow.

The central aspect of the overall narrative constellation of the novelle is, in my view, the attempt to interpret the unusual event or sequence of events in the context of a generality of human affairs and their understanding. The interpretative intention has to be present—even if it fails. It is this crucial undertaking that distinguishes the novelle from another short form that, it could be argued, is the legitimate twentieth-century successor to the nineteenth-century novelle—the *Kurzgeschichte* or short story. The latter has been defined as a "moment become word,"[47] as a momentary aperçu of a tiny segment of reality. Obviously, the Novelle too can function as a glimpse of human experience, but the crucial difference resides in the interpreta-

---

[46] *Die deutsche Novelle von Goethe bis Kafka*, vol. 1, p. 15.

[47] Quoted in R. Hinton Thomas, ed., *Seventeen Modern German Short Stories*, London, 1965, p. 21.

tive claims that both forms make. The point can be made most economically by juxtaposing two definitions of the respective genres. Bernhard von Arx sees the following process as central to the novelle: "A unique, often chance event is interpreted, because this one thing is typical, it seems to be a pointer to the nature of the world."[48] Erika Essen writes of the short story: "As material, reality should be left open: it should be shown, not interpreted. Because in reality temporal flow knows neither beginning nor end, but each moment is, in itself, a focus of reality, the short story can take up each moment and depict it as it appears in its openness to the two directions of past and future."[49] The crucial difference resides, then, in the fact that the novelle attempts to establish some kind of overall interpretative relationship to the event or events it describes, whereas the short story has abandoned any such pretentions to interpretative mediation. It offers an isolated aperçu that remains isolated. However helpful this distinction may be, one should not fall into the trap of arguing with simple linear historicism that the nineteenth-century novelle is an unproblematic form, serenely able to interpret the remarkable event and encompass it safely within a known and manageable universe, while the twentieth-century imagination, confronted by a world that increasingly disintegrates into little, intractable fragments, contents itself with expressing the uninterpretable strangeness of those isolated glimpses of the world.[50] The danger here is that one makes a crude distinc-

---

[48] *Novellistisches Dasein*, p. 173.

[49] Quoted in J. Kuipers, *Zeitlose Zeit*, p. 80.

[50] Ludwig Rohner seems to me to fall into this trap in his *Theorie der Kurzgeschichte*. See especially pp. 73, 157, 178, 222.

Only after this study was completed was I able to read Judith Leibowitz, *Narrative Purpose in the Novella*, The Hague, 1974. Her concern to define the genre as a "narrative shaping purpose" (p. 15) is very close to my own. Moreover, her characterization of the novelle as "microcosmic viewpoint with macrocosmic relevance" (p. 82)—which produces the "double effect of intensity and expansion" (p. 16)—seems to me to stress, quite rightly, the overriding question of the interpretative focus of the genre.

found. The notion that morality consists above all else in restraining one's desires rests upon a somewhat undifferentiated understanding of human emotions and their problematic relationship to moral values. Indeed, morality becomes simply equated with a rejection of intensity and passion, whereby self-limitation is seen to be the highest good. All problems are soluble: "Once we have acknowledged the good and mighty self, which dwells so calmly and quietly within us and which, until at last it gains the upper hand, constantly makes its presence felt through gentle hints and reminders" (185). The individual, then, only has to overcome the specific aberration that threatens him in order to find the permanent security of knowing himself, of being in command of his life. In the *Unterhaltungen* the threat to the ordered world is something specific, usually a particular passion or infatuation that clearly is of disastrous consequences for the character both as an individual and as a social being, and this can be overcome by his voluntary act of *Entsagung*, "renunciation."

I want to argue in my analysis of the *Novelle* that this work is, both stylistically and thematically, infinitely richer than the stories of the *Unterhaltungen*. For this reason I have chosen it for detailed analysis—despite the undeniable literary-historical significance of the *Unterhaltungen*. Furthermore, because Goethe's endeavors within the novelle genre are so much the starting point of the German novelle, I have broken with chronology and decided to treat the *Novelle* before *Peter Schlemihl*, although it in fact appeared some thirteen years after Chamisso's story.

One of the most striking characteristics of Goethe's *Novelle* is its obliqueness. If one summarizes the plot, one gets nowhere near the web of implication that sustains the story. If one asks who is the main character, one again finds it difficult to answer with any authority. According to most critics, Honorio is the obvious candidate. Yet it is remarkable how little we know about him. Why is his infatuation with the Fürstin only hinted at? Why are we told so little about his thoughts and feelings? The first reference to any sort of love on Honorio's part occurs when the Fürstin leaves the residence to go for a ride with the *Fürst-Oheim* (the Prince's uncle) and Honorio: "The Fürstin hurried to mount her favorite horse, and led her half-reluctant, half-acquiescent companion not through the back gate up the hillside, but downward through the front gate; for who would not have gladly ridden at her side, who would not have gladly followed her! So, too, Honorio had willingly forgone the otherwise so desired hunt in order to be exclusively at her service" (496).

Clearly, Honorio is delighted to be able to devote himself exclusively to the service of his mistress. Yet the intrusion of the rhetorical question—"who would not have gladly ridden at her side"—would seem to indicate, even allowing for ironical undertones, that there is nothing particularly unusual or socially unacceptable in his feelings. The scene between Honorio and the Fürstin after the death of the tiger does unmistakably reveal the intensity of the former's passion. Once again, however, his feelings are only hinted. Emil Staiger makes this point in his analysis of the story: "The conversation of the Fürstin with Honorio is discreet to the point of being incomprehensible."[2] Staiger attributes this reticence to the restraint dictated by social convention. While I agree that the narrator is part of the society he is describing and hence shares its conventions, it seems to me he could reveal Honorio's passion more explicitly— particularly in terms of its disastrous social implications— without forfeiting his position within this society. The point is that the narrator does not *choose* to explore Honorio's passion fully because he is concerned to show a much more fundamental threat to human society in all its subtlety and pervasiveness. To state it explicitly would be to falsify it. The narrator therefore continues to hint at Honorio's infatuation for the Fürstin. We see his pride in offering her the tiger's skin "with glowing cheeks" (503). We sense his delight in kneeling before her and hearing her

[2] *Goethe*, vol. 3, p. 184.

thrice-repeated "stand up" (503), and the narrator tells us—with characteristic obliqueness—of Honorio's sadness when she promises to grant his request to leave court. The extent of Honorio's passion is, of course, made explicit in the words addressed to him at the end of the story: "Hurry now, do not delay, you will conquer. But first conquer yourself!" (510). Interestingly, however, it is not the object of Honorio's love who administers these words of advice (as it is the *Prokurator* who educates the merchant's wife in the *Unterhaltungen*), but the mother of the boy who by his music tames the lion.

Clearly, Goethe is very much at pains to understate the importance of Honorio's love for the Fürstin. We seem to be concerned not so much with a specific aberration that threatens Honorio, but rather with a less clearly definable, and therefore more insidious, threat to the apparently secure social world within which the events take place. In fact, the threat to society Goethe is portraying here is one against which *no* member of that society is proof—neither the *Fürst* (the Prince), the Fürstin, the Fürst-Oheim, nor, of course, Honorio. It is on this point that I find myself in considerable disagreement with those interpreters who have confined the moral concern of the *Novelle* to Honorio alone.

What, then, is the nature of this threat? The story, in my view, embodies the insight that even the most sophisticated and ordered of societies is attracted, albeit in spite of itself, toward savagery and violence. Indeed, it is in large measure because of its sophistication and self-discipline that the society depicted in the *Novelle* craves to experience the complete antithesis of its own way of life. Hence, the members of that society—both individually and collectively—create images of an elemental, anarchical world. It is not sufficient to say, for example, that the tiger represents the unruly passions in Honorio's heart. The tiger is completely tame. Its significance lies in the discrepancy between what it is in reality and what society wants to see in it. In this story human society oscillates between the two poles of mature, civilized attitudes on the one hand and a strange indulgence in specious images of the violent on the other. The story opens early one autumn morning when preparations are in hand for a hunt. The narrator begins by describing the lively to-ing and fro-ing of the huntsmen, horses, and dogs as they wait for the Fürst to appear and lead them. The mention of the Fürst leads to a description of the perfect harmony that prevails between him and his young wife. Their happiness seems to be reflected in the serene give-and-take that is the secure basis of the society over which they rule. This ideal of social life that allows opposites to coexist, that gives people a time to work and a time to enjoy themselves, is mirrored in the scene at the marketplace to which the Fürst had a few days previously drawn his wife's attention, stressing how mountains and plains met in happy concord.

At this point, however, we are brought back to the scene with which the work opened, for mention is made of the "hunting master . . . in whose opinion it was impossible to resist the temptation, on these ideal autumn days, to undertake an already postponed hunt" (491f.). The preparations for the hunt, as we have seen in the first paragraph, breathe an air of excitement and vitality: "People were adjusting their knapsacks, while the dogs impatiently threatened to pull along by the leash their handlers, who were trying to restrain them. Here and there a horse showed its high spirits, impelled by its fiery nature or by the spur of its rider who even here in the half-light could not resist a certain vain desire to show off" (491).

We later read: "The Fürstin was loath to stay behind; the intention was to penetrate far into the mountains in order to disturb the peaceful denizens of the forests there by an unexpected act of war" (492). Gradually we realize that a contradictory element has entered the ordered social world that our narrator has been at pains to evoke. If the scene on the marketplace showed the perfect interchange of mountains and plains, we are now witnessing an invasion, an attack on the peace and calm of the natural world of the mountains from the town. The hunt is described, in the passages already quoted, as a *Versuchung*, a "temptation," as a *Kriegszug*, "an act of military aggression." The hunt is a scene of savagery and splendor. All this is suggested in the vitality and defiance of the horse, a defiance in which its rider fully acquiesces ("impelled by its fiery nature or by the spur of its rider"). The appeal of the hunt is, moreover, something felt not only by the men, but also by the Fürstin; she knows full well the nature of the proposed hunt, and she too would dearly like to take part in this "act of war."

As the Fürstin's gaze follows the departing hunting party, she catches sight of the old castle on the hillside, and this ruin is the subject of her ensuing conversation with the Fürst-Oheim. He describes the site as a remarkable place, where the man-made and the natural are locked in bitter battle. However, plans are in hand for a restoration of the castle. The power of nature is not to be suppressed, but the whole site is to be carefully reorganized to preserve it as it is. The aim is to preserve the fusion of the work of man and the natural world, and yet to remove the element of tension and struggle from the scene. It is to be maintained as it has been depicted in the artist's drawings, as a scene where the two opposed forces are seen to be not so much in conflict, but rather held in balance. The Fürstin not unnaturally wishes to see in reality what the artist's sketches have depicted. The Fürst-Oheim, however, resists her suggestion with surprising vehemence. It is almost as though he senses that there is something unsettling in the present condition of the castle and its surroundings, in the spectacle it affords of a mighty, man-made structure being slowly overcome by the forces of nature.

The Fürstin agrees to abandon the project of visiting the castle, but insists on their going for a ride and suggests that they should make a point of crossing the marketplace. She clearly has been much struck by the harmony, by the balance and fusion of different worlds, which, as her husband had pointed out to her, is to be seen in the hurly-burly of market day. The mention of the marketplace, however, brings an unfortunate memory to the mind of the Fürst-Oheim: a memory of an appalling night when a fire broke out and the marketplace was engulfed by flames. Indeed, so horrifying is the impact of this memory that the Fürst-Oheim is about to recount it to the Fürstin. She, however, prevents the retelling: " 'Let us not waste the beautiful hours,' the Fürstin interrupted him, as the worthy man had already on several occasions terrified her with a detailed description of this disaster" (496). The implications of this are important: the old man has had this terrible experience, and yet in a strange way he enjoys recounting it over and over again—and in full detail. His behavior in this context is interesting, indeed paradoxical, in the light of his later remarks about the strange fascination that horror exerts on the human mind.

The riding party sets off across the marketplace; the people are delighted to see the Fürstin, delighted to be reminded "that the first lady in the land was also the most beautiful and gracious" (497). Once again we seem to be in a world of total harmony, where the preferments of social status coincide with natural gifts. However, as so often in the story, the world of ordered harmony is shown to be threatened. Beyond the marketplace are various cages containing wild animals; our narrator comments that the roar of the lion sounds particularly terrifying in the context of a civilized society. Yet the terror inspired by the lion's roaring does not prevent the group from advancing to the cages. Indeed, it is almost as if there were something irresistible in the voice of savagery in an ordered world. This impression is reinforced by the description of the various placards and posters in front of the cages; they are lurid and portray the savagery of the animals—the tiger is about to maul a black man: "As they approached the booth, they could not overlook the colorful, colossal pictures that portrayed with violent colors and powerful images those strange animals at which the peaceful citizen apparently feels an irresistible craving to look. The ferocious, massive tiger leaped at a Moor and was about to tear him to pieces" (497).

The Fürst-Oheim is at pains to point out the discrepancy between the actual tiger in the cage and its depiction on the hoardings. This is a point that is taken up later in the confrontation between Honorio and the tiger. The animal is tame; it does not constitute a threat to the world of human society. Here nature has been tamed just as it will be tamed in the restoration of the castle. However, society does not want to see this aspect of the tiger; it wants the thrill of being confronted with something violent and terrifying. The Fürstin expresses a wish to inspect the wild animals on her way home. The Fürst-Oheim resists her suggestion— just as he had resisted her previous wish to visit the ruined castle—and once again, for good reasons: "It is strange that man always desires to be excited by the terrifying. Inside, the tiger lies quite peacefully in his cage, but here he has to be shown attacking a Moor so that people are led to believe they will see the same sort of thing inside; there is not enough murder and slaughter, fire and destruction: the ballad singers must repeat it at every corner. Dear old mankind wants to be intimidated, in order afterward to feel with full force what a fine and laudable thing it is to be able to breathe freely" (498).

Clearly, the Fürst-Oheim is right in his analysis of the appeal wild animals have for a sophisticated society. One wonders, however, how far he is trying to rationalize and excuse something that has more disturbing causes than he is prepared to admit. Do the people want to see—and indeed create—such spectacles in order to be able to appreciate the security that the social order gives them? Is it not rather that the sight of something savage and bloody never loses its appeal for man, however sophisticated and self-aware he may become? The Fürst-Oheim clearly senses that there is something undesirable about this sort of interest in savagery. Yet, he himself, although he would presumably not admit it, finds a certain pleasure in telling

with the world of nature. Nature is at peace; it is traditionally the time of day when Pan sleeps and nature holds its breath so as not to disturb him. Yet the calm is almost immediately shattered as Honorio catches sight of a fire that has broken out in the marketplace. Despite his efforts to calm her, the Fürstin finds her mind filled with the terrifying images—the *Schreckbilder*—of the Fürst-Oheim's stories. The horror of the scene resides not in what is actually happening, but in her mental picture and interpretation of it. Significantly, the narrator now gives what is clearly the Fürst-Oheim's description of the fire on the marketplace; we are allowed to hear the narration which has so impressed itself on the Fürstin's mind. The language here is different; it has a restlessness and violence that distinguishes it from the narrator's own voice. This is a depiction of the scene through the eyes of an actual witness and recounted as he would tell it. Certain phrases suggest a very personal response on the part of this eyewitness. He does not simply report facts, but deliberately tries to recreate through images the horror of the scene: "below the elemental force raged ceaselessly"; "as though evil spirits in their element, constantly changing their shape, were trying to consume themselves in an exuberant dance, to reemerge here and there from out of the glowing heat"; "strongwilled men ferociously resisted the ferocious enemy" (501). In all these passages the fire is personified as a malevolent demon, and one is not surprised that the Fürstin did not relish a frequent hearing of this account of the fire. Once the Fürst-Oheim's narration is over, we return to the present time of our narrative—a fact marked by the repetition of the adverb *"leider,"* "unfortunately"—and our narrator stresses the disastrous consequences of the Fürst-Oheim's story for the mental state of the Fürstin. Such is her fear that she becomes totally alienated from the real world around her: "Unfortunately the ugly turmoil now took possession again of the lovely mind of the Fürstin, now the happy morning vision was shrouded, her eyes were troubled; forest and meadow had a wondrous, fearful aura"

68

(501). It is at this moment, and in the scene that follows, that the discrepancy between the real world and man's perception of it is at its greatest.

Yet one wonders whether, in the light of what follows, the Fürstin is not perhaps right; one wonders if reality is not the horrific nightmare she has seen. The tiger, set free in the tumult of the marketplace, suddenly bounds toward her. Yet our narrator is at pains to stress that it is her (and Honorio's) image of reality that is at fault. It is the dubious depiction of horror (the Fürst-Oheim's narration, the placards by the animals' cages) that leads them astray: "Bounding toward them, as she had recently seen him in the painting, he approached—and this picture, allied to the terrible images that were engaging her attention, made the strangest impression" (502). As Staiger quite rightly points out, it is only after Honorio has fired a shot at the tiger that the animal is angered. It is the fact of Honorio giving chase that "seemed to excite anew and to spur on his energies"— "*schien seine Kraft aufs neue anzuspornen und zu reizen*" (502). The metaphor of the spurs recalls a detail from the opening scene of the story (the horse rearing up as the hunt is about to start) where, as here, a man provokes and excites an animal. Honorio shoots the tiger, kneels on its dead body, and as the Fürstin gazes at her rescuer she realizes how beautiful he is. Her mind associates this beauty with his skill in riding, in swordsmanship, in all manner of military exercises and games: "The young man was beautiful; he had galloped up as the Fürstin had often seen him do in the lance and ring games. This was just how, on the riding track, he would fire his bullet into the Turk's forehead right under the turban as he galloped past the stake; this was just how, at a swift gallop, he would pick up from the ground the Moor's head on the point of his shining saber. He was skilled and naturally at home in all such arts" (502f.).

The beauty of Honorio is linked with the savagery that he has just displayed. This beauty is something primitive, sadistic. It is the beauty of the hunter and as such it is pre-

69

cisely the same beauty as that of the tiger on the placards. In the Fürstin's mind the image of Honorio as slayer of the tiger is linked with his beauty as a swordsman and warrior. As Seuffert suggests,[3] the *Mohrenhaupt*, the mock Moor's head, which Honorio can so neatly impale on his sword in the cavalry games, surely reminds us specifically of that earlier depiction of the tiger as portrayed on the crude poster: "the ferocious, massive tiger leaped at a moor, was about to tear him to pieces" (497). Both Honorio and the tiger on the placard have the same power, the same terrible beauty. Significantly, Honorio's beauty is one of the threads running through the story and it embodies its thematic progression. At the beginning, reference is made to him as "a well-built young man" (492). His beauty is at first stated simply as a natural gift. In the course of the story, however, we see that his attitude toward the natural world—and toward his own nature—conditions his beauty as a person. This beauty can be something serene and controlled as in the closing pages of the story where it is referred to twice in the space of a few lines. The woman addresses him as "*schöner junger Mann,*" "beautiful young man," and later we read that "she believed she had never seen a more beautiful young man" (510). At this moment Honorio is absorbed in the glory of the setting sun and he finds the peace that comes from maturity and renunciation. Immediately after he has killed the tiger, however, it is the savage aspect of his beauty that is stressed, as when he offers the Fürstin the skin of the slaughtered beast, specifically likening his action to that of the victor in war parading with the spoils of conquest.

The spell of the scene, the moment of attraction between Honorio and the Fürstin, is broken by the arrival of the mother and boy who are responsible for the wild animals. The conversation that ensues between the strange family and the Fürst, who has appeared with the hunting party, is interrupted briefly by the arrival of the watchman from the

3 B. Seuffert, "Goethes *Novelle*," p. 138.

castle. He has seen the other animal that has escaped, and his attitude is reminiscent of Honorio's treatment of the tiger for he instinctively regrets that he does not have his rifle with him; if he had, he could have gained a splendid trophy—a lion's skin.

Yet violence is not necessary. The family shows how the lion, like the horse, is part of God's ordered world—and hence is ordained to be harnessed by man, whom God has created in His own image. Man, if he is in tune with God's purposes, if he offers to God a *"frommen Gesang,"* a "pious song" (508), he can, like Daniel, tame even the most apparently savage of beasts. In the same way Honorio can find his full beauty as a person by making his desires and passions compatible with his knowledge of the true and perfect harmony God has ordained. It is this ordering principle that is expressed in the boy's song; and because of this, the young boy, truly the "image of God," can tame the lion.

Thematically, the ending of the story represents in Goethe's terms a *Steigerung*, in which two intensified opposites are raised to a fruitful synthesis, are raised to a different experiential plane where order and harmony are attained. The intensification of opposites is made clear in the scene where the young boy takes the thorn from the lion's paw and binds the wound. It is childlike weakness that liberates the animal to full life and yet at the same time tames and orders its vitality. In the same way, it is the boy's childlike openness before the world as God has created it that embodies that ordering principle by which the mature adult world seeks to live. This perfect seeing is only possible because his mind is uncluttered by those fantasies to which the sophisticated adult mind is prone. It is interesting to note in this context how even the boy's parents are susceptible to being drawn into society's collective fantasies. The father is presumably responsible for the lurid posters that surround the tiger's cage; and the mother, when she witnesses the boy removing the thorn from the lion's paw, cannot help reverting to her role as a circus performer. We read: "In her joy, the mother stretched out her arms and leaned back, and perhaps she would, as was her wont, have clapped and applauded if the watchman, gripping her arm, had not reminded her that the danger was not yet over" (512). In her almost involuntary action here she reveals the function within civilized society into which she and her husband become almost unwittingly drawn; they find themselves providing the social world with a thrill of horror—and it is for this service that society is prepared to pay them money. Their function as figures from a mythical world who have the power to tame animals is tainted by their being subordinated to the needs of society. Only in the boy with that openness of childhood does the ordering principle that the family represents reveal itself in all its fullness and purity.

As Goethe himself saw, the thematic *Steigerung* of the final stages of the story required a stylistic *Steigerung*, a transference to a different plane of artistic creation. Prose of necessity gave place to lyric poetry: "An ideal, indeed lyrical conclusion was necessary and had to come; for after the pathos of the man's speech, which is already poetic prose, there had to be an intensification. I had to move over to lyric poetry, in fact even to song."[4] The plane of experience in which this intensified synthesis is attained transcends the social. It represents the source of order and balance to which human society aspires without ever fully achieving it within the context of the social world. Goethe, as he himself tells us, was very careful to prepare for this final *Steigerung*. He describes the structural progression of his story as a plant growing upward, its green leaves and shoots finally culminating in a flower: "the flower was unexpected, surprising, but it had to come; indeed, the green foliage was only there for its sake, and would not have been worth the trouble but for the flower."[5] Yet most of the story as we possess it is concerned with "the green foliage of the absolutely real exposition"[6]—and we know that

---

[4] Goethe to Eckermann, 18 January 1827.
[5] Ibid.   [6] Ibid.

Goethe took a great deal of trouble over the real world that was to constitute the exposition. He carefully reworked it so that it would, while remaining "absolutely real," embody those tensions in human society that will properly find balance and synthesis in the higher world of the boy's song. The final *Steigerung*, for all that it is the necessary and inevitable outcome of the tensions at work in the society depicted in the story, goes beyond the experiential world of the narrator. He is concerned with a society that in its maturity represents both security and threat.

This duality accounts for the subtlety of Goethe's insight into human society. For all their indulgence in questionable images of the anarchical and the violent, the characters depicted in the *Novelle* are in no sense monsters of depravity. They represent a social maturity and wisdom to which we are clearly required to assent. The adjectives of approval that the narrator bestows on the Fürst-Oheim— such as "worthy" and "admirable"—are not simply to be taken ironically. Rather, it is basic to the story's meaning that the Fürst-Oheim should be seen in an ambivalent light. On the one hand, he is an intelligent person who instinctively feels the questionableness of the crude posters near the animals' cages, who is aware of the powerful appeal of the ruined castle and of what must be done if it is to be properly restored. On the other hand, this same man can be disastrously led astray—and can lead others astray, as is the case in his frequent recounting of the marketplace fire. We, the readers, are made to perceive both the admirable qualities of the characters in the story, and the fact that their moral stability and security is something that is constantly being called into question, something that can never be taken for granted. At one point the narrator refers to "the group . . . which we know" (504). Surely we do know the members of the group—not simply because the narrator has described them to us, but because they are part of the real world of social man. Frequently the narrator designates the social group as *"man"*—"one"—(as in the opening description of the hunt), whereby he maintains a certain distance from the social world he is describing; but occasionally the perspective becomes *"wir"*—"we"—whereby the narrator includes himself and his readers: "as tends to happen to us as we look around from such a high vantage point" (499). The use of the verb "tends to" (*"pflegen"*) asks for assent to the fact that these people belong to our world, that their experiences and problems overlap with ours.

The tone in which the narrator writes is unmistakably that of a mature, sophisticated social being. His voice embodies the reticence, the sense of order and propriety that is so much the hallmark of the society he evokes. It is only in spite of themselves that the members of this society give way to occasional moments of emotion. When her husband leaves to go hunting, the Fürstin "could not prevent herself from waving her handkerchief again" (493); later we read that she "did not refrain from producing the embroidered handkerchief and covering her eyes with it" (509). Again, one thinks of the huntsman who "could not deny himself a certain vanity" (491). Precisely the same attitude is implicit in the way the narrator writes. One thinks of the moment when he summarizes the boy's song, almost embarrassed by its beauty and poetic intensity, by those qualities that set it apart from the world of social convention. He recounts how the boy "began his soothing song, whose repetition here we, too, cannot deny ourselves" (511). The formulation is crucial here, for it serves to identify the narrator as part of the social world he so compassionately and so critically depicts. Human society is shown to rest on a number of assumptions shared by the narrative voice itself. Both the society portrayed and the tone of its narrative evocation represent that discipline that was the center of the moral teaching expressed in the *Unterhaltungen deutscher Ausgewanderten*. Yet in the *Novelle* Goethe shows how the ethos of restraining one's passions, while on the one hand giving security and order, on the other can lead to a craving for vicious imaginative outlets for the natural vitality that is being so firmly held in check. The import of the *Novelle* is underlined and enacted at every turn by the way the story is told. Its narrative perspective is a real tour de force in the way that it remains within the social world while at the same time indicating its inherent inadequacies. In this story, the tone of the narration is an essential part of the overall thematic argument.

At the end of the story, the narrator confesses that his language is not adequate to express the supreme source of order embodied in the boy's song, and, hence, he leaves us to listen to the pure language of the strange family, rendering its meaning as best he can into "our" language: "A natural language, brief and staccato, made itself insistently and movingly felt. In vain would one try to translate it into our speech; but we must not conceal the approximate sense" (510). The narrator, because he is part of the social world, is inadequate when he has to state the absolute source of harmony and order in the world. Hence, he withdraws his voice almost completely. The closing perspective, in which a mythical world enters the real one and orders it, is clearly something the narrator esteems profoundly. Yet, fundamentally, however much he assents to it, this is not his perspective. He remains the man in society, the man who talks of human society in terms of the moral values implicit in a human community. It is because of his maturity and insight that he sees the dangers threatening Honorio, the Fürstin, and the Fürst-Oheim, although they themselves are unaware of them. The narrator's tone is an embodiment of and judgment on the nature of human society and the tensions to which it is prone.

The "unprecedented happening that has actually occurred," which is the essence of Goethe's famous definition of the novelle, could be identified in this story as the moment when the young boy through his music tames the escaped lion. However, it is not the actuality of the event that matters, but its interpretative value in context. The event is clearly unprecedented in the sense that it is a manifestly unusual, even magical, happening. It is, however, "actual" not just in the simple sense that it is portrayed as an event that genuinely took place. Rather, it is actual in that it is an event that derives its meaning from the ordinary social universe as commonly interpreted and lived in. In an exceptional, radical way, the magical conclusion to the story expresses the conflicts that permeate the real social world of the exposition, and blends them into a higher synthesis. Such a synthesis is not possible in the everyday world of man as a social being. For this reason, the closing scene is intimated as strange, unusual—as foreign to the ordinary human universe. Yet, for all its marginality, the mythical ending to the story is a comment on those conflicts to which real men and real societies are prone. Interpretatively, then, this experience is both distinct from and also embedded in the very stuff of social living. It is both strange and familiar, both unreal and real, both exceptional and yet inescapably central.

IV. Chamisso: *Peter Schlemihl**

As a boy of nine, the young French nobleman Louis Charles Adelaide de Chamisso had to leave his homeland in order to escape the French Revolution. He settled in Berlin where he was educated for the Prussian military service. The emergence of his literary gifts coincided with his growing commitment to the German language as the vehicle for his art. Adalbert von Chamisso, as he is known in German literature, is remembered chiefly for his lyric poetry—and for his superb tale *Peter Schlemihls wundersame Geschichte* (*Peter Schlemihl's Wondrous Story*, 1814). It is a work that has often been interpreted in biographical terms. The hero's homelessness is seen as the cipher for Chamisso's loss of his native country, and the conclusion of the story is linked with the world journey that Chamisso undertook between 1815 and 1818—and with the fact that he finally made a career for himself as a botanist. In more general terms, the story has frequently been seen in the context of German Romantic prose writing. Particularly its realistic elements have led critics to see *Peter Schlemihl* as a parody of the Romantic tale with its cult of the wandering, footloose hero. Yet, for all its anti-Romantic qualities, the story is not by any standards a work of down-to-earth realism.

Chamisso's tale raises with particular urgency the problem of how one classifies Romantic short prose writing. The literature of German Romanticism is spectacularly rich in short prose narratives—and for this reason alone it is tempting to assume that the novelle comes to particular prominence at this time. Any such assumption is, however, deeply problematic in view of the immense popularity of

* This chapter is a revised version of my paper "Mundane Magic: Some Observations on Chamisso's *Peter Schlemihl*," *FMLS* 12 (1976). I am grateful to the editors for allowing me to draw on this material here.

another form of short prose narrative—the *Märchen* or fairy tale. The critic soon finds himself wrestling with the knotty question of whether any given Romantic narration is to be accounted a novelle or a *Märchen*. The difficulty is further compounded by the fact that many Romantics produced their own exercises in the *Märchen* form (such stories are usually referred to as *Kunstmärchen* in order to distinguish them from the traditional *Volksmärchen*). Brian Rowley, in a most stimulating discussion of these issues, suggests: "The Romantic 'Novelle' is distinguished from the 'Märchen' by the fact that its action plays in a precisely identified and physically characterized world. This precise orientation, established at the very beginning of many of these stories, is strikingly different in effect from the opening sentences of earlier 'Märchen,' which begin in the 'once upon a time' world of *Der blonde Eckbert*."[1]

While the distinction Rowley makes here has much to commend it, there is the added problem that many Romantic *Kunstmärchen* draw on a traditional narrative convention (the *Volksmärchen*)—but only in order to play a set of highly sophisticated variations on this simple narrative form. It is, for example, very dubious whether stories such as Tieck's *Der blonde Eckbert* or Brentano's *Kasperl und Annerl* sustain that intactness of *Märchen* convention that would allow them to "operate entirely within a magical world."[2] Very frequently we find that Romantic narrative (one thinks particularly of a writer such as E.T.A. Hoffmann) embodies an interpretative dualism, one in which the real and the magical are made not only to coexist but also to overlap. For this reason it could be argued that many Romantic *Kunstmärchen* are in certain vital respects closer to the novelle than they are to the traditional *Volksmärchen*. Even so, it would be very unwise simply to equate *Kunstmärchen* and novelle. Rowley rightly insists that we must distinguish between *das Unerhörte*, "the unprecedented" and *das Wunderbare*, "the supernatural"[3]—although in my view we must

---

[1] "The Novelle," p. 121.   [3] Ibid., p. 121.
[2] Ibid., p. 125.

fatherland, national identity, the social persona, the world of appearances, the integrity of the personality, solidarity with the human community, participation in bourgeois society. While the story certainly does invite this kind of reading, one feels that a degree of violence has to be done to the work in order to transform it into an explicit allegory. Furthermore, the shadow poses certain interpretative problems. My objection to the overtly symbolic readings is that they tend to overlook the crucial interpretative ambiguity of the shadow itself. The shadow, as it functions in the story, is both a nothing and a something, both worthless and infinitely precious. No reading that ignores this dialectic can do justice to the story. Moreover, the shadow acquires meaning not in and of itself, but entirely within the context of people's attitudes to it. Its meaning resides in what it tells us about the people who react to it, who interpret it, who notice it. In itself, it is—and remains—simply a shadow. For this reason it is not, strictly speaking, a symbol. It does not reliably embody anything apart from its own insubstantial existence. This is not to say that it is devoid of overall interpretative significance within the story. If the kind of distinction I have in mind sounds like hairsplitting, one can perhaps clarify the point by means of a comparison. Hugo von Hofmannsthal's *Die Frau ohne Schatten* (*The Woman without a Shadow*) is also concerned with shadowlessness. Yet Hofmannsthal's story operates with a consistently sustained allegorical intensity (and clarity) that Chamisso never achieves. In Hofmannsthal's work the attainment of a shadow is, interpretatively, a known quantity throughout: it represents the acceptance of—and entry into—full humanity. There is no trace of the kind of ambiguity that pervades Chamisso's story. Furthermore, the high seriousness of allegorical intention in *Die Frau ohne Schatten* is apparent in the style, in the narrative tone, in the depiction of events. There is none of the humor, none of the down-to-earth, almost mundane treatment of the magical such as we get in *Peter Schlemihl*. Indeed, actual social reality has little place in Hofmannsthal's story (although it

would seem to be very much part of its theme), precisely
because Hofmannsthal will not allow himself to document
a specific social world in the way that Chamisso does. In *Die
Frau ohne Schatten* everything is handled allegorically; the
characters move through an overtly denotative landscape.
The magical elements are symptomatic of the story's whole
detachment from concrete realities, while in *Peter Schlemihl*
the supernatural is obliged to exist in and work through
the everyday social world. This is the source of much of the
humor in *Peter Schlemihl*—and of its deepest import. The
dialectic of the real and the magical, of the concrete and
the abstract, informs the whole of Chamisso's story and
prevents it from operating at the level of unrelieved allegorical abstraction.

An analysis of the opening pages of *Peter Schlemihl* will, I
hope, suggest some of the specific qualities of this remarkable story and the narrative control with which they are
handled. The story begins with a preface that consists of
three letters, one from Chamisso to his publisher Hitzig,
one from Hitzig to Fouqué, and one from Fouqué to Hitzig. The letters tell us how the story of Peter Schlemihl—
told in his own words—came to be published. It transpires
that both Chamisso and Hitzig knew Schlemihl; Chamisso
on one occasion even took him along to one of his publisher's literary teas. Peter, having written down his life
story, leaves it one night for his friend Chamisso. The latter is obviously touched by what he reads, although he
cannot help feeling that much more could have been made
of it if the tale had been entrusted to a professional
writer—such as Jean Paul. However, as it stands, it has the
authority of personal confession. Fouqué apparently
shares Chamisso's admiration for the story—and has it
published. Obviously, this introduction serves one overriding purpose. It asserts that the story we are about to read is
true, that the man who wrote it actually lived; he was a
friend of well-known German authors and publishers.
Therefore the magical events that he describes did, in fact,
occur in the recognizable world of North German society

in the early years of the nineteenth century. Indeed, it is made clear that when Schlemihl delivered the manuscript to Chamisso's house, he was wearing his seven league boots at the time, a fact that accounts for his rather strange attire—"and in the damp, rainy weather, wearing slippers over his boots" (410).[5] It follows, then, that magic can exist in the world of early nineteenth-century literary Berlin, a world whose objective existence we can verify from standard histories of literature. It is important to note that this opening, which functions as a kind of frame, serves to underpin not only the authenticity of the tale we are about to read but also its interpretative relevance to an unmistakably real social world. Moreover, although the narrative frame (*Rahmen*) is only very brief, consisting as it does of three letters, it continues as an implicit presence throughout Schlemihl's narration. Time and time again he refers to "my dear Chamisso," thus reminding us of the real world that will see fit to publish his manuscript. Hence, the whole urgency of the moral teaching he seeks to express is both derived from and relevant to the society that exists as an objective historical entity. The function of the *Rahmen* is, then, fulfilled here with the most economical of means, for the device is used with its characteristic implications. We are concerned with the interpretative interrelationship between the world of which the narrator tells and the world to which he tells his story.

We then begin with Peter's narration. He describes his arrival in Germany after a long and wearisome sea voyage. His first contact with the bustling, lively society around him occurs when he tries to find hotel accommodation for the night: "I asked for a room; the servant sized me up with a glance and led me to the attic" (413). This encounter sets the seal on what is to follow. Peter has arrived in an acquisitive, money-conscious society from which his relative poverty excludes him. He immediately sets off for Thomas

[5] References throughout are to *Chamissos Werke*, vol. 1. ed. Heinrich Kurz, Hildburghausen (Verlag des Bibliographischen Instituts), 1870.

CHAMISSO: PETER SCHLEMIHL

John's residence, armed with his letter of introduction. He has no difficulty in recognizing the wealthy owner of the mansion: "I recognized the man immediately by the brilliance of his portly self-satisfaction" (413). The formulation here is noteworthy: it derives wit and satirical energy from the surprising yoking of abstract and concrete, and this is a register that will be sustained throughout Peter's narration. The satire is continued in the very next sentence: "He received me very well, as a rich man does a poor devil" (413). We find ourselves in a world dominated by money, by worldly concerns. Furthermore, it is significant that in this story, which is so full of magical events, including even several appearances by the Devil himself, the first reference to the Devil is completely without metaphysical resonance. Schlemihl is a "poor devil" ("*armer Teufel*"). The Devil exists as a component in the colloquial speech of wealthy, leisured society—and as a metaphor expressing the attitudes inherent in that society. Peter manages to give Thomas John the letter of introduction, and the latter receives it with manifest casualness and lofty self-assurance. The patronizing quality in his behavior is suggested by a witty formulation, a formulation which once again unites abstract and concrete, metaphorical and physical: "*Er brach das Siegel auf und das Gespräch nicht ab*" (413f.). ("He broke the seal open—without breaking off the conversation.")

The company moves toward the garden amidst social chatter: "There was flirting and joking, people sometimes spoke seriously of trivial things—and often trivially of serious things" (414). Here the behavior of the society receives explicit moral evaluation; the important becomes trivial and the trivial important. Yet the full implications of this are something to which Peter is largely blind; he is infatuated with the glittering world around him and is dominated by a burning desire to participate in it (as we see from his full-blooded assent to Thomas John's remark that whoever is not a millionaire is a scoundrel—a remark that involves a simple equation of worldly success and moral value). Peter, then, is in an ambivalent situation; he is dazzled by a world of which he is not yet a part. He has the detachment that enables him to feel—and to see—the strangeness of the way of life this society embodies, and yet it is a detachment that is not allowed to ripen into a fully critical attitude because he desperately wants to become part of the world he observes.

At this stage in the story, the man in gray makes his first appearance. One of the ladies scratches her hand on a thorn, and requests sticking plaster. A somewhat insignificant man whom Peter has hitherto not noticed produces the desired article—"and gave it to the lady with a devoted bow. She took it without thanks—and without paying any attention to the giver" (414). This incident is the first of many; the man in gray shows a quite remarkable ability to minister to the needs of the company. He produces a Dollond telescope (the mention of the make underscores the point that the gray man is the inexhaustible purveyor of the practical articles and manufactured goods by which this society sets such store). The telescope is used by the company—but it is not returned to its owner. He then provides "with a modest, indeed humble gesture" (415) a Turkish carpet, which is accepted by the servants as a matter of course. Only Schlemihl is astonished at the gray man's inexhaustible supply of goods, and yet he is uncertain what to make of his own surprise "especially as no one found anything remarkable in it" (415). His attempts to find out more about the gray man fail; nobody seems to know him, nor even to want to know him. His remarkable powers are taken for granted. One of the guests now turns to ask if he has a tent with him, and the man, "as though he were the recipient of an undeserved honor" (416), produces even this. This is the first time that anyone has spoken to the man—and, characteristically, it is a request for further goods. The gray man obliges—"and nobody found it at all unusual" (416). Peter becomes more and more troubled: "For some time now I had been feeling unsettled, yes frightened" (416). Yet there is more to come, and the gray man produces three horses from his pocket. The hapless Peter can only reassure the friend for whom he is writing the story (Chamisso) that all these things really happened, that he saw them with his own eyes. Schlemihl feels so unsettled that he decides to leave the party, but he is foiled by the gray man.

Before one analyzes the conversation that ensues, it is appropriate to summarize the interpretative implications of the behavior of the gray man up to this point. First, one should notice that the magic is introduced gradually into the story; only when the gray man produces the carpet from his pocket does the reader begin to suspect that he is some supernatural figure. Quite apart from the fact that the opening feats involve deeds that are well within the realm of physical possibility, we do not suspect anything unusual about the gray man because he is so much anchored in a carefully documented social role—that of the servant. That social role is not changed in the slightest even when the tasks he performs become more and more prodigious. He continues to behave as the perfect servant, ready to fulfill any and every whim of his wealthy masters. It is because the framework of his behavior is one of social normality that none of the guests at Thomas John's garden party thinks twice about the physical impossibility of his last two actions. This is a society that is used to having every conceivable wish granted immediately. It is a society that is completely dependent on the ready supply of goods and services, that is used to the fact that physical difficulty and practical obstacles can always be overcome, provided one has enough money. Everything—the physically possible and the physically impossible—exists on the same level, the level of instantaneous availability. The man in gray (the Devil) knows that the society is vulnerable in terms of its complete dependence on an army of servants who will carry out every command and fulfill every wish. Hence, by assuming the role of perfect social servant, he gains power over the members of that society. He himself does not draw attention to the prodigies he performs—this would be inappropriate in terms of his chosen social function. He behaves with the silent, devoted deference that the society expects, and for this reason he stifles any possible awareness on the part of the social world that there is something unusual or sinister about him. Only Peter, who is not yet a member of that society, notices how unusual the behavior of the man in gray is. Yet his infatuation with the wealthy society around him prevents him from drawing the necessary conclusions from this perception; he does not see that if the gray man's behavior is sinister, then the kind of social ethos it serves and helps to reinforce is also sinister. There is one particularly revealing moment in the scene when Peter comments—in an untranslatable pun—that he was almost more afraid of the servants than he was of the masters: *"ich fürchtete mich fast noch mehr vor den Herren Bedienten als vor den bedienten Herren"* (415). The verbal wit, the neatly turned pun is, as I have already suggested, typical of much of the narration. It involves not simply gratuitous linguistic exuberance, but an important perception of the particular social situation before him. The servants are, in fact, as much "masters" as the masters whom they serve. This is to develop into one of the major themes of the story.

Because the gray man has noticed Schlemihl's overwhelming desire to join the acquisitive society from which he is at present excluded, he approaches Peter and suggests a bargain to him. In proposing the bargain, he adopts precisely the register that he has already employed with such effectiveness: "He at once removed his hat and bowed more deeply to me than anybody had done before" (416). Peter is terrified and responds in the same vein: "I took my hat off too, bowed again, and stood there, bareheaded in the sun, as though rooted to the spot" (416). The man in gray then intensifies the expressions of his subservience: "He himself seemed to be very embarrassed; he did not lift his eyes from the ground, bowed frequently, approached me and spoke in a quiet, uncertain voice, roughly in the tones of a beggar" (416f.). This section reads like a kind of comic ballet. Both participants seem to be ter

concludes that the man in gray is not just odd—he must be mad. This crucial step forces him into a role of superiority: "He must be mad, I thought, and with a different tone that accorded better with the humility of his, I therefore replied: 'Come, come, my good man, is your own shadow not sufficient for you? That's what I call a proposition of a very strange kind' " (417). The arrogant tone, the inherent loftiness is the sign that Schlemihl has lost the battle. The sheer charm of being superior, of having someone of the gray man's extraordinary capabilities at his disposal, proves too much. The Devil makes his proposal that in exchange for the shadow he will offer Schlemihl some of the many treasures he has in his pocket. The mention of the pocket recalls to Schlemihl what he has seen only minutes before, and he regrets his patronizing tone. Instinctively he tries to get out of the present dangerous situation in which he has placed himself by returning to the subservient role: "I spoke again and endeavored to repair the damage by being immensely polite" (417). When he speaks, he refers to himself as the "most humble servant" of the man in gray. Yet he makes one crucial mistake: instead of repudiating the bargain that has been proposed, he asserts its impracticability. As we have already seen, physical difficulties are no problem for the man in gray: "I would only ask your gracious permission to pick up this noble shadow here on the spot and to pocket it; how I shall do it can safely be left to me" (417). The objection on practical grounds allows the Devil to interrupt with the simple assertion (so much a part of his role) that such difficulties are no problem for him. With the subservience of the good salesman he lists the various articles he has to offer, culminating in the offer of a "free trial." Schlemihl pulls gold coins out of the bag and without any further hesitation accepts the bargain. The Devil shakes his hand, and "with admirable skillfulness" (418) he lifts the shadow from the grass, rolls it up, folds it, and puts it in his pocket. The ending of the first encounter between Schlemihl and the man in gray is as unspectacular, as ordinary, as bound to the practicalities of concrete exist-

abstract and the concrete, of the grandiose and the every-day. The tension between these two registers means that the story never loses contact with the simple facts of social experience. One remembers the curiously puncturing quality of the following description of Schlemihl's despair: "Oh, what would I not have given then for a shadow! I had to bury my shame, my fear, my desperation in the depths of my carriage" (427). What we expect here is the phrase "in the depths of my heart." What we read is the relentless reminder of the sheer unrelieved *practicality* of the problem; Schlemihl has to hide his grief where no one will notice his shadowlessness.[7] More important are those moments where the strangeness of Schlemihl's situation makes the language he uses comment on itself. When our hero encounters a shadow running along without an owner, he concludes that the man in question must be wearing the magic bird's nest. He introduces his explanation with the following words: "Now the whole occurrence became naturally explicable" (441). Obviously, the explanation given is—on our terms—anything but "natural," but, in the context of Schlemihl's existence, it is perfectly "natural." The language here reminds us that what is natural is largely a question of interpretative context—and not of factual possibility or impossibility. A similar effect is achieved when the Devil refers to himself as "a poor devil" (437), or when he justifies his behavior with the time-honored phrase "the devil is not as black as he is painted" (449). Both the tone—and the sentiments expressed—are in keeping with the undaemonic gray man; he is, after all, only an impeccable social servant, a man who has power insofar as the prevailing social ethos allows him to be power-ful. Indeed, at one point, he sounds like a thoroughly reliable pawnbroker: "Allow me to show you that I do not let the things that I buy accumulate mold; I look after them well, they are in good hands" (438). In such moments of linguistic subtlety Chamisso sustains that interplay of the

---

[7] See Stuart Atkins's argument that *Peter Schlemihl* is a satire on the lacrymose effusions of contemporary novel-writing ("*Peter Schlemihl* in Relation to the Popular Novel of the Romantic Period").

magical and the mundane, of the foreign and the familiar, that is central to the story's meaning.

The function of the shadow is consistent with the dialectic that informs both the events and the language of the story. Interpretatively, the shadow is linked with a whole series of supernatural occurrences and is at the same time embedded in the moral and social attitudes of real people. In this sense, it conveys a whole complex of meanings— without in itself being the reliable symbol "for" any one thing. Indeed, the shadow fulfills an ambiguous function within the context of people's attitudes to Peter's plight. At one level, all the characters with whom he comes into contact sense that there is something wrong about his lack of a shadow. In part at least, their judgment stands as an indictment of the main character, as a reliable indication of his betrayal of his own humanity. On the other hand, much of their instinctive revulsion reflects not simply on Peter but on themselves; they seem spiteful and small-minded, as in the self-righteous, uncaring reaction of the boys: "Decent people are in the habit of taking their shadows with them when they go walking in broad daylight" (419). The shadow may be important, but it is not all-important. Precisely this dialectic is embodied in the attitude of Bendel, who is both critical and compassionate. His first comment is: "Woe is me that I was born to serve a shadowless master!" (424). Then he modifies this to "Whatever the world says, I cannot and will not leave my kind master because of a shadow" (424), and thus distances himself from the uncharitable and prejudiced views of worldly wisdom.

The essential point about the shadow is that while Peter's ability to dispose of it is, by definition, a magical event, the implications of this action (both before and after the event) are moral and social—rather than metaphysical. Of course, the metaphysical dimension does enter the story when the man in gray offers Peter the traditional Devil's pact (involving the soul of his victim). However, interpretatively, this confrontation represents a metaphorical underpinning of the moral vision that is the substance of the story.

What Chamisso offers us is much more than a straightforward social satire, much more than a simple assertion that "money is the root of all evil." Rather, he conveys the confusion, the psychological and moral uprootedness that the inherent paradoxes of this specific kind of society implant in the individual. Early in the story, when Peter has for the first time experienced the unpleasant consequences that his shadowlessness brings, he reflects that on earth the shadow is prized more highly than gold, and that gold, in its turn, is felt to be worth more than justice or decency: "That here on earth, by as much as gold is felt to be more valuable than achievement or virtue, by so much is the shadow rated more highly even than gold" (419). Schlemihl is here talking not of his own personal attitudes—but of the consensus of worldly opinion. The crucial term is *schätzen*—"to rate." Society's *Schätzung* is ambivalent. On the one hand, people rate money far above moral virtue (in that they are prepared to sell even human values and relationships—Minna's parents will make sure that their daughter is married off to the highest bidder). On the other hand, money can only be worshiped with impunity in certain socially acceptable contexts. Marriage is one, profitable evasion of creditors is another; one thinks, for example, of the "businessman, who had gone bankrupt in order to add to his wealth, who enjoyed general respect, and who cast a broad, although somewhat pale shadow" (430). Schlemihl's moral guilt is one that is shared by most of the people with whom he comes into contact. What distinguishes him is the radical consequences of his attitude, consequences that are extreme to the point of involving magic. The actual sale of the shadow puts Schlemihl beyond the pale. Yet, in moral terms, the damage done to other people by his thoughtless action is much less than that done by the many "acceptable" bargains. Here we come to one crucial aspect of the shadow in this story: when the Devil first proposes his transaction to Schlemihl, he says: "For this invaluable (*unschätzbar*) shadow I consider the highest price too low" (417). Once again, we have the notion of *Schätzung*. It is in this whole question of evaluation within both social and moral value scales that the central meaning of the shadow—and of Chamisso's story—resides.

In the word *unschätzbar* two value scales—and their largely contradictory relationship to one another—are suggested. Within the context of the practical, monetary value scale of the acquisitive society portrayed in this story, the shadow is quite simply worthless. Yet in terms of a different, less easily definable value scale, the shadow is priceless, it is invaluable precisely because it is of a different order from those things that can be assessed in terms of quantifiable exchange-value, of price. The social universe to which Peter so eagerly desires access is almost exclusively dominated by the first scale. And even when it notices Peter's shadowlessness and repudiates him for it, it does so at the debased—and reified—level of Minna's father who says: "I will give you three days' grace in which you might care to cast around for a shadow" (436). One notes the use of the indefinite article here; any shadow will do, it does not have to be Peter's. The people impute a false value to the shadow when they conceive of it as a thing, as something one owns, as part of one's socially necessary equipment (like money, clothes, possessions). Hermann Weigand makes the interesting point that the shadow, once handled by the Devil, assumes magical properties in that "it can be manipulated, rolled up, and unfolded for display, like a substantial physical object."[8] Everything the Devil touches becomes reduced to the level of a barterable object. When Peter refuses the final exchange the man in gray offers him, he vindicates the scale of values to which he has hitherto been blind, the value of the *unschätzbar*. At this point he distances himself from the norms of the society around him. For the obsession with material possessions, with goods and services, affects the quality of life of the members of this society. Everything is, as it were, for sale; everything is potentially available. The only distinctions are those of quantity (of how many currency units article A

[8] Hermann J. Weigand, "*Peter Schlemihl*," p. 210.

costs as against article B). There is no awareness of ultimately qualitative distinctions, of the fact that article A may
be of a different order from article B. This involves a dras-
tic reduction of man's possible evaluative responses to the
world in which he lives. In a strange way—for all the mate-
rialism of the society—reality is converted into something
weightless and abstract.[9] Ready exchangeability removes
distinctions; above all, it removes the human capacity to
perceive and act upon distinctions. Hence, the entry of
magic into this social world constitutes a radical expression
of the kind of human ethos that prevails; in no sense does it
suggest a transcendence of the materialist ethos.

When Peter sells his shadow for money, he disposes of
one part of the simple clutter that surrounds human existence on this planet. He sells part of the *donnée* of the
human universe, a part that cannot be evaluated in terms
of practical use or monetary significance. By doing so he
starts on the path toward selling his soul. Yet Peter is able
to call a halt to this process; he instinctively recoils from the
final exchange possibility, although the Devil's arguments
are splendidly persuasive and consistent. The Devil offers
him, in essence, a repeat of the first bargain: the opportunity to exchange something of no demonstrable value for
something that is of immediate practical use. The only
change vis-à-vis the first bargain is that the shadow has now
become the "solid" piece of goods—the soul is the useless
appendage:

> And, if I may ask, what sort of a thing is it, this soul of
> yours? Have you ever seen it, and what do you propose
> doing with it once you are dead? You should be grateful
> that you have found an enthusiast, someone who is pre-
> pared, during your lifetime, to pay for the residue of this

[9] Compare Benno von Wiese's telling point: "In spite of—or perhaps
precisely on account of—this social function, money becomes something
chimerical, fluid, and inconstant—and, therefore, something unreliable"
(*Die deutsche Novelle von Goethe bis Kafka*, vol. 1, p. 111). See also Ralph
Flores, "The Lost Shadow of Peter Schlemihl," pp. 576–577, for a fine discussion of Peter's money as wealth unearned by labor.

X, of this galvanizing force or polarizing energy—or whatever else the silly thing is supposed to be—with something real, namely with your own, actual shadow, by means of which you can obtain the hand of your beloved and the fulfillment of all your wishes (437).

The language here subtly stresses the pragmatic value scale. If the soul is not a thing of demonstrable usefulness (and only *things* are of demonstrable usefulness), then it can simply be disposed of. The Devil argues that, whereas the soul is not a "*Ding*," a "thing," the shadow is in every sense "*leibhaftig*," "actual." Furthermore, the Devil reasserts his role of the eager servant-cum-buyer; Schlemihl should be glad to find someone who is prepared to offer substantial payment for such an insignificant trifle as the soul. (The appeal has been used before in the first bargain when the Devil comments on the casualness with which Schlemihl performs the task of casting a good shadow.) Yet this is one attempt at salesmanship where the Devil fails— although his defeat is due more to deeply engrained, instinctive responses in Schlemihl than to any precise understanding of the issues involved.

It is, in my view, important to insist on the predominantly social reading of the story that I have given above, because it helps to account not simply for the sequence of events in the work but also for its narrative mode. It also highlights the importance of certain carefully articulated themes. I have, for example, already insisted on the frequency with which the Devil plays the role of impeccable servant. The relationship of master and servant is a vital concern in the story. The wealthy society to which Schlemihl gains access is dependent upon being served by both people and goods. Moreover, in this process the "masters" become the slaves of the "servants." It is important to note that when Schlemihl is betrayed, it is by the one figure who has real power over him—the servant Raskal. Hence, Schlemihl needs the offices of his good servant Bendel at every turn in order to keep unpleasant consequences at bay. This is, at one level, the simple result of practical difficulties that stem from his shadowlessness. At another level, however, much more is involved. The story of Schlemihl's life is a radical enactment of implications inherent in the social experience of his time; and his utter dependence on being protected by his servant is symptomatic of the encapsulated existence led by the wealthy figures who gather at Thomas John's garden party. Whole dimensions of human experiences (and of human responses) have to be kept at bay, and the welter of servant figures expresses the sheer timorousness, the existential fragility of the world that their masters inhabit. Ultimately, Schlemihl is able to repudiate and break out of this world. The ending of the story is conciliatory in that Schlemihl, while remaining an outcast, is enabled by the lucky acquisition of some seven league boots to find a purpose in life. This purpose seems, at first sight, a rather peculiar one. Obviously, the hero's ability to travel, to explore the natural world, is a source of comfort to him; but one must note the specific nature of the exploration that is involved. Schlemihl is not concerned to observe spectacular natural phenomena; rather, his relationship to nature is as prosaic as the slippers he has to wear over his magic boots. He becomes a scientist, a cataloguer of natural phenomena, who lists not the great wonders of the world, but simply the ordinary stuff of which this planet is made up. Literary-historical explanations of the ending (which refer us to the *Biedermeier* ethos, to the basically conservative mood that succeeds the excesses of Romanticism) are not, in themselves, sufficient to account for the ending to this story. Purely within the context of the work, however, the ending in my view makes perfect sense. If Schlemihl's sin in selling his shadow concerns the inability to cherish the simple, and, in itself, unremarkable and unimportant clutter of life on earth, then surely his career as a botanist is the sustained enactment of the lesson he has learned. The Schlemihl of the closing pages of the story is someone who devotes his life to the careful, reverent cataloguing of the facts of this world. These facts are not in themselves significant; but they acquire significance in terms of the kind of response they can elicit from man. As with the shadow, the human attitude is all-important, and is the source of meaning. A reverent cherishing of such things implies the awareness of a value scale that operates completely without reference to notions of monetary quantifiability—or of practical usefulness. Schlemihl's botanizing activities are the assertion of the value of the *unschätzbar*, of the worth of the invaluable.

In Chamisso's story, the whole complex of themes is brought into interpretative focus by means of the shadow. That shadow is a nothing and a something, an insubstantial factor within man's existence, but one that can have value nonetheless; it is a human attribute—but of an utterly intangible kind, an absence and a presence. Within the money-conscious society of this story the concrete facts of man's life are rendered insubstantial by their interchangeability, whereas money, that very agent of interchangeability, that abstraction from actual goods and objects, becomes the one and only hard fact. In this blurred and topsy-turvy world the shadow—and the interpretative problem it poses for us the readers—functions as the paradigm for that uncertain moral and social situation that the story so brilliantly explores.

Peter's selling of his shadow is, in terms of novelle theory, an obvious example of the unique and unprecedented event that embodies the central concern of the story. Yet the story is also imbued with an awareness of practical reality, of the utterly familiar conventions and values of money-conscious society. The friction between—and the interlocking of—these two worlds, the magical and the mundane, is the raison d'être of the story. The narration makes us realize that, paradoxically, the magical, exceptional event is the most radical enactment of what is *potentially* inherent in the set of given social attitudes. In our reading of the shadow we come to realize

V. Büchner: *Lenz*

Georg Büchner's was a short life; he died at the age of twenty-four in 1837. His literary work, although it is anything but bulky (consisting of three plays and one novelle), came to be recognized late in the nineteenth century as a prodigious achievement. Büchner has been hailed as one of the seminal writers of the post-Romantic era: as a superbly tenacious realist, a man deeply aware of the extent to which history and society shape the fate of man; as a writer who constantly articulates the sense of a world bereft of any metaphysical anchorage; as a master of thoroughgoing psychological insight. In many of his works Büchner portrays the individual in the grip of forces (be they historical or psychological) that are outside his control. His one novelle *Lenz* is no exception. In this story Büchner concerns himself with a mind whose hold on reality becomes ever more precarious as the sparse events that constitute the plot unfold.

The story opens with a description of Lenz's journey through a mountainous landscape. The first mention of his reaction to this natural world is: "Indifferently, he walked on; the path he took, now ascending, now descending, did not matter to him. He felt no tiredness; only it occasionally irked him that he could not walk on his head" (79).[1] A few sentences later we read: "Everything struck him as so small, so near, so damp; he would have liked to stow the earth behind the stove. He did not understand that it should take so long to climb down a slope, to reach a distant point; he thought he should have been able to cover everything in a few steps" (79). Both these statements serve to define Lenz's psychological condition at the beginning of the story. Two points should be noted: first, the dislocation and

[1] References throughout are to Georg Büchner, *Sämtliche Werke und Briefe*, vol. 1, ed. W. R. Lehmann, Hamburg, 1967.

boredom, the indifference (*Gleichgültigkeit*); second, Lenz's wildly unfocused perception of the world around him, the sense of the closeness and smallness of everything—a sense that is contradicted by his actual experience of how long it takes him to get from one point to another. A further response to the natural world is suggested a few sentences later when we are told of moments when "he felt he must draw the storm to himself, take everything into him, he stretched himself out and lay over the earth, he bored his way into the All, it was a pleasure that hurt him" (79f.). From such passages the reader gains a clear picture of the state of mind in which Lenz arrives at the house of Pastor Oberlin. It is a mind already unhinged, in the sense that there is no coherent and sustaining relationship to the world. Instead there are periods of utter indifference when the world becomes a small, indeed negligible entity, there are periods when it becomes a massive, physically assaulting experience. Lenz's mind moves uneasily within this spectrum of possible responses. This restless movement is symptomatic of his incipient madness, of his alienation from the world as binding reality.

The story Büchner tells grows with terrible and inevitable logic from this opening portrayal. However much the story enters Lenz's mind and renders with sharp immediacy the inner turmoil of the man, it does not simply become an uncontrolled series of "mood pictures." Büchner argues out the process of mental disintegration with great thematic and stylistic tautness.[2] He shows how his protagonist is increasingly torn asunder by the various possible relationships to the world inherent in his psychological state. The concluding register is the one with which the story opens—indifference. Except that, at the end of the story, there is no struggle left any more, no tension, no friction. The mind succumbs to a total loss of relationship to the world, and ceases even to know the enormity of its loss.

---

[2] Of the several structural analyses of the story I would single out particularly Erna K. Neuse, "Büchners *Lenz*," and Heinz Fischer, *Georg Büchner*, pp.18ff.

Lenz's calm at the end of the story is the calm of living death.

The process by which Lenz moves from the precariousness of his opening state to irrevocable collapse is argued by Büchner in terms of a series of tensions to which his hero is prone, tensions in which one perception of world conflicts with another. At the simplest level, this involves a sustained interplay of dialectics in the story, as Lenz oscillates between loss of contact with the world on the one hand and desperate, self-lacerating surrender to its physical presence on the other. There are also image patterns of cold and heat, dark and light, emptiness and fullness, isolation and communion, boredom and pain.[3] The violent oscillations are symptomatic not only of Lenz's alienation from the world, but also of his frantic attempts to answer the deadness that threatens to engulf him by making himself feel in touch with the world through hurtful exposure to shock. Hence, as Stern has argued, pain becomes the last-ditch proof of his own—and the world's—actual existence.[4] Yet the very extremism of the two poles means that the dialectic that encompasses them becomes stretched to breaking point. Gradually, in terms of the color imagery of the story, the grayness of boredom swallows up even the vivid red of pain, gradually even the nameless, blinding *Angst* gives place to utter indifference.

As a depiction of madness, *Lenz* is remarkable for the combination of structural control and imaginative empathy with which the subject matter is handled. The balance of intimacy and detachment is central to the overall impact that the story makes, and it is mediated through the narrative perspective. Obviously, the fact that the story is a third-person narrative means that we, the readers, are made—at one level—to stand outside the protagonist, to

[3] One could also add to this list the dialectic of stasis and movement, of *Geborgenheit* and *Unruhe* (see Peter Hasubek's perceptive study, " 'Ruhe' und 'Bewegung.' ")

[4] J. P. Stern, *Re-Interpretations*, pp. 104ff. Throughout this paper I am indebted to Stern's profoundly illuminating study.

view him through the eyes of a dispassionate observer. Thus there is a curiously sober, factual register that recurs throughout the story. It allows us to know as facts the world through which Lenz moves, to see as facts the actions he performs.[5] And, of course, much of the narrative is indebted to Oberlin's account of Lenz's behavior. Büchner remains close to this source material without attempting to play down the extent to which it is clear, sensible reportage. What Büchner adds to the Oberlin account is the whole depiction of the world as perceived through the distorting agency of Lenz's unhinged mind. At times this is achieved by the straightforward introduction of indirect speech, at times it is conveyed by means of a construction such as "*ihm war*" ("he felt"), at times it is attained by the use of "*erlebte Rede*" (free indirect speech) whereby the narrator simply adopts Lenz's perspective without comment. There is, then, a whole spectrum of narrative modes that allows the factual report to be colored by the protagonist's own highly charged response to the world around him—while never obliterating the register of sober reportage. At first sight, the net result might seem to be a curiously dislocated set of possible perspectives, but the overall import is anything but fragmented. We are never asked to forget that Lenz's is a mind unhinged, and this surely is central to Büchner's meaning; if madness is loss of relationship to the world, is alienation from the facts of experience, then the narrative must consistently intimate the binding presence of those facts upon which Lenz's hold becomes ever more tenuous. Furthermore, it must also intimate not simply the concrete reality of the objects present, but also the possibility of valuable and sustaining moral activity for human beings. In this sense, the real world that the narrator constantly acknowledges is affirmed both philosophically and ethically. Yet this is not all that Büchner wishes to convey. His

---

[5] On the crucial implications of the narrative perspective in this story (and on the transformation of the Oberlin source) see H. P. Pütz, "Büchners *Lenz* und seine Quelle." See also Herbert Lindenberger's persuasive analysis in his study *Georg Büchner*.

analysis of the mad mind is anything but a simple case history, anything but an unproblematic assertion of the discrepancy between reality on the one hand and the individual capacity for psychological aberration on the other. The narrator does not choose to remain consistently outside the mad mind; hence, he will not allow his readers to remain outside that mind. In a feat of extraordinary imaginative empathy the narrative voice enters the mad mind and makes us share the devastating intensity of human response of which that mind is capable. It is an intensity that derives not from an exuberantly solipsistic fantasy, not from the endless creation of dream-worlds, but from a kind of helpless, unprotected exposure to certain kinds of—albeit dislocated—sense impression. Lenz's mind is defenseless before those sharp fragments of the world that pierce through his alienation. He is unable to hold what he perceives in any kind of perspective; distant things suddenly come up close, nearby things can withdraw into extinction. Yet what is involved here is both perception and interpretation. Because Lenz finds himself existing outside the perceptual framework of ordinary humanity, he is excluded from the normally interpreted, habitable universe. Once one admits the possibility that common human certainty rests on an interpretation of the facts that surround the individual mind, it follows that Lenz's perception becomes *another* interpretation, one that may reveal things that are normally obscured by accepted conventions. It is in this sense, as Stern has so brilliantly argued,[6] that Büchner makes use of the mad mind to comment on the accepted universe, that Lenz's viewpoint acquires a kind of existential relevance. This is not, of course, to say that he is indulging in a simple inversion whereby the sane mind is mad and the mad sane. There is never any doubt in the story that Lenz *is* mad—and this leads to a powerful note of regret for the sheer human waste involved. Yet the mad mind is made to relativize the accepted human interpreta-

[6] *Re-Interpretations*, pp. 137ff.

tions. Paradoxically, the mad or alienated mind is able to *see* precisely by virtue of its alienation, precisely because it does not have recourse to the prejudgments of the commonly accepted interpretation. The strangeness of Lenz's perception helps us, the readers, to see afresh. One is reminded of Brecht's aim of presenting an alienated image of the social world in order to peel away the "stamp of the familiar" from experience.[7] One is also reminded of Aldous Huxley's comment on the perceptual gain—and the threatening implications—of the drug-taker's perspective: "The fear, as I analyze it in retrospect, was of being overwhelmed, of disintegrating under a pressure of reality greater than a mind accustomed to living most of the time in a cosy world of symbols could possibly bear."[8] It is on these terms that the alienated mind matters to us; and in Büchner's story this is conveyed through the narrative presentation. Furthermore, if we ask by what stylistic means this story is able to intimate the relevance of the alienated mind, the answer must reside in the sheer imaginative and linguistic intensity with which Lenz's perception is presented to us. It is crucially important to note that Lenz's vision thereby acquires a *poetic* intensity and persuasiveness that is the deepest source of its significance. For this reason, the whole nature of artistic—and poetic—seeing and expression is one of the deepest concerns of this story (involving much more than the overt formulations of the *Kunstgespräch* section, the discussion about art).

The point can be made most clearly by specific analyses, and to this end I wish to look in some detail at two passages, both of which are concerned with description of the natural world. The first is taken from the first page or so of the story. The opening sentences are completely sober, laconically sketching in the necessary details: "On January 20 Lenz went through the mountains. The peaks and high mountain slopes snow-clad, down the valleys gray masses of stone, green patches, rocks and pine trees" (79). We

---

[7] Bertolt Brecht, *Kleines Organon für das Theater*, sect. 43.

[8] Aldous Huxley, *The Doors of Perception*, Harmondsworth, 1960, p. 46.

begin on a note of sparse reportage, with no particular stylistic intensity or pressure. However, the urgency soon enters the story as a personal note is struck and an emotive response to the landscape is hinted at: "It was wet cold, the water trickled down the rocks and bounded over the path. The boughs of the pines hung heavily down in the damp air. Gray clouds tracked across the sky, but everything so thick, and then the mist rose up as steam and moved slow and damp through the undergrowth, so lazy, so dull" (79). Strangely, however, these sentences contain no explicit mention of Lenz himself; the emotive response—the sense of excessive heaviness, of oppressiveness in the land-scape—would, then, appear to be attested to by the narrator. Syntactically, these are *his* observations. Hence, the first few sentences of the story establish the two regis-ters within the narrative voice—that of sober reportage and that of emotive evaluation and response.

Almost immediately, the descriptive energy is intensified as we read: "At first his heart felt constricted when the stone broke away like that, when the gray forest shook under him and the mist now concealed outlines, now half-revealed mighty limbs" (79). The construction here is im-portant, because at the simplest level the syntax of the sen-tence suggests that Lenz's reaction results from objective happenings in the natural world, that Lenz is not imposing his own responses onto—and thereby distorting—the nat-ural world, but that his responses are *produced* by external facts. Of course, we are in uncertain territory here. We suspect that the narrator is—without admitting it—rendering Lenz's perception at this point. We may conjec-ture as much; but the fact remains that the narrator simply offers *his* description of those events that so oppress Lenz. The same is true of the enormous sentence that dominates the first page or so of the story:

> Only sometimes when the storm hurled the cloud masses
> into the valley and the steam rose up from the forest and
> the voices awoke and rebounded from the rocks, now
> like distant fading thunder, and then roaring mightily

upward as though with their clamor they wanted to celebrate the earth in their wild tumult, and the clouds
galloped toward him like wild neighing horses, and the
sunshine came and went between them and passed its
shining sword over the snow-covered slopes so that a
bright, dazzling light cut its way over the peaks and into
the valleys; or when the storm drove the cloud masses
downward and tore open a light blue lake in them, and
then the wind died away and from down below, from the
chasms, from the tops of the pines sent its humming upward like a lullaby, like a peal of bells, and a gentle red
climbed up the deep blue, and small clouds sailed along
on silvery wings and all mountain peaks, sharp and clear,
shone and sparkled far over the land, it tore at his heart,
he stood, panting, his body bent forward, eyes and
mouth wide open . . . (79).

Once again, the depiction of the natural landscape is given
with the authority of what seems to be the narrator's perspective; Lenz's anguish is produced by certain phenomena that are described and evoked by the narrator.
On the other hand, the sentence is only completed syntactically at the moment when it catalogues Lenz's reaction to
the violence of the storm. It is, therefore, essentially concerned with the protagonist's responses, and we may therefore suspect that the seemingly objective cause-and-effect
sequence is nowhere near so clear-cut as the narrator
makes it appear. Yet we must remember that the narrator
is prepared, elsewhere in the story, to enter Lenz's mind
and to signal quite clearly the fact that he is writing not
from his own but from the protagonist's perspective. Presumably, therefore, if he does not adopt this method in the
opening section of the story, he chooses not to do so. It is
almost as though he is prepared to allow his voice—and
perception—to overlap with Lenz's but without ever getting to the point of forfeiting his own separate identity.
Why should this be? The answer, in my view, lies in the
crucial problem of the "poetic" relevance of Lenz's an-

guished vision. The narrator allows himself an imaginatively charged description of the storm to suggest the level at which—for all its hallucinations—Lenz's mind will matter to us, will be utterly and terribly relevant. The narrator in this story is not just a cataloguer of facts, an observer of what actually happens. He is also a poet who will attempt to interpret what he depicts, who will render not just actualities but the meaning facts acquire by becoming part of man's interpreted universe. The narrative voice—at its most poetic—reminds us of those passages that explicitly re-create the delusions that pass through Lenz's mind. For this reason, we find ourselves unable to keep the mad mind at a safe distance, we are forced to acknowledge our common ground with the hapless protagonist. Yet, of course, the narrator's description of the storm-filled landscape also intimates the difference between the poetic description of the world and the delusions of a madman. In the narrator's description of the storm one notices the recurrence of images, and in these images resides the creativity, the poetic power of the passage. Some of these images make explicit the introduction of analogues: "now like fading thunder," "as though with their clamor they wanted to celebrate the earth," "clouds like wild, neighing horses," "like a lullaby." Other images do not explicitly signal this analogizing process; they anchor it without comment in the very stuff of the experiences they evoke: "the voices awoke and rebounded," "when the sunshine passed its shining sword over the snow-covered slopes." Of course, none of this is in any way unfamiliar to us. We are perfectly used to this kind of writing, we have technical terms such as *simile* and *metaphor* that designate the figures of speech used. This is poetic language; but it is not only poetic language, it is also "our" language, human language. We are able to understand simile and metaphor when a poet uses them—for the quite simple reason that we use them ourselves, that we know of these resources from our own experience of language. For all the overlap, however, between the figurative use of language and the manic power of Lenz's visions, there is an important difference to be observed, a difference that is nonetheless valid for being one of degree and not one of kind. The narrator's images attempt to evoke the sheer animation of the scene he is describing, the analogues partake of and sustain the reality, whereas in Lenz's outbursts the analogues so take possession of the real that they tend to obliterate it to the point where we feel that mind and world are no longer interacting. Indeed, we feel that the mind has made reality the cipher for its present state: " 'Now I feel so confined, so confined, you see, it is sometimes as though my hands were knocking against the sky' " (92). Or again: "So he came to the top of the mountain, and the uncertain light spread down to where the white masses of stone lay, and the sky was a silly blue eye, and the moon stood quite ludicrously in it—stupid" (94). Or again: " 'Do you hear nothing, do you not hear the terrible voice that screams round the whole horizon and that is normally called silence? Since I have been in this peaceful valley I hear it always' " (100).

All these perceptions of the world are not intrinsically foreign to our experience; we could be persuaded of them as a poetic truth about the world we all inhabit. Yet they have in common a certain radicalism, a forcing of the perception to the point where the link with our world is stretched to breaking point. The story forces us into an ambivalent situation with regard to such statements; it asks for both our assent and our rejection, for association and dissociation. In just the same way, the narrative perspective is ambivalent in its interpretative relationship to the protagonist. It can be dissociated in that it adopts the register of the factual report, viewing Lenz's behavior from the outside; it can be associated in that it allows itself a poetic rendering of the natural world whereby it comes close to the kind of linguistic vividness and stylistic intensity that characterize Lenz's anguished visions.

A brief discussion of a second passage—the closing

rator's evocation of the sunset. For the last time in the story, the narrator's poetic register sounds as he conveys to us the sheer replete glory of the moonlit night. We notice the all-important presence of images. The narrator is not simply being factual here; he is interpreting the scene, he is giving it meaning by entering it imaginatively. The mountains are "like a deep blue wave of crystal," the earth is "like a golden goblet over which the golden waves of the moon ran foaming." The imaginative intensity of the narrator's description here would seem to contrast strangely with the spare, laconic account of Lenz's resignation and indifference. One asks oneself why the description is there, above all why the narrative should become so dramatically charged for these few sentences. Far from being an irrelevancy, a stylistic excrescence, this descriptive passage in my view unmistakably belongs to the argument of the story as a whole. At one level, it serves to heighten the poignancy of Lenz's utter emptiness. If madness in this story is shown as alienation from the real world, then the closing scene shows that splendor of which the protagonist is now irrevocably denied all knowledge. The sense of loss, of deprivation, is almost unbearable. At another level, the narrator's description reminds us for the last time of a thread that has been running through the whole story, of the theme of a poetic reworking of the world. Lenz, of course, is an artist; his loss of contact with the world is the measure of his loss of artistic creativity. The narrator's use of images to convey the glory of the sunset reminds us that we can be persuaded of the poetic truth of even the most idiosyncratic perceptions of the world, that we are not literal-minded to the point of being mere observers of facts. If we can be made to feel that the earth is a golden goblet, then *potentially* we can be persuaded of even the validity of Lenz's perceptions that the sky is a "silly blue eye," that silence is a voice screaming through an emptied world. Once we admit to ourselves that reality is not just objects present, but is something that partakes of—and indeed demands—a humanly interpreted context, then we admit the possible validity of poetic interpretations of the world. Then, on frequent, uncomfortable occasions, Lenz's madness feels like poetry. The text itself constantly reminds us that the protagonist of Büchner's story is an artist. Indeed, the one lengthy discursive statement that Lenz makes in the whole work occurs in the famous *Kunstgespräch*, conversation on art, in which he gives us his artistic credo. The passage is not simply a piece of, as it were, *Sturm und Drang* local color.[9] It has meaning in the story not only by virtue of the arguments it advances but above all because of the function of these arguments in a work where the artistic relationship to (and interpretation of) reality is one of the central themes. Lenz argues against any kind of idealist art, insisting: "The dear Lord has presumably made the world as it should be, and we therefore cannot put anything better together; our sole intention should be to copy the work of His hands. I demand in everything life, the possibility of being, and that is all; it is not our business to ask if it is beautiful or ugly, the feeling that what has been created has life takes precedence over these two qualities and is the only criterion in matters of art" (86).

What Lenz asserts here is a kind of realistic principle behind artistic creation. Yet realism must not be understood as simply fidelity to facts and to external appearances. Rather, Lenz stresses the intense creativity of realistic art, a

[9] Nor does it seem to me adequate to attribute the views expressed in the *Kunstgespräch* section to Büchner himself. One must ask after their function in this particular story. I have derived great pleasure and profit from Ronald Hauser's analysis in his study *Georg Büchner*, pp. 56ff. However, his application of the principles expressed in the *Kunstgespräch* to the actual story suffers, in my view, from a certain schematism, although he has telling points to make about the narrative technique. I agree with Hauser that Lenz's "fears are well founded in the human condition as Büchner sees it" (70), but one needs also to show how these fears are founded in the human condition *as the story makes us see it*. In his detailed discussion of the *Kunstgespräch* Peter Jansen suggests that this section gives the protagonist a spiritual stature that renders his degradation and collapse all the more poignant ("The Structural Function of the 'Kunstgespräch' in Büchner's *Lenz*").

creativity that allows such art to satisfy the one criterion that ultimately matters: the end product shall be vibrantly, tinglingly alive. Indeed, Lenz throughout his remarks insists on the primacy of imaginative empathy; this is the one true aesthetic principle. At one point he makes it clear that no amount of factual details, of externals, will be able to bring the work of art alive. Realism is not to be equated with a simple allegiance to empirical facts; rather, it involves the recognition that man *creates* reality out of the dynamic interaction of the self and the world. The figures in a truly successful work of art, then, generate their living reality from within themselves: "One has to love humanity in order to be able to penetrate into the unique being of each person; nobody can be too humble, too ugly for us— only then can one understand mankind; the most insignificant face makes a deeper impression than the mere sense of the beautiful, and one can allow the characters to emerge out of themselves without slavishly copying externals where no life, no muscles, no pulse swell and throb toward us" (87).

The crucial opposition here is that between externals (*"das Äussere"*) on the one hand and the living principle of an art that cherishes the outgoing creativity of the individual self (*"aus sich"*) on the other.[10] Realism is concerned with a world whose every fact is alive with the dimension of human significance. This credo is implicit in the poetic intensity of the narrator's descriptive passages. Furthermore, Lenz's alienation from the world is intimated as precisely the inability to know and hold fast to the vital meaning of the created reality that man inhabits. Lenz finds either the hideous absence of this living agency—or the overwhelming presence of a power whose very intensity threatens to tear him asunder. Yet his anguish centers upon—and derives from—the desperate attempt to affirm the immanent

[10] In my reading of this passage I find myself in disagreement with M. B. Benn who renders the *"aus sich"* as referring back to *"man,"* i.e. "one— the artist—can let the figures proceed out of oneself" (Georg Büchner, *Leonce und Lena and Lenz*).

poetry of the real. His anguish at his loss is anguish at the loss of human substance. Moreover, because his visions grope for the very stuff of poetry and art, they are related to—yet ultimately separate from—the narrator's capacity for poetic description. Hence, the *Kunstgespräch*, the conversation on art, clarifies the fact that madness, because it is alienation from reality, involves also an alienation from the preconditions of artistic creativity. Moreover, the *Kunstgespräch* also serves to underpin the thematic significance of one whole strand within the narrator's stylistic handling of his material. If the story establishes the existential relevance of the mad mind, it does so by arguing this link through the narrative medium of artistic interpretation and expression. The narrative process becomes, then, part of the story's theme. No attempt is made to play down the precariousness of Lenz's mental state, to suggest that he is not "really" mad. Lenz is so radically distanced from our world that he exists at the very periphery of the commonly understood universe. Yet the story, through its all-important narrative perspective, is able to endow even the marginal mind of the protagonist with such an interpretative implication for us, the readers, that that mind acquires a nagging existential centrality. The disturbing mediations involved in this process are, in my view, characteristic of the novelle genre. Moreover, it is those mediations that make this particular story one of the great literary explorations of madness.

VI. Grillparzer: *Der arme Spielmann**

Franz Grillparzer was born in Vienna on January 15, 1791. He studied law at the university, and from 1813 to 1856 he was employed as a civil servant, finally reaching the post of *Archivdirektor*. His was not a life rich in spectacular events; there were, admittedly, occasional visits abroad (to Italy, Germany, France, England, Greece), but on the whole, irresolution and timorousness prevailed (as in his agonized relationship to Katharina Fröhlich, the "eternal fiancée" whom he was never to marry). His career as an artist began with the considerable public success of *Die Ahnfrau (The Ancestress)* of 1817, but it was a triumph that was not to be repeated. The disastrous reception accorded to his comedy *Weh dem der lügt (Woe unto the Liar)* of 1838 so embittered Grillparzer that he never again attempted to have his plays performed publicly (although he continued to write for the stage). Both as man and artist Grillparzer was prey to nervous indecision and uncertainty; his relationship to his artistic calling was profoundly ambivalent, sometimes curiously arrogant, sometimes self-lacerating in its despair. Over and over again his art expresses his fear of passion, of intensity, of great and decisive activity, and upholds the values of a contained and tranquil life. Yet there is an intellectual toughness and honesty about Grillparzer that prevents him from becoming the philistine apologist for the values of "peace and quiet." In his story *Der arme Spielmann (The Poor Musician)* of 1848 he gives us the obliquely tender portrait of one man, the poor musician of the title, whose humility and serenity are both strength and weakness, both sublime and questionable.

In outline, at least, *Der arme Spielmann* is a character

* This chapter is a revised version of my paper "The Narrative Perspective in Grillparzer's *Der arme Spielmann*," GLL 20 (1967): 107–116. I am most grateful to the editors for allowing me to use this material here.

study, concerned with the life and death of Jakob, a poor street musician, whom the narrator happens to meet one year at a fair (*Volksfest*) in Vienna. Much of the work is taken up with Jakob's narration of his own life story, and at one point in that narration he describes the death of his father—and adds the following comment: "One day I hope to find him again where we will be judged by our intentions, and not by our works" (65).[1] In these words Jakob expresses the ambivalence that informs everything he tries to accomplish in this life. He is a man of infinite goodwill, of sublime intentions, who finds it impossible to translate his inner integrity into terms at all meaningful to the world in which he finds himself. It is precisely this split between the inward (*Innen*) and the outward (*Aussen*) that renders him incapable of performing even the most menial of clerical tasks and that ultimately destroys his relationship with Barbara. The high point of this relationship is a kiss, a kiss given through a pane of glass. For all the genuineness and intensity of his love for Barbara, Jakob can never put his love into practice—he can never convert his inner feelings into a workable human relationship.

Such is the picture that emerges of the *armer Spielmann*, "the poor musician," from his own narration. Although Jakob is without self-pity and his narration is utterly devoid of any attempts at self-justification, clearly one must ask oneself how valid this picture is. On his own admission, Jakob finds it difficult to communicate his inner feelings to the world outside, and hence we must have more evidence before we can accept his account of his life as in any sense valid. Here the narrator has a vital role to play. One notices immediately that the impression of Jakob that emerges from his own narration corresponds very closely to the narrator's assessment of the old man. Indeed, if one examines the narrator's opening description of the Spielmann, one sees that it is precisely because of the contradic-

---

[1] References throughout are to Franz Grillparzer, *Sämtliche Werke*, vol. 13, ed. A. Sauer and R. Backmann, Vienna, 1930.

tions in his behavior—the poverty and the nobility, the commitment to music and the technical incompetence—that the narrator is so intrigued by him. When the narrator engages the Spielmann in conversation about his music, he is immediately struck by the contradiction between *Innen* and *Aussen*, between the Spielmann's ideals and their concrete expression in the music he actually plays. The narrator speaks of his "surprise at hearing the man speak of the very highest levels of art, who was at the same time incapable of giving a recognizable rendering of the simplest waltz" (43). Clearly, therefore, the narrator's estimation of the Spielmann's character is very much in accord with that of the old man himself. Moreover, certain aspects of the Spielmann's narration can be and are checked by the narrator. Particularly the relationship with Barbara is crucial. Does she in fact feel anything more than pity for Jakob? It would obviously be possible that Jakob, because of his feelings for Barbara, could offer a falsely colored picture of their relationship in order to compensate for his complete inadequacy in terms of their practical relationship. The structure of the story, the closing scene in which the narrator goes to see Barbara, means that the world of the Spielmann's narration is examined by the narrator, and hence we are enabled to test the validity of Jakob's account of himself. His death is at once sublime and foolish. Barbara's son *is* called Jakob; Barbara does weep for the dead Spielmann, and she cherishes his violin as an almost sacred relic of his existence on earth.

Hence, from what the narrator and the Spielmann tell us, and from the occasional glimpse they both give us of Barbara, we can build up a fairly consistent picture of the Spielmann's character. The contradiction between his inner intention and its outward expression, between "the goodwill and its profane realization"[2] lies at the very heart of his being. Yet is this all that needs to be said about the story? Does the work do no more than state the ambiva-

---

[2] J. P. Stern, *Re-Interpretations*, p. 61.

lence of the Spielmann's situation? Are we given any evaluative perspective that tells us whether to judge according to intention (*Absichten*) or according to actual achievement (*Werken*)? The Spielmann can be seen either as a saintly figure whose practical failures are the measure of his commitment to an unattainable ideal or as a fool who erects a pretentious superstructure of impossible ideals to compensate for his inadequacy before the demands of everyday living. Do we, the readers, simply take our choice, or does the story help us at all in our evaluation of the Spielmann? If there is an answer, it can only lie in the narrative perspective, in the attitude of the narrator to his central character and, above all, in *our* evaluation of that narrator and his viewpoint.

When the narrator first meets the Spielmann we read: "I had, in order to observe the oddity undisturbed, withdrawn some distance on to the side of the embankment" (41). The implications of this are symptomatic of the narrator's whole attitude toward the Spielmann. Most commentators on the story have drawn attention to the narrator's laconic, ironical tone.[3] As J. P. Stern puts it, "As far as the narrator is concerned he merely reports but never identifies himself with the unheroic hero's point of view."[4] Could one not, however, go further than this and say that, far from identifying himself with Jakob, the narrator makes every effort to distance himself from him, while at the same time remaining strangely fascinated by him? His attitude is rather more complex than might appear at first sight. Indeed, one is tempted to say that there is something profoundly paradoxical in the narrator's overall relationship to the Spielmann, and the paradox is reflected in his remarks about himself and the *Volk*, the common people. The narrator describes himself as being a passionate lover of human beings (although we see remarkably little evi-

[3] See especially Heinz Politzer, *Franz Grillparzers "Der arme Spielmann."* Politzer stresses (pp. 8f.) that the narrator's loftiness masks both diffidence and uncertainty.

[4] *Re-Interpretations*, p. 67.

117

dence of this love in the story he tells): "as a lover of human beings, I say, especially when they come together in masses, for a time forgetting their own wishes and becoming part of that wholeness in which ultimately the divine resides" (39).

Hence he is delighted by the fair, that one event in the year when individuals and social classes are absorbed into the sea of people all enjoying themselves. When one examines the narrator's description of the fair, however, one finds that he does not merge with the common people. Rather, he remains detached and aloof: an observer rather than a participant. Furthermore, he writes, as Richard Brinkmann puts it, "with a condescending, but clear, slightly intellectual distance."[5] Indeed, at times the irony seems to express not simply detachment but also criticism, an awareness of something violent and destructive at work in the spectacle before him: "the stream of the people, released from the containment of the bridge, a massive, roaring sea, pouring out and flooding everything" (37). It is perhaps significant that the only other time in the story when the narrator describes a crowd scene (the occasion of another deluge, the flooding of the Leopoldstadt) this, too, is something horrific. Its horrific quality resides unmistakably in the fact that it is a *mass* spectacle, with rows of bodies laid out for inspection by the authorities.[6]

The narrator's description of the crowd at the fair becomes intensified to grotesque proportions, as he narrows his field of vision from "the pleasure-hungry mass" to various beggar musicians who are attempting to entertain the passersby: "A lame, misshapen boy, he and his violin form-

---

[5] *Wirklichkeit und Illusion*, p. 96. John M. Ellis makes the same point, but his analysis suffers, in my view, from his undifferentiated denigration of the narrator figure. What he describes as "lack of sincerity" (p. 123), as "wanton self-gratification" (p. 125) is, in my view, symptomatic of a much more complex interpretative unease (*Narration in the German Novelle*).

[6] On the implications of the narrator's distaste for the masses see especially Wolfgang Paulsen, "Der gute Bürger Jakob," and Hertha Krotkoff, "Über den Rahmen in Franz Grillparzers Novelle *Der arme Spielmann*."

ing one inextricable tangle, who turned out endlessly unfolding waltzes with all the hectic violence of his twisted
chest" (40). For all the horror of such performers, they are
more at one with the crowd than is Jakob, the poor musician. This is made explicitly clear by the reactions of the
crowd who simply laugh at the old man, giving him no
money. Yet, suddenly the whole world of the fair fades and
the narrator's attention is focused on Jakob:

> an old man, at least seventy, in a threadbare, but neat
> broadcloth coat, with a smiling, self-congratulating ex-
> pression. He stood there, his bald head bared, having
> put, as these beggar musicians do, his hat on the ground
> before him as a collecting-box; and he was belaboring an
> old, very cracked violin, marking the beat not only by
> raising and lowering his foot, but also by the concerted
> movement of his whole bent body. But all this effort to
> bring unity into his performance was fruitless, for what
> he played seemed to be an incoherent sequence of notes,
> without shape or melody. Yet he was totally absorbed in
> his work; his lips twitched, his eyes never left the sheet
> music in front of him—yes, in all truth, sheet music!
> (40f.).

The contrast with the description of the other musicians
is unmistakable. The whole tone of the language changes
and the irony becomes more kindly: the mood is more re-
laxed, even good-humored, one of relief after the horrors
that have preceded it. The quality of the language suggests
that in the Spielmann the narrator finds an individual who
attracts rather than repels him. Furthermore, it is significant that the narrator is attracted to the Spielmann not
simply because he is unusual (the other musicians are unusual), but because his unusualness so manifestly divorces
him from the whole quality and atmosphere of the fair.
Suddenly the crowd is forgotten and only the Spielmann is
of interest. This would seem to be somewhat inconsistent
with the narrator's avowed purpose in attending the fair.
Indeed, looking back on the narrator's praise of the fair,

do we not detect a certain strain, an element of self-deception in the language—does not our narrator perhaps "protest too much"? "From the altercation of tipsy carters there runs an invisible, but uninterrupted thread up to the quarrel of the sons of gods, and in the young maid, who, half-unwillingly, follows her eager lover away from the mass of the dancers, are to be found, in embryo, the Juliets, Didos, and Medeas" (39). Is he really involved in the fair and all it stands for? If so, it is odd that he should be so easily deflected from his purpose by the meeting with someone who is, if nothing else, a complete outsider.

This is not, of course, to imply that our narrator immediately identifies himself with the Spielmann. The description of Jakob is ironic ("was belaboring"), with a touch of comic surprise ("yes, in all truth, sheet music!"). Yet, because of the tone of the passage and particularly in the light of what precedes it, one feels that the narrator is potentially more sympathetic to the Spielmann than he is to the general spectacle around him. Almost immediately, however, this gentle hint of some sort of involvement is negated by the rather pompous sentence: "The whole being of the old man was as though expressly designed to excite my anthropological hunger to the utmost" (41). It is almost as if the narrator were ashamed of a moment of weakness for the Spielmann—and immediately adopts an ironic and consciously withdrawn tone in order to distance himself from him.

The crowd now obscures the Spielmann and the narrator admits what has been implicit in his description of their meeting—that only the old man is of interest: "the lost adventure had taken away all my pleasure in the fair. I explored the *Augarten* in every direction, and finally decided to return home" (42). The fair, this inherently "divine" spectacle, is no longer worthy of the narrator's attention. Yet even this admission of the Spielmann's importance for the narrator is not without its distancing effect. Their meeting is described as an adventure, something out of the ordinary, but no more than that. Suddenly, however, the narrator hears the sound of the old man's violin: "I accelerated my pace and, lo and behold, the object of my curiosity stood playing for all he was worth before a circle of some boys who were impatiently demanding a waltz of him" (42). Once again, the language here is interesting. The narrator admits to a certain exultation and excitement at the prospect of seeing the Spielmann again. Yet lest we should mistake his feelings for sympathy and emotional involvement, he once again distances himself from the Spielmann by the way he describes the meeting—the self-conscious "lo and behold" (*"siehe da!"*), and the aloof "object of my curiosity" (*"Gegenstand meiner Neugier"*).

A conversation takes place between the two of them, a conversation the narrator decides to terminate as it is getting late. Almost instinctively he accompanies his words with the offer of further money. Yet here, too, any possible overtones of sympathetic involvement with the old man are neutralized by the narrator's stressing the diffidence and awkwardness of the old man's leave-taking: "And then, with a curious kind of aristocratic ease, he made a rather awkward bow and went off as fast as his old legs would carry him" (45). Even so, the Spielmann is uppermost in the narrator's mind as he pauses on his way home for a drink. The thought occurs to him that he is near the Spielmann's house, and having made inquiries, he abandons his route home and turns off toward the *Gärtnergasse* where the old man lives. It is repeatedly stressed that the *Gärtnergasse* is not on the narrator's way home. We are told that, after leaving the inn garden, our narrator walked toward the town (46), whereas the *Gärtnergasse* "ran toward the open fields. I followed that direction" (46).

Furthermore, it is worth noting that, from the moment of his first meeting with the Spielmann, the narrator—in terms of his physical movements on that day—removes himself farther and farther from the crowd, from the flood of common humanity.[7] Once again, however, the narrator

---

[7] I am grateful to my colleague Professor Ilse Graham for drawing my attention to this point.

negates any suggestion of sympathy by the way he describes his thoughts as he enters the *Gärtnergasse*: "In which of these wretched huts could my oddity live? Typically, I had forgotten the number" (46). The insertion of the word "typically" ("*glücklich*") here is intriguing. It implies that the narrator is irritated with himself for his forgetfulness, that he resents the thought that he might lose another opportunity of gaining insight into the Spielmann and his way of life. All this might seem to imply that there is an instinctive—almost spontaneous—involvement on the part of the narrator. Yet we are never allowed to forget that the present narrator is looking back on what he describes; he is reporting events that took place "two years ago" (39), and from the vantage point of his present narrative perspective he is able to play down his personal involvement at the time. Indeed, at times he is ironic at his own expense—as when he reports his journey home after finding the *Gärtnergasse*: "Only finding my way with difficulty in the unfamiliar streets, I embarked on my homeward journey, and I, too, improvised, but disturbing nobody, only in my head" (47). The irony here lightheartedly implies that an affinity existed between the Spielmann and the narrator of two years ago.

This curious half-identification occurs again when the narrator visits the Spielmann a few days later: "There has been almost an excess of reference to the ugly notes produced by my, and I almost fear that he is only my, favorite, that I will spare the reader the description of this hellish concert" (48). There is perhaps an implication here that the story of the narrator's encounters with the Spielmann is only of interest to the two people concerned—almost as if only the narrator could possibly be concerned with the doings of the strange old man. It is at this point that the Spielmann embarks on his narration. At first the narrator makes several comments, but only in order to fill in background detail (on the Spielmann's father) or to describe the Spielmann as he settles himself to tell his tale. Gradually, however, the narrator's interpolations become fewer and fewer until the old man is allowed to dominate the narrative completely. This whole scene is, then, remarkable for its lack of distancing commentary on the part of the narrator.[8] Once the Spielmann's narration is ended, the narrator reasserts his usual laconic mode. Two sentences describe his leave-taking; no word is said about what the Spielmann has just told him. Several months are passed over in a few terse sentences—the narrator goes on a journey and only remembers the Spielmann when he hears of the terrible flooding in the Leopoldstadt. He decides to offer some help "to the address most of concern to me" (78). Once again, as with the description of that earlier flood—the people at the fair—the narrator offers a catalogue of horrors: "on all sides weeping, funeral bells, anxiously searching mothers and lost children" (78), before passing on to the specific case that interests him. The narrator arrives in time to witness Jakob's funeral. Without actually telling us as much, he clearly takes part in the funeral procession, or at least follows it at some suitable distance; from the concrete details of his description it is clear that he is present at the cemetery to witness the actual burial.

There then follows the closing scene—the meeting with Barbara—which brings together all the narrative features I have discussed, and which, in that reticent and understated way that is typical of the whole work, crystallizes the narrator's response to the Spielmann:

A few days later—it was a Sunday—I went, impelled by my psychological curiosity, to the house of the butcher and took as my pretext that I wished to possess the old man's violin as a souvenir. I found the family together—with no particular impression left on them. Yet the violin hung on the wall, with a kind of symmetry, next to the mirror and opposite a crucifix. When I ex-

---

[8] On the importance—and the hermeneutic cohesion—of Jakob's account of his own life and on the significance of the narrator's withdrawal into silence see Roland Heine, "Ästhetische oder existentielle Integration?"

plained my intention and offered a relatively high price, the man seemed anything but disinclined to conclude a good deal. But the woman leaped up from her chair and said: "Whatever next! The violin belongs to our Jakob, and a few Gulden more or less do not make much difference to us!" She took the instrument from the wall, looked at it, turning it round in her hands, blew the dust off it and put it into a drawer, which she, as though fearing burglary, shut violently and locked. Her face was turned away from me so that I could not see what it might have expressed. As at this point the maid came in with the soup, and the butcher, without being embarrassed by the presence of the visitor, began to say grace in a loud voice—in which the children joined their shrill voices—I wished them a pleasant meal and went out of the door. My last glance fell on the woman. She had turned around and the tears were pouring down her face (8of.).

The paragraph opens with what is by now almost a familiar refrain: "impelled by my psychological curiosity." Surely, this sort of comment has by now become something repetitive and mechanical. Why does the narrator feel that he must explain his motives every time? Do we need to be constantly reminded that his curiosity is purely scientific? Indeed, could not the very obtrusiveness of such comments indicate to us that the narrator is trying to deceive himself—and us—about his true motives? Furthermore, for somebody who claims to have an insatiable scientific curiosity, the narrator is remarkably reticent about giving any psychological *interpretation* of the old man's life. Indeed, he does not allow himself one analytical statement about the Spielmann. In view of the repetitive references to "psychological curiosity" ("*psychologische Neugierde*"), one cannot help wondering whether he wants to see the old man only in order to prove to himself (and to us) that he is able—despite his fascination—to maintain a scrupulous detachment. This accounts for his obliqueness. He goes to see

Barbara on the pretext that he wishes to buy the old man's violin. If this is only a pretext, we must ask ourselves what his real motives are. Psychological curiosity? But curiosity about what? After all, he has already seen Barbara on the day of the funeral; he has learned that she insists on paying the burial costs. He knows, therefore, that she does still feel something for the old man, that she has not forgotten him. Yet, presumably, he wants to know more. We must assume that the extra information he wants can only be elicited by the direct approach of offering to buy the violin.

He finds the family "with no particular impression left on them. Yet the violin hung on the wall, with a kind of symmetry, next to the mirror and opposite a crucifix." Here one must note the conjunction "yet" ("*doch*") by which the narrator fleetingly betrays his—almost embarrassed— intuition that he and a member of the family he is visiting have responded to the Spielmann in the same way. The other person is, of course, Barbara. That the narrator is embarrassed by his intuition is revealed in his attempt to understate the importance of the violin's position on the wall ("with *a kind of* symmetry"). The full significance of the violin is made abundantly clear by subsequent events. When the narrator offers money for the violin Barbara refuses violently. Her first, and instinctive, reaction is physical: she leaps to her feet. She then has to say something, to give reasons why it would be wrong to accept the narrator's financially favorable offer. She gives, in essence, two reasons for her refusal. First, "the violin belongs to our Jakob"—the violin belongs to their son Jakob and as parents they would be wrong to sell it. Second, "a few Gulden more or less do not make much difference to us"—they are not in need of the money. Of course, both these arguments could be perfectly valid reasons for her rejection of the narrator's offer. However, her subsequent actions suggest something very different: "She took the instrument from the wall, looked at it, turning it round in her hands, blew the dust off it and put it into a drawer, which she, as though fearing burglary, shut violently and locked." This sentence implies two things. In the first place, the fact that the violin has acquired dust on the wall suggests that her son has not played it, that it is not really *his* violin. Second, the violence with which she locks away the violin indicates that to her it is beyond price. Barbara's actions suggest the full importance the violin has for her, the importance of a sacred relic. Her actions intimate this—and yet, the statements she makes imply very different considerations on her part. They give mundane, practical reasons why the violin should not be sold. In other words, the truth of Barbara's feelings about the violin (and about the Spielmann) is something that she cannot say—perhaps because she does not fully understand it herself, perhaps because, even if she does know what she feels, she is convinced that nobody would comprehend the nature of her involvement with the old man, would understand why she so cherishes the last relic of his life on earth.

As a result of his pretext—his offer to buy the violin—the narrator finds out something important about Barbara. The funeral had told him that she grieved for the old man. What he needed to know was at what level she laments this loss. Pity? Nostalgic memory of her youth? With his offer to buy the violin, the narrator applies the crucial test to Barbara—and he discovers that she cares for the Spielmann in a way that she will not and cannot express. She asserts possession of the violin not simply against her family and the narrator, but ultimately against the real world, which in its unyielding material existence makes a mockery of her involvement with the "ideal" world of the Spielmann. The narrator knows—before he visits Barbara— that this is a possible response to the old man; hence he insists on seeing her again, on posing the crucial question. He senses this response, because at an unspoken—and unsayable—level of his being, this is his response to the Spielmann, a response that he masks as "psychological curiosity."

We now come to the narrator's last glimpse of Barbara. She has turned away and the narrator cannot see her face.

is made explicit by Barbara in the words she speaks to the old man. They are words of total assent; for the first and only time the *du* is used. Also, the words are not simply expressions of human tenderness—they have religious connotations. Barbara asks for God's blessing on the man whom she is rejecting. It is this response that binds Barbara to the memory of the dead Spielmann, it is this same response that binds the narrator to the old man. In spite of what unites them, however, there is no communication between Barbara and the narrator in the closing scene. This is surely because, by definition, there can be no community of those who have assented to the sheer saintliness of the old man. The violin may hang with a certain symmetry opposite the cross; but there can be no brotherhood of believers because the Spielmann's life—unlike Christ's passion—is not the story of a mediation between spirit and world. Rather, Jakob's life asserts the unbridgeable gulf between intention (*Absicht*) and work (*Werk*), between values and facts.

If one traces the religious references throughout the story one finds a significant pattern at work. The narrator praises the fair as a mass spectacle "in which ultimately the divine resides" (39). He tries to assert the presence of absolute values in the mass of common, ordinary humanity. However, he is deflected from the pursuit of this immanent divinity by his meeting with one man, a man whose efforts to make music are for him a link with the divine, who speaks of his art as a prayer, as "playing the dear Lord," a man for whom the Christian heaven is a world "where we are judged by our intentions and not by our works" (65). It is to that divinity, a divinity denied any substantial realization in the world that both Barbara and the narrator subscribe with part of their being. Both of them know that by this assent they threaten to isolate themselves from the real world, from any hope of human fulfillment deriving from practical achievement. Yet Barbara will not relinquish her hold on this world. She is an efficient wife and mother, she has practical good sense, she belongs to the world of the family, of impatient customers, of the simple, uncouth prayer spoken before a meal. Still, potentially the assent to the Spielmann is there. Similarly, the narrator, although manifestly different from the Spielmann in his intellectual sophistication and his social standing, displays an implicit affinity with the old man. When, for example, he first sees him at the fair, the narrator withdraws from the crowd "on to the side of the embankment" (41). At this moment both the narrator and the Spielmann stand apart from the crowd in total isolation. Both are oddities in the sense that they do not share in the merrymaking of the crowd. It is because of this strange affinity between them that the narrator is so fascinated by the Spielmann, and it is because he knows of—and is embarrassed by—this affinity that the narrator adopts a stance of ironical distance from the Spielmann. Yet in so doing he lays bare his own uncertainty, he emphasizes the irony of his own precarious position.[9]

Many critics have interpreted this story in autobiographical terms. Quite clearly, Grillparzer is here examining with terrible and unflinching honesty his own agonizing self-doubts as a man and as an artist. Both Barbara and the narrator, however much they resent it or are embarrassed by it, subscribe with part of their nature to Jakob's world, to his ceaseless—and necessarily doomed—struggle to express the inner ideal in outward terms. Their resentment, their ambivalence is part of the honesty of the story. This is no facile affirmation of the idealist in a cold, materialist society. Barbara and the narrator know that to adopt Jakob's perspective fully is to negate the meaningfulness of life in the physical world, of family, of art created with material things. It is the specifically artistic aspect of the Spielmann's dilemma that is pertinent to the narrator's own situation. Unless he can believe that the "divine" does, potentially, reside in the mass, that "the unrestrained burst of applause from a fully packed theater" is "interesting, indeed instructive" (39), he condemns his art to a terrible isolation and to

[9] For a telling discussion of this affinity see Peter Schäublin, "Das Musizieren des armen Spielmannes."

utter unrealization; he condemns himself to write for those few oddities who know that the "divine" has withdrawn into pure inwardness, who know that practical failure may be the measure of ideal intention. This involves so radical a devaluation of the real that the narrator must make himself repudiate it. He continues to repudiate it by his *present* act of narration, by insisting that his attitudes to the common people—and to the fair—have not changed despite the meeting of some two years previously with the Spielmann. It is, for example, significant that toward the beginning of his story he asserts his credo in the present tense: "I do not lightly miss this festival. . . . as a lover of human beings, I say, especially when they come together in masses, for a time forgetting their own wishes and becoming part of that wholeness in which ultimately the divine resides, indeed God himself—as such a person I find that every popular festival is actually a festival of the soul, a pilgrimage, an act of worship" (39). With this strident credo— affirmed as his present position—the narrator aligns himself with the real world of practical achievement. Accordingly, the perspective he adopts throughout his narration gives firm allegiance to externals, to the familiar universe of facts and events. That other interpretative possibility— of assent to the Spielmann—has to be implied, not stated, has to be intimated through irony, and not declared unambiguously. This is because any such explicit declaration to this effect would involve another credo—precisely that artistic and human credo that would render nugatory the attempt to write this story or any other story, for that matter.

The Spielmann, for all his reticence and self-depreciation, is both a radical and a disturbing figure. The confrontation with him—however much the narrator tries to play it down—is a shock, a shock to which he continues to subject himself in order to be able to withstand it. One is reminded here of Grillparzer's great contemporary, Baudelaire, and especially of the role of shock meetings in his work. Walter Benjamin argues that Baudelaire's decisive experience is that of the artist living within (but alienated from) the metropolis.[10] He distills the experience of the city—and its critique—from shock confrontations with the odd, the quirky, the freakish. The critique is channeled through an artistic concentration on the oddities that mass city life presents. Paradoxically, in the marginality of his human and social situation—and in the marginality of his thematic concern—the artist explores the central issue of the ruthlessly competitive, individualist society around him. This, too, behind all the oblique irony, is central to Grillparzer's vision in *Der arme Spielmann*.

It is a disturbing story, disturbing in the fact that it implies a deeply dangerous hermeneutic possibility: that we, its readers, may be tempted to relate to the Spielmann in the way that Barbara and the narrator, in spite of themselves, do. This central relationship of association and dissociation, of affinity and detachment, is perhaps put most succinctly, and with desperately appropriate ambiguity, by Franz Kafka in the *Briefe an Milena*. Kafka sends the story to Milena with the obliquely disparaging comment: "I am sending you *Der arme Spielmann* today, not because it has great meaning for me—it did once have it, years ago. I send it because he is so Viennese, so unmusical, so heartbreaking, because he looked down upon us in the *Volksgarten* (on us! You were walking beside me, Milena, just think, you walked beside me), because he is so bureaucratic, and because he loved a girl who had a good business sense."[11] Clearly, Milena's reaction to the story is a positive one, and Kafka replies to her with a more detailed commentary on his relationship to the work. Significantly, however, the more detailed commentary is no less ambiguous than his first statement. What Kafka does is to deepen the dialectic, to intensify both his acceptance and his rejec-

[10] In Walter Benjamin, *Schriften*, ed. T. W. Adorno, Frankfurt am Main, 1955. For an English version see Benjamin's *Illuminations*, pp. 157ff. See also Benjamin's *Charles Baudelaire: Ein Lyriker im Zeitalter des Hochkapitalismus*, ed. R. Tiedemann, Frankfurt am Main, 1969.

[11] Franz Kafka, *Briefe an Milena*, ed. W. Haas, Frankfurt am Main, 1966, p. 61.

tion of the story. In so doing, he reenacts, as we do, the central dilemma of both Barbara and the narrator:

> Everything you say about *Der arme Spielmann* is right. If I said that it did not mean anything to me, it was out of caution, because I did not know how you would get on with it, and then also because I am as ashamed of the story as if I had written it myself. And actually it does begin wrongly, has a number of things that are false, ludicrous, dilettante, grotesquely affected (especially when reading it aloud one notices it, I could show you the passages); and especially this kind of musical performance is surely a pitiably laughable invention, designed to make the girl so irritated as to throw everything, the whole shop, at the story, in a towering rage, in which the whole world, myself especially, would share, until the story, which deserves no better, would perish from within. Admittedly, there is no more beautiful fate for a story than to disappear—and in this way. The narrator, too, this comic psychologist, would fully agree with this, because he is probably the true poor musician who plays this story for us in the most unmusical way possible, thanked for his pains in an excessively abundant way by the tears from your eyes.[12]

Seldom has any novelle had such a devastatingly attuned reader.

---

[12] Ibid., p. 77.

VII. Stifter: *Granit*

Adalbert Stifter was born at Oberplan on the Moldau in the Bohemian forest in 1805. He studied in Vienna and was, for some time, a private tutor in various aristocratic houses. Finally, he became a school inspector in Linz, Upper Austria. His life was, in outward terms, as resolutely uneventful and provincial as his art, on first reading, appears. He was, as his choice of profession implies, a pedagogue—committed to upholding certain values, those of stability, continuity, self-restraint, which he felt to be threatened by the contemporary world—most notably by the events of 1848. The collection of stories entitled *Bunte Steine (Colored Stones)* of 1853—together with their famous Preface or *Vorrede*—are Stifter's answer to the provocation of his times. Yet, like all his art, they have a remarkable intensity that raises them above the level of unproblematic provincial idylls (of which there is no shortage in nineteenth-century German literature).

It is probably no exaggeration to say that the *Bunte Steine* collection is known less for the stories it contains than for its renowned Preface. The *Vorrede* has acquired a sacrosanct place in literary history, and has often been seen as the manifesto of *Biedermeier* literature or of Poetic Realism. However much justification there may be for such pigeonholing, the fact remains that many of the arguments in the Preface have been sadly neglected, and that the *Vorrede* as a whole has been reduced to the status of an unequivocal and somewhat timid apology for the literary— and moral—celebration of the "little things" of life. The danger is that the emphasis here becomes too restrictive. One easily forgets that this one argument is part of a larger scheme, as well as the fact that the stories themselves can deepen and fill out the implications of the overtly tendentious program. Furthermore, one has to remember that

Stifter wrote the *Vorrede* in answer to attacks that had been made on him (by the dramatist Friedrich Hebbel). Stopp has argued that we should therefore allow for the possibility that the polemical intention behind Stifter's reply produces a certain stridency and one-sidedness in his formulation of artistic aims, that the statement of principle can be much more unequivocal than is the realization of that principle in the fiction that Stifter actually produced.[1] Eugen Thurnher has, however, countered Stopp's arguments by showing that the *Vorrede* was in no sense a sudden and ill-considered reply, but that both the ideas—and, indeed, many of their actual formulations—had been very much in evidence well before the decision to compose the *Vorrede*.[2] Thurnher insists: "The tone of the argument is the even flow of sober discussion."[3] He sees the *Vorrede* not as a "credo for his art" but simply as an "article of faith."[4] Now while, clearly, Thurnher is right to insist that there is much more to Stifter's art than the simple realization of the views expressed in the Preface, he is, in my view, unwise to discount the presence of a polemical intention behind the Preface. After all, Stifter begins by referring to—and by summarizing—the attacks that have been made on him. In other words, he himself is careful to invoke the existence of a polemical context. Furthermore, the quiet tone to which Thurnher refers is, in my view, a carefully manipulated polemical weapon.

If there is, then, a certain tendentiousness to the *Vorrede*, one must, I think, stress that it is a tendentiousness that derives with a certain logic from the curiously radical nature of Stifter's art. Whatever Stifter was or was not, he was an uncompromising writer, and he insists on precisely this uncompromising quality in the *Vorrede*. One notices this in the first two sentences: "It has on one occasion been held against me that I only portray small things and that my

---

[1] F. J. Stopp, "Die Symbolik in Stifters *Bunten Steinen*."
[2] "Stifters 'sanftes Gesetz.'"
[3] Ibid., p. 391.
[4] Ibid., p. 395.

characters are always ordinary people. If that is true, I am now in the position to offer my readers something that is even smaller, even more insignificant—all manner of diversions for young people" (5).[5] Here Stifter seizes upon the *Bunte Steine* stories as radical exemplars of something that he is prepared to formulate as his artistic—and human—credo. He then goes on to offer a consistent understatement of his art. The stories, he tells us, contain no overt teaching, they are concerned with neither the great nor the small. They simply are what they are: their aim is to give modest pleasure to a certain number of like-minded friends. Indeed, Stifter disclaims the title of *Dichtung* for his art; for him, true art comes immediately after religion in importance, the great artist is one of the "benefactors of the human race" (5). If his works are not in this sense *Dichtung*, "yet they can surely be something else that is not devoid of all justification" (5). The understatement is unmistakable here, and it is sustained in the first tentative assertion of real worth that he makes on behalf of his art: that, by giving pleasure to friends both known and unknown, it may be able "to contribute a small grain of goodness to the edifice of the Eternal" (5). The diminutive here—"*Kornlein*," "a small grain"—is very much part of the mode of understatement. Stifter continues almost as an afterthought: "But while we are talking of great and small, I will put forward my views which probably diverge from those of many other people" (6). Only after this disarming opening does he launch into the major statement of that philosophy for which the Preface is so well known.

One has, I think, to ask what the point is of this extended—and deliberately low-key—opening. In view of the understatement of these introductory remarks, in view of their constant assertions of reticence, modesty, humility, one would expect—in terms of rhetorical registers—that

[5] References are to Adalbert Stifter, *Bunte Steine, Späte Erzählungen*, ed. Max Stefl, Augsburg, 1960 (which contains the *Vorrede, Granit*, and *Der Waldgänger*), and to Adalbert Stifter, *Studien II*, ed. Max Stefl, Augsburg, 1956 (which contains *Abdias* and *Der Hagestolz*).

Stifter would ask for the overall assent of his readers to the fact that these modest human dimensions are the framework within which we all live our lives, that he would, as it were, get us on his side by implying that we are most at home with works that give us—"*eine vergnügte Stunde*"—"a pleasant hour" (5). Surprisingly, however, he does not indulge in such buttonholing. Rather, he does the opposite. He suggests that the humility of his art will only appeal to those who are "like-minded" ("*gleichgestimmt*"), that most of us will look for something different in the literature we read. In other words, Stifter, having once divorced himself and his work from the elite circle of *Dichtung*, goes on to suggest that the low-key humility of his art will only appeal to an intimate group, that his readers will be a circle of friends, not the mass of the reading public. The opening page of the *Vorrede*, then, suggests one of the crucial directions of Stifter's artistic endeavor: that he is writing *against* common expectations, *against* popular taste, *against* generally held views of human—and artistic—value. If Hebbel's attack implied that Stifter was only concerned with the mundane, the everyday, the trivial, Stifter replies by accepting the criticism and by arguing that such a concern is anything but mundane, everyday, or trivial: it is utterly exceptional. From this starting point, Stifter goes on in the *Vorrede* to suggest the rightness and the human substance of his perspective. Insofar as he captures our assent, we become one of the "like-minded friends" ("*gleichgestimmten Freunden*"), we are persuaded to revise our artistic and moral value scale. Indeed, the crucial notion is *revise*. Stifter is uncompromising, and he knows it. The uniquely strenuous demands he places on the reader are interpretative demands; and if we assent to his interpretation, then, by implication, we dissociate ourselves from the common interpretation.

Stifter begins by discussing natural phenomena. He takes the established value scale of what constitutes a "great" natural event, of what constitutes a "small" natural event and seeks to invert it. He does this in various ways. At

one level he argues in terms of physical greatness or smallness. He says that the power required to account for the
total phenomenon of "the moving of the air, the rippling
of water, the growing of the corn, the flowing of the sea,
the greening of the earth, the glowing of the sky, the shining of the stars" (6) is greater than that required for "the
majestically approaching thunderstorm, the lightning that
shatters houses, the storm that lashes the surf, the mountain belching forth fire, and the earthquake that buries
whole countries" (6). This is because, Stifter argues, events
of the former category take place all the time, everywhere
in the world, whereas the latter phenomena are exceptional, occurring at one moment in time and at one specific
place. In the list of these two categories, Stifter's formulation is particularly significant. The first category consists
exclusively of verbal nouns, with no accompanying descriptive epithets. They are, then, simple, unchanging processes
with no beginning and no end. The second list consists
of specific nouns—"thunderstorm," "lightning," "earthquake"—and are all accompanied by descriptive epithets.
We note the subtle hint in "the majestically approaching thunderstorm" that most people would reserve such
terms as "majestic" for just such events, events that lend
themselves to vivid description. Yet Stifter is saying that
these need to be described much less than do the unexceptional, recurring processes. Moreover, he is suggesting that we need a new vocabulary for depicting the nature
of being; we need to celebrate the uninterrupted continuity of those things that are omnipresent, to celebrate
the fact that they *are*, rather than cataloguing the attributes
of unique—and therefore ephemeral—situations and
events. The second level of Stifter's revaluation of the accepted value scale of great and small concerns human perception of greatness (significance) or smallness (insignifi-
cance). Here he draws a distinction between the "glance of
the uninitiated," which is fascinated by uniqueness, by
manifest spectacle, and the "sovereign vision of the scientist," which is concerned with "the whole, the generality"

(6). The eye of the scientist, then, perceives the law that binds together individual phenomena as great because it alone sustains the world as we know it: *"weil es allein das Welterhaltende ist"* (6). The law emerges as the result of human effort, of an interpretative relationship to the specific phenomena that surround man. The same is true of the work of the artist; he, like the scientist, must add detail to detail in such a way that he builds up a coherent interpretation of the real world. He works in this way because "we in our workshops can always only portray the individual, never the general—for that would be creation itself" (7). The artist cannot, in other words, portray pure, self-renewing being; he can only intimate this as an interpretation of, as a perspective on, the specifics of any given reality, whether natural, social, or psychological. Later in the *Vorrede* Stifter suggests how this can be achieved.

From a discussion of the world of natural objects, Stifter turns his attention to the sphere of human activity. He attempts to draw parallel conclusions: "As it is in outward nature so it is in inward—in the nature of the human race" (7). Greatness resides in a "life full of uprightness, simplicity, self-mastery," whereas smallness is to be found in such "mighty emotional upheavals as anger or desire for revenge" (8). The latter manifestations of the human spirit are *"einseitig"*—"one-sided"; they are not part of "the gentle law by which the human race is guided" (8). The great qualities are sustaining—both for the individual and for the human totality. Hence, man's moral response is part of this great and good law; by exercising his ethical capacities, he contributes to the well-being of the generality (human society) of which he is part, and the individual who feels himself part of this greater order partakes of a human totality. When we understand our lives in this way, Stifter argues, we are part of the generality of mankind. This fundamental human attitude becomes, for Stifter, a crucial component in all great works of art. Tragedy is uplifting "because the whole takes precedence over the individual component" (10), and in a similar way the epic voice attains to sublimity when it views human affairs as part of one mighty unending stream: "When we see humanity moving through history like a calm silver river toward a great and eternal goal, then we experience the sublimity of—most usually—the epic vision" (10). Here Stifter returns to the crucial point he has made earlier: human beings must concern themselves with specific facts; the artist must write about concrete situations and people, but in such a way that the reader perceives the vital significance of the recurring, the ordinary, the everyday. Stifter concludes the *Vorrede* by summarizing the process through which man develops to ethical maturity; this development expresses itself above all in a change of perspective, from an intimate concern with the specific to the unfolding of an "*Überblick über ein Grösseres*"—"an overview over a greater whole" (11). A people in decline, he argues, lose precisely this sense of proportion; they pursue the contingent, the limited—not the general and abiding. This decay can be noted in the art that is produced: "In their art the one-sided is depicted—that which is valid from only one standpoint" (11).

This concludes the general argument of the *Vorrede*. In the closing section, Stifter reverts to the understatement with which he began. He insists that the general remarks that he has made are not really appropriate to the youthful audience for whom the *Bunte Steine* stories are intended, and he now invites us to turn to the "harmless things" that follow. The Introduction that follows as a second preface asserts the unpretentiousness of the stories, likening them to the colorful collection of stones that the author in his youth so eagerly accumulated. However disarming such statements sound, they have a certain sting and urgency. The stories manifestly are not intended for children; and if we fail to recognize this, we have, by implication, given our allegiance to a widespread—but questionable—view of human affairs.

I have summarized the substance of the *Vorrede* at what may seem excessive length. However, I think that, by following the various stages of Stifter's argument, one can highlight a number of important—and often over-looked—points. It is essential to notice that Stifter does not attempt to deny the existence of violent, unusual, exceptional events. They do take place, and of necessity they claim man's attention. What he suggests, however, is that such events should be viewed and interpreted from a human perspective that sees them as part of an overall sequence. The notion of human—and of artistic—interpretation is all-important here. Moreover, in terms of Stifter's own prose fiction we could say that the essential ingredient to which the *Vorrede* directs our attention is the narrative perspective. It is, in other words, possible for a writer to present events—however violent or terrible—in such a way that he locates them in a greater generality of interpretative context. We remember Stifter's remarks about the sublimity of the epic mode. The epic view will, of course, have to concern itself with specifics, with individual people and their experiences; but it will see the specifics as embedded in the great river of humanity that has one eternal, unchanging goal. In precise terms, this means that the narrative voice in Stifter's stories will over and over again—and very frequently at the end of the individual work—attempt to place what has been described in the overall sequence of human generations, and will ask what the experiences amount to when viewed in this context. The overview "over a greater whole" of which Stifter speaks as the keynote of a mature human attitude is frequently (but, as I hope to show later, by no means always) the basis of the narrative perspective he adopts. In this sense, then, the *Vorrede* represents not so much the statement of a rather timid philosophy of life, but the articulation of a crucial artistic—and above all *narrative*—attitude.

The second point about the *Vorrede* that deserves comment is the whole question of the link between natural and human phenomena. The link is at best a problematic one—and the degree to which it is problematic is shown by the fact that Stifter's work is devoted to the unremitting exploration of this central issue. Man's ethical behavior is

not governed by a law in the way that the changes of the
seasons can be said to obey the laws of the physical universe. The point is that, if man esteems the sustaining
laws of the natural world more highly than he does freak
individual phenomena, then he is not thereby making an
inherently *moral* choice, but simply expressing an interpretative relationship to the natural world. The law may
indeed be world-sustaining—*welterhaltend*—but this can
only be understood in the concrete sense that it is the uni-
fied organization of being that allows certain individua-
tions to take place. While such an attitude, such a perspective, when applied to the sphere of human conduct, *can* be
a moral one, it does not *have* to be a moral one. This is because the human debate about moral values cannot be re-
solved by such simple categories. There are different kinds
of morality, and they can often come into conflict. There is,
for example, the morality of being true to oneself and the
morality of being true to other people; there is the morality
of adherence to principle and the morality of human flexi-
bility and adaptability. Furthermore, there is also the problem of the interpretation of specific circumstances: morals
involve the human capacity for weighing certain modes of
behavior, for interpreting according to various value
scales. They involve a complex dialectic of the specific and
the general. What Stifter attempts to do in the *Vorrede* is to
understand the notion of world-sustaining both as a physical and a moral category, and the coupling will not work
with any reassuring consistency. To put it most obviously,
"self-mastery" and "effective work within one's circle" may
be, in the first sense, world-sustaining. Yet they do not have
to be morally right. One needs to know *which* world is being
preserved and by what criteria that world is known to be
worth preserving. Indeed, one asks oneself if the notion of
the unbroken chain of human generations has anything to
do with moral values. Perhaps it simply represents the fact
of self-renewing being, a notion to which the narrative perspective of some of Stifter's stories can assent unreservedly
but which the perspective in other stories will see as mas-

sively indifferent to human suffering, to any attempt at moral understanding of the world.

The *Vorrede* is, then, a more complex and more problematic statement than has often been allowed. It is also a more helpful one in that it suggests the spectrum of human possibilities and of their interpretative expression that sustains Stifter's work as a whole. I propose to look at one story in detail, and to suggest by brief reference to other works how the implications of that story recur throughout Stifter's *oeuvre*. I am not hoping to prove thematic—or technical—conformity. Rather, I am attempting to show that there is a recurring constellation of human and artistic possibilities in Stifter's art and that this constellation allows of a great variety of possible meanings.

Granit, from the *Bunte Steine* collection, is a *Rahmenerzählung*, a story with a narrative frame. It begins by describing a granite block that stands in front of the narrator's childhood home. The narrator recalls how one day, while he was sitting on this stone, a trick was played on him by Andreas, the *Schmiermann* (seller of grease and pitch). The boy allows his feet to be smeared with cart grease—and runs into the house to show his mother. She is furious at the mess he makes on the clean floor; in her anger she refers to him as "unholy and obstinate" (20), and carries him into an outhouse where she beats his legs with branches and twigs. She then leaves him to ponder his misdeeds. The boy is heartbroken at the terrible turn of events; the ordered, familiar world has fallen about his ears. However trivial the incident may seem, within the boy's perspective it is a catastrophe of world-shaking proportions. This is reflected by the uproar in the house, by the frantic activity of the maids, by the fact that the "swallow flew screaming in and out of the door because of the constant disturbance below its nest" (23). However, comfort arrives in the person of the boy's grandfather, who washes his feet clean and then takes the boy for a walk. During their walk, he tells him a story from the past of the region through which they are passing. It is a story that took place many years

142

previously and that centers upon a freak and terrible event—an outbreak of the plague. The grandfather begins his narration proper as follows: "In all these woods and in all these settlements long ago a strange thing happened—a great misfortune descended upon them. My grandfather, your great-great-grandfather, who lived at that time, often told us about it" (30).

The opening is symptomatic of the narrative perspective that is sustained throughout the telling of the plague story. The grandfather asserts both distance from and closeness to what he recounts. The events lie well in the past; they occurred at the time when the grandfather's grandfather was alive. They are, then, four generations removed from the little boy. Yet the very fact of family continuity and tradition—that the grandfather heard the story from his grandfather and is now passing it on to his grandson— gives the sense both of authenticity and of connection. Furthermore, the events took place in the natural world through which the grandfather is now walking with his grandson; the same landscape that surrounds them was the scene of the various terrible events recounted. We return frequently to the frame and are reminded of the continued existence of the world in which the plague once wrought such terrible destruction. This dual sense of distance and closeness is central to the meaning of the story which the old man tells. The story opens with a description of the unexpectedness of the plague. No reason can be found for the outbreak, and the human suffering is appalling. Furthermore, all social cohesion is lost, all moral dictates are forgotten, although the natural world continues to fulfill its cycle as always. The cherries and the corn ripen, but no one bothers to harvest them. It is from the natural world that salvation finally comes. A peasant hears the magic song of a bird, and the words of the song are a recipe against the plague. The word is spread around, the people follow the advice, and gradually the epidemic disappears.

The grandfather then comes to the specific details of the story he has to tell: it concerns a pitchman's family that, on the orders of the father, withdraws from the community and takes to the woods in the hope of escaping the plague. All their precautions are in vain, however, and the family is destroyed—with the exception of the little boy. He knows how to support himself from the wild life around him, and his skill saves not only his own life, but also the life of a little girl whom he discovers by chance. When he meets her, she is gravely ill from the plague, but he manages to nurse her back to health. Many years later the two of them marry, and the boy becomes one of the most prosperous and respected members of the community. At the end of the story, we return to the present of the narrative frame. When grandfather and grandson return home, all traces of the disturbance have faded. Peace reigns in the house— and in the swallows' nest "the young swallows twittered in their sleep" (52). As the boy is falling asleep that night he is aware of his mother coming into the room, and she makes the sign of the cross over him as an expression of her forgiveness. The angry condemnation of him as "unholy" (*"heillos"*) has been retracted, the sacred order has reasserted itself.

The plague story is, in itself, not a particularly remarkable or challenging tale. It has very much the feel of a local legend or a *Märchen*, and it expresses a simple moral lesson. For this reason, it is tempting to dismiss *Granit* as a work of harmless didacticism. Yet one must remember that Stifter's story, as we possess it, has a particularly extended frame. Indeed, more time is spent on the frame situation (*Rahmensituation*) than on the inset story (*Binnenerzählung*) itself. We have to ask ourselves why this should be—and whether this is a defensible narrative constellation. In the first place, one must note the care and the frequency with which Stifter establishes explicit links between the inset story and the frame. There is, for example, the fact that the grandfather has inherited the story from his grandfather—and is continuing the line of family continuity by passing it on to his grandson. There is also the fact that Andreas, the *Schmiermann*, is descended from the pitchman of the inset story.

There are also, in the frame situation, references to the columns of smoke, to the fact that there are nomadic groups of people who live in the woods. This mode of existence—and the smoke that signals it—plays an important part in the plague story. There are, then, many specific links of this kind that can be made. Yet one has the feeling that this is only scratching the surface of the problem, that the answer must be more substantial, more fully integrated into the import of both frame and inset story. One notes that pages go by before the grandfather begins his actual story—and that there are frequent interruptions to his narrative as we return to the *Rahmensituation*. Passages such as the following exchange between grandfather and grandson abound:

"And what is that which stands in front of the Alp?" he asked again.
"That is the Hütten forest," I answered.
"And to the right of the Alp and the Hütten forest?"
"That is the Philippgeorgsberg mountain."
"And to the right of the Philippgeorgsberg?"
"That is the Seewald, the forest with the dark, deep lake."
"And again to the right of the Seewald?"
"That is the Blockenstein and the Sesselwald."
"And further to the right?"
"That is the Tussetwald" (27f.).

Details of the landscape are referred to over and over again. The passage quoted above is an example (and it is by no means the only one) of the relentless naming of the landscape, of a stately exchange of question and answer. We have to account for the frequency of such passages— and for the length and stylistic weightiness that is assigned to them. Obviously, the presence of such passages implies much more than a concern on Stifter's part with local color, more even than a realistic intention. In a dialogue such as the one quoted above we have a degree of stylization that suggests quite specifically the rhythm of a litany. Such passages are a credo, a reverent saying of articles of faith. The landscape is the source and embodiment of the security that pervades the story; it is the unexceptional, but utterly reliable, guarantor for the fact that the horrors of the plague do not in the last analysis disturb the even and sacred continuity of life as a total—or, in Stifter's sense, "epic"—continuity of being. Indeed, even during the time of the plague, the landscape keeps faith with man. It continues to give of its treasures; the corn ripens as always. When the plague has passed, men discover that the natural world is unmarked by the horrors that have occurred. Hence, the continuing, self-renewing presence of the landscape is central to the meaning not only of the frame, but of the story as a whole; and herein resides the persuasive power of *Granit*. It could be argued that in this story—as elsewhere in Stifter—the portrayal of specifically human experience is somewhat limited. However, the depiction of nature brings us to the heart of Stifter's vision, to its overall epic weight and grandeur. Indeed, for Stifter, man finds strength and shelter by anchoring himself as fully as possible in the measured rhythm of the natural order. The naming of the landscape is part of a much larger attempt to know and to assent to the unspectacular details of what abundantly and sustainingly *is*. The lesson that this natural world teaches those who approach it with the reverent absorption of the grandfather is one in which the general triumphs over the particular, the ordinary over the exceptional, the timeless over the temporal.

This lesson is vindicated in the closing section of the frame. The exceptional event—the collapse of family harmony—may dislocate the secure order for a while. Yet ultimately, that order proves too strong; the disturbance passes, and the simple world is left as vigorous as ever. The implications of the grandfather's story are borne out by the events of the frame story. This vindication takes place at a level that goes much deeper than any overt didacticism. Obviously, the import of the story the grandfather tells can comfort and sustain the little boy in his present unhappiness. Still, one must not overestimate the explicitly pedagogic force of the old man's narration. It is not because he has acquired certain insights that the boy is reconciled with his mother. He is already forgiven by the time he returns home. The reconciliation comes about because the capacity for reconciliation, for overcoming conflict and disturbance, is inherent in the whole nature of creation as Stifter portrays it. Time is the great healer, because it is the dimension that allows everyday normality to digest and to encapsulate the freak event. By the time the boy returns home, the temporal law has done its work; the discord is now a thing of the past, securely vanquished by the sheer resilience of ordinary reality. Hence, time is a crucial factor in the story, and its narrative structure intimates a time scale that encompasses both present (the frame) and past (the inset story), and that allows the two to interlock in such a way that we can distinguish the lasting from the temporary. The things that are frequently dismissed by man turn out to be the things that last, whereas the things that are frequently of overriding concern turn out to be purely localized phenomena. Furthermore, the time scale in the story is even greater than this summary suggests. The story opens and closes with a mention of the granite block that stands in front of the house. This stone has a temporal dimension that far exceeds even the collective memory of the human family: "The stone is very old, and nobody remembers having heard of a time when it was laid" (17). And at the end of the story we return to our starting point: "Since then many years have passed; the stone still stands in front of my father's house, but now my sister's children are playing on it" (53). The narrator is now grown up, but he has never forgotten the story his grandfather told him. He passes the story on to us, to another generation of hearers. The stone still stands before the house, and a new generation of children play around it. The human continuity is sustained, and behind that continuity stands the even greater continuity of the natural world, of forests, lakes and hills, above all, of the enduring block of stone that is

story suggests the presence in the human mind of a speculative construct, of a cosmic chain of cause and effect that can help man to locate any given event or set of events in an overall context. The narrator writes of the possibility that:

> A serene chain of flowers hangs through the infinity of the universe and sends its shimmer into human hearts; it is the chain of cause and effect. And into the human mind was planted the finest of these flowers, reason, the eye of the soul, in order to be the anchoring point for this chain—so that one could count flower by flower, link by link right back to that hand in which the end rests. And if, at some future time, we have counted correctly, and if we can survey that count, then chance will cease to exist for us—there will only be necessary sequences, there will be no more misfortune—only retribution . . . (6).

This is a possibility—and no more. One notes the conditional mode—if we have counted correctly and if we can survey the whole sequence of things counted, then the world order becomes meaningful. However, the narrator goes on to argue that the condition is one that man cannot fulfill—nor can we conceive of his ever being able to fulfill it: "Events still flow past us like a sacred riddle, pain still comes and goes in the human heart—perhaps it too, in the last analysis, is itself a flower in that chain? Who can ever know?" (6). The perspective of overall viewpoint, the ability to take in at a glance a whole sequence of generations, these possibilities are embedded in the narrative perspective of *Granit*; but they are excluded from the narrative perspective of *Abdias*. Indeed, the opening to *Abdias* makes clear that the very laws that were felt to be sustaining in *Granit* are here a source of anguish, of existential helplessness: "But truly there is something horrific in the impassive innocence with which natural laws work. . . . For today with the same lovely face blessing is dispensed and tomorrow the terrible occurs. And when both have passed, then nature is serenity itself, as before" (5). The serenity ("*Unbe-fangenheit*") after the plague is the source of comfort in *Granit*, because that serenity is integrated into a human attitude, an epic narrative perspective. *Abdias*, however, is a story that observes with fascinated, horror-struck intimacy the series of disasters that destroys the main character. The narration, bereft of the ability to stand back interpretatively, can only suggest that there is an indifference to man's world in the laws of nature, an indifference that in certain lives amounts to a malignancy of cosmic proportions. The world continues its way, being constantly renews itself, but the core of the process is the "*Unvernunft des Seins*"—the "irrationality of being" (6)—a kind of ruthless, blind will that is reminiscent of Schopenhauer's *Wille*.

At a cosmic level, then, the story can offer no interpretative certainty; and at the human—and moral—level, the story can likewise do no more than conjecture. When Abdias's home is pillaged by Melek, we are given a possible interpretation of what has happened. Yet it is Abdias's neighbors who express the conviction of his moral guilt. We have no authoritative statement from the narrative voice: " 'Because you walked about in their arrogant clothing, they suspected your wealth, the wrath of the Lord found and crushed you' " (22). It would at first sight seem as though the neighbors are right, for Abdias learns a lesson from his misfortune. He finds intense happiness in the life of his child, a happiness that unites him again with his wife. Abdias himself interprets the event that has overtaken him as the "beginning of his salvation" (26). However, the ray of hope—and of interpretative understanding and insight—is not sustained. Deborah bleeds to death shortly after she has given birth to Ditha. All the narrator can offer is a laconic statement of the sheer perversity of what happens: "She [Deborah] had little good fortune in this marriage, and when her luck changed she had to die" (38). Abdias moves to Europe and settles in Austria. His way of life has changed completely; he is now peaceful and contented, absorbed in reverent love for his daughter. Yet

Ditha does not develop normally. It is almost as though perversity is the guiding principle in Abdias's life. Again, the narrator can give us no interpretation. He simply states the bare, horrific fact that "she was a lie" (73). The only interpretation we are given is, as before, a conjecture made by other people: "They attributed the misfortune of his daughter to the just verdict of God who wanted to punish the boundless avarice of the father" (78). Such an interpretation implies an overview (*Überblick*) that the narrator cannot share. His comments on the senseless killing of the dog are typical of his perspective throughout: he sees it as a "misfortune—as though in this man's life it had to happen that things interlocked to form the strangest adversities" (79). The perversity is heightened by the tormenting glimpses of happiness and fulfillment. Ditha is struck by lightning—and regains her sight. The thunderstorm destroys the roof of Abdias's house and ruins the crops of the neighboring farms—and passes, leaving behind it a shimmering rainbow as a last glimpse of its strange power. The gentle flowering of Ditha's personality after the miraculous restoration of her sight is an idyll of infinite beauty. Yet it is of limited duration, for another thunderstorm occurs, and Ditha is killed. Once again, the narrator can only share Abdias's paralyzed horror at what has happened, his battered disbelief that this inert form is his daughter: "He stared at the being before him and did not believe that this thing was his daughter" (103). Abdias loses his sanity after this last terrible blow, and lives on for many years in vacant helplessness. At the end of the story, our narrator intimates the bare fact—which in *Granit* was a source of comfort and certainty—that life goes on. Here in this story, where even the narrator is excluded from that interpretative perspective that would allow him to draw comfort from the fact that natural and human worlds continue undisturbed, this same fact becomes the ultimate expression of the sheer indifference of the world order. We read: "The thunderstorm, which with its soft flame had kissed the life away from the girl's head, poured out on that same

drama as an unending chain of being, as a massive, timeless cycle of generations in the context of which individual fate (however heartrending) emerges as largely irrelevant to the overall design. In terms of human attitude, this means that the individual seeks to obliterate his own individuality by embedding himself in the continuity of village life, of family tradition, so that the relentlessness and indifference of the self-renewing chain of being becomes a kind of reliable—and total—ontological shelter. There may, of course, be much wrenching, much renunciation involved, but the process can work, and can represent real human fulfillment. On the other hand, it can fail. There are people who cannot—or who are not allowed to—subdue their existence and their emotional needs as individuals.

In a story such as *Der Hagestolz* Stifter combines a whole spectrum of human possibilities in one work. The uncle— the *Hagestolz* or embittered bachelor of the title—exists as an irreducible parcel of wounded individuality, as a man whose suffering, loneliness, and deprivation can be healed neither by the passage of time nor by the "gentle law" of the natural and human world. The story also shows, however, how the healing process can work. Ludmilla (like Risach and Mathilde in *Der Nachsommer*) can find fulfillment and contentment in the later years of her life, her sorrow can be safely insulated in the past, and the young Viktor can be helped (as Risach can help Heinrich in *Der Nachsommer*) to avoid the mistakes of youth and to recognize simple and abiding happiness when it offers itself to him. The story ends with a characteristic narrative comment in which the "epic" time scale is invoked—and shows the uncle as ruthlessly excluded from any participation in the great stream of human continuity:

> Then the sun shines down always and always, the blue sky smiles from one millennium to the other, the earth dons its time-honored green and the generations follow their path down the long chain to the youngest child; but he is eradicated without trace because his existence has

left no imprint, because his offspring do not move down the stream of time. But if he has left other traces, they too fade as everything earthly fades—and when in the ocean of days finally everything, everything is swallowed up, even the greatest, the most joyous of man's experiences, so he disappears the more swiftly, because everything about him is dying even as he breathes and lives (351).

Here the narrative voice balances both endorsement and rejection of the "epic" perspective on human affairs in that it speaks in terms of that pluralism of experiential possibilities the story has explored. The cruelty and indifference is there—the old man is tossed aside as an irrelevancy, and ultimately the cycle is about the death and extinction of each specific, created being. On the other hand, there is the sense that to those who partake of human continuity, who are part of the abiding sequence of family life, the sting is taken out of the universal principle of transience, for to them is granted as much immortality and rootedness as man can ever know.

This story, then, would seem to be a kind of overall summation of the view of human life in all its various possibilities that Stifter seeks to convey through his art. Yet not even this can be asserted unequivocally, for such a concern with the continuity of human generations, when implemented as a philosophy, as a recipe for right living, can be disastrous. This is shown with great power in *Der Waldgänger*. Georg and Corona have been happily married for a number of years. They are deeply in love, but they decide to separate because their marriage has proved childless. They sacrifice their happiness to the notional fulfillment promised by involvement in the sacred law of family continuity. However, the decision is a disaster. What destroys these two people is not just freak external occurrences (as in *Abdias*), but their own ruthless attempt to assert principle as a source of fulfillment—rather than trusting their actual experience. For Corona, the attempt quite simply founders in her inability to carry out the proposed course of action; her love for Georg has become the inalienable foundation of her being, and she cannot erase this without erasing her own existence. Georg is, in practical terms, more successful: he does remarry and he has two children, but in the long run this does not provide him with a sense of security or fulfillment. Rather, it gives him a precise and inescapable sense of his own loneliness. At the end of this story, when the narrator once again formulates the overview (*Überblick*) perspective, the evaluative coloring is, as one would expect, a somber one. The law of family continuity becomes the law of individual expendability. Children grow up and leave the parental home and make their own separate way through life. Also, as the opening section, "*Der Waldgänger*," shows, there is no way around this ineluctable law. Georg adopts a little boy—the *Hegerbub*—and teaches him all he can. Still, eventually the boy has to go away to school. In one sense, then, the general law can only yield a sustaining human interpretation as an abstract principle, as a construct. Yet it has to be enacted by specific individuals, and there is no guarantee that the sustaining force of the generality will be embedded in the facts of their specific experience of life. For Georg and Corona, the general law simply guarantees the presence of loneliness and deprivation as their experiential bedrock:

> Georg is alone again, as he had to be in the eyes of the children whom he so desperately craved—the bough, left to itself, withered, as the new shoots grow upward in their strength and youth toward the new air, as they look upward to their blue sky, their clouds, to their sun—and never backward to him from whom they grew. These sons will one day receive the same letter telling them that their father has died, just as their father, absorbed in his studies, had learned that he no longer had parents living and both were buried in the earth. And so it will con-

tinue, as it did, starting with his parents, as it continues in the lives of his sons—and as it will continue in the *Heger-bub*. He may take up a handicraft, a trade, he may turn to the wide sea of scientific research on which he will sail away until he too will be abandoned by his son and will stand alone on the ship as it sinks (468).

The overall view here, as applied to the specific lives depicted, expresses a despairing ruthlessness for which the traditional literary-historical image of Stifter scarcely allows. Yet it is a perspective that grows organically from the story told, a perspective that represents yet another possibility within the experiential universe of Stifter's fiction. The range of Stifter's art derives from his recognition of the uneasy relationship between individuality and generality that can allow of both profound fulfillment and of unrelieved despair.[8]

In Stifter's narrative art the act of interpretation, of establishing perspective, is part of the central theme. Stifter explores the hermeneutic challenge that is so characteristic of the novelle—the friction that results when the specific is pitted against the general, the exceptional against the recurrent. He faces the full implications of this interaction with a generosity of human response and with a corresponding differentiation of narrative perspective that makes him a writer of real breadth and stature. For all the excellence of his two novels, he is most successful as a writer of novellen, because the form itself invites the kind of interpretative tension that his theme demands. Of course, Stifter spends much of his time attempting to exorcise the unheard of, the unique, the intractably individual by expending narrative length and intensity on things, on details of the natural landscape, simply because they have reliable, unproblematic being. Stifter may indeed long for man to attain to just such a state of being. Yet this does not

[8] In attempting to define the range of Stifter's art, I have derived great pleasure and profit from the studies by Gelley, George, Müller, Seidler, Steffen, Stern, Weiss listed in the bibliography.

lead him to betray the human drama, to portray it as more soluble or more manageable than it is. Stifter's universe is one that admits of both hope and despair, of hope for the generality of mankind and of despair for any number of specific individuals.

VIII. Keller: *Die drei gerechten Kammacher*

Gottfried Keller was born in Zurich in 1819. As a young man he intended to pursue a career as a painter. He spent two years studying art in Munich, only to find that he had mistaken his vocation. He returned home to Switzerland, penniless and without a profession, but a scholarship enabled him to spend the years from 1848 to 1850 studying in Heidelberg. Here he came under the influence of Feuerbach; he was impressed by the passionate affirmation contained in the latter's atheism—by the notion that the world is meaningful in its own right, precisely because it is not validated from without (by some metaphysical agency). In the early 1850s Keller went to Berlin and his career as a prose writer began. In 1855 he returned to Zurich and became a civil servant, remaining the *erster Staatsschreiber* until his retirement in 1876. In many ways, Keller remains a complex and elusive figure; part of him, certainly, was the forthright pedagogue, concerned with imparting the values of common sense, of unequivocal allegiance to effective practical work in society. Yet, at his best, he is not a philistine realist; his works contain much irony—and a humor that can be both conciliatory and, at times, genuinely uncomfortable. Moreover, he also had an unremitting sense that individual people can deny themselves—or be denied—a fulfilling relationship to the practical world, and can, as a result, find themselves inhabiting an increasingly lifeless universe. He is certainly at his best when taking issue with the social experience—and values—of his times. The collection of tales entitled *Die Leute von Seldwyla* (*The People of Seldwyla*) embodies this aspect of his art most clearly.

Die drei gerechten Kammacher (*The Three Upright Combmakers*) belongs to the first volume of Seldwyla stories (1856).

Keller prefaces this volume with an introductory statement about the setting—the imaginary Swiss community of Seldwyla—and he analyzes the sense in which Seldwyla constitutes both a physical and a spiritual climate whose presence can be felt in all the stories that he tells.[1] Seldwyla, he asserts, has changed very little over the last three hundred years; indeed, it remains the same little backwater—*"immer das gleiche Nest"* (1).[2] Resistance to change would appear to have been very much part of the intention of the founding fathers who placed it "a good half hour away from a navigable river . . . as a clear sign that nothing should come of the place" (1). It does, however, enjoy great natural advantages: a good wine and extensive forests, the latter constituting the principal source of income for the community. It is a given wealth the inhabitants take very much for granted. This enjoyment of well-nigh automatic financial security accounts for the dominant characteristic of the people—their *Gemütlichkeit*, their easygoing cheerfulness and geniality. The ethos of Seldwyla is, however, not without its ambiguities and tensions. The young people, we are told, are very much the advantaged section of the community. They tend not to work themselves, but to employ foreign labor, "and use their profession for the pursuit of a lively traffic in debts, which constitutes the basis of the power, glory, and jollity of the gentlemen of Seldwyla" (2). However, the paradise is of limited duration, for once youth gives place to middle age, the Seldwyler finds himself excluded from this "credit paradise" (2). Many of them will choose to leave Seldwyla. Some will go abroad in order to learn to tighten their belts and will, on their return to Seldwyla, be among the best "drill sergeants in Switzerland" (3). Others will continue their easygoing way of life in foreign parts, and Keller assures us that the world has its fair share of Seldwyler whose

---

[1] For a discussion of the historical and social factors listed in the preface see Hans Richter, *Gottfried Kellers frühe Novellen*, pp. 48ff.

[2] References throughout are to Gottfried Keller, *Sämtliche Werke*, vol. 7, ed. Jonas Fränkel, Zurich and Munich, 1927.

principal claim to fame is that they have impeccable social manners. Those who remain in Seldwyla are curiously without any profession or trade; they devote themselves to various kinds of odd jobs and casual labor. However, the rich forests continue to provide for basic necessities, and the Seldwyler retain their contentment and good humor. In addition, they have one great hobby that is the source of endless entertainment: politics. They have a remarkable capacity for "political mobility" (3), for changing their colors as an automatic protest against whatever party happens to be in power. Yet the greatest source of their good humor is, we are told, their wine and apple juice. The grape and apple harvest can prove a time when the whole community is incapable of any solid work.

Keller concludes this summary of the characteristics of the Seldwyler with a straightforward opposition between the ethos of the community and that of the outside world: "But the less a Seldwyler is able to make good at home, the better does he get on, strangely enough, when he goes abroad" (6). Here Keller suggests what proves to be one of the central concerns of the Seldwyla stories: the relationship between this specific community and the ethos by which it lives and the wider human community outside its walls and the kinds of ethos by which it lives. This opposition is at the heart of Keller's most challenging exploration of Seldwyla, because it allows him, as narrator, to be very much part of Seldwyla, without however succumbing to the narrowness of its outlook. As the introduction makes clear, Keller is by no means uncritical of Seldwyla and what it stands for. He links the irresponsibility of the people with economic irresponsibility, with indiscriminate buying on credit, with thoughtless squandering of the natural resources of the area. Indeed, the *Gemütlichkeit* on which the citizens so pride themselves is intrinsically problematic. It is an eroding ethos, and those who succumb to its influence either have to make a clean break both with their physical and moral environment or they will end their days eking out a pathetically improvised living. Even those who do break out either continue in their flaccid easygoing ways, or they become men of iron discipline, definitive military disciplinarians. What Keller suggests, then, in his introduction to the Seldwyla tales is both the questionableness and the charm of the Seldwyla ethos. Keller also suggests, by implication, that the experience of the outsider who enters this community, or, conversely, the experience of the insider who is forced to break with his home community, is the decisive area where this little Swiss world yields its full moral and social implications. As the stories themselves show, it is this marginal area—both literally and metaphorically—that will provide Keller with the material he recounts. It is in these terms that Keller himself defines the thematic interest of the stories he narrates. He points out that, given the character of the Seldwyla community, there can be no shortage of strange life histories. However, he continues: "Yet in this little volume I do not want to tell such stories as are inherent in the character of Seldwyla as I have described it—but rather a number of strange oddities, which happened from time to time, exceptions as it were, but they could only occur in Seldwyla" (6). Perhaps we should push Keller's argument a stage further and suggest that these experiences are typical precisely because they are exceptional, precisely because they involve the radical and explicit enactment of what is always latent in the workings of the community. We should add a further layer of paradox: the marginal experience is central to the interpretative undertaking that Keller announces in the preface because at the margins of this society the deepest implications of its sustaining ethos are laid bare. They are concretized in lived experience that our narrator can both recount and comment upon. Marginal experience—whether in the form of the alienated outsider or of the alienated insider—constitutes a challenge to the Seldwyla ethos. The radicalism of this challenge—interpretatively—is the measure of Keller's own honesty in confronting the problem he has set himself.

Die drei gerechten Kammacher opens with a general introduction that recalls to the reader's mind several of the arguments advanced in the preface to the stories. We are told that the Seldwyler have shown that frivolous people can just about get along together—whereas the three *Kammmacher* (combmakers) prove that three upright, "righteous" men cannot live under the same roof without getting on each other's nerves. Here, Keller immediately defines the prevailing ingredient of the Seldwyla ethos—"*Ungerechtigkeit*" ("unrighteousness") or "*Leichtsinn*" ("frivolity"). He goes on to indicate that the three combmakers are "righteous" ("*gerecht*"): they embody an ethos that is diametrically opposed to the lighthearted, frivolous climate of the town. Keller is careful to introduce an immediate qualification of the notion of *Gerechtigkeit*— "righteousness." It is, we are told, neither divine righteousness, nor the "natural righteousness of the human conscience," but it is "that bloodless righteousness which has removed from the Lord's Prayer the sentence 'and forgive us our debts as we forgive our debtors'—because it never makes any debts" (259). Two notions are important here: first, the bloodlessness of the ethic that dominates the Kammacher, a bloodlessness that will be reflected in their character and behavior; second, the modification of the Lord's Prayer that the ethic of the combmakers implies. The sentence from the prayer is concerned with moral and spiritual guilt, but, for the Kammacher, guilt is no such complex commodity: it means debt, quantifiable, i.e. monetary debt. In this touch of ironic commentary Keller suggests how the combmakers are reduced human beings, reduced because they know only one value scale, that of hard work with a view to monetary advancement. Guilt, for them, is a sin against this ethos—the sin of "getting into debt." In the radicalism of their creed, the combmakers not only diminish their own existence as human beings, but they also function as catalysts who bring to the fore all that is latent in the Seldwyla ethos. For example, it will be remembered that Seldwyla is particularly renowned for its *Schuldenverkehr*, its irresponsible and wholesale dependence on credit. The Kammacher are three people for whom the repudiation of this way of life is nothing short of an obsession.

Keller goes on to give further examples of the creed of *Gerechtigkeit* that is to play such an important part in the story. It involves joyless commitment to hard work and the obsessive hoarding of money. *Gerechtigkeit* is an inherently individualist, competitive ethic, and its practitioners derive sustenance from the degree to which they can be seen to surpass all others in their ascetic aloofness from the shallow worldliness of a frivolous society. Thus they seek out a community "where there are a great number of—in their terms—unrighteous people" (259). In many respects this creed recalls Max Weber's definition of the Protestant ethic. In this story, Keller with a precise artistic and social sense confronts this ethic with the easygoing ethic of Seldwyla. That he should find the code by which the combmakers live monstrous and horrific is scarcely surprising. However, the greatness of Keller's story resides in the careful dialectic that it sustains, whereby the *Gemütlichkeit* of the Seldwyler, for all its appealing qualities—particularly when compared to the existence of the Kammacher—is ultimately no more a genuinely humane value than is the righteousness that it so strenuously—and rightly—repudiates.

The opening paragraph is both a witty and precise introduction to the theme of the story, suggesting as it does the all-important confrontation between *Gerechtigkeit* ("righteousness") and *Leichtsinn* ("frivolity"). Yet this paragraph is important in a deeper sense: it serves to establish a narrative mode that is to be of central significance to the story as a whole. This mode is one of moral evaluation. The first paragraph is full of interpretative statements that express human judgments. We are, for example, told that the combmakers see the world as "a huge, well-managed police institution" (260). This first paragraph is, of course, concerned principally with the ethos of the Kammacher, and it is on this that judgment is passed. The *Leichtsinn* of Seldwyla is used—at this stage of the story—simply as a foil, as a contrasting possibility that serves to highlight the monstrousness of the combmakers. However, Keller is careful not to claim too much for Seldwyla; he makes only one statement in this paragraph—"a whole town of unrighteous or frivolous people can just about get along" (259). This is hardly to be accounted unreserved enthusiasm, and one notes the qualifying phrase "just about" ("*zur Not*").

In the second sentence of the story, the narrator makes it quite clear that what he rejects is not *Gerechtigkeit* as such, but the specific form of righteousness that is practiced by the Kammacher. There is such a thing as "the natural righteousness of the human conscience" (259), and it is with this yardstick in mind that the narrator judges both the Kammacher and the Seldwyler. Indeed, it is essential to the radicalism of the confrontation between these two ethics that there is no middle ground left, that a polarization takes place. This is superbly suggested in the narrator's telling phrase that the Kammacher "make their home where there are a great number of—in their terms—unrighteous people" (259). The combmakers seek out a community that is the overt antithesis of all they stand for. By their aloofness, by their repudiation of this community, they will force it to be radical in *its* repudiation of them, to become more and more "unrighteous—in their terms."

With the interpretative framework of his story thus established, the narrator embarks on the process of introducing his main characters to the reader. This he does at great length, paying unremitting attention to the details of their behavior and attitudes. Jobst is the first to arrive. He is an "orderly and quiet apprentice" who "worked like an animal and was not to be got rid of, so that he finally became a lasting fixture" (261). If the first two epithets suggest positive evaluation, the images that follow intimate a degree of

criticism: Jobst is likened to an animal (*"Tierlein"*), to a fixture (*"Hausrat"*) within the business. What is here suggested, of course, is human degradation. Moreover, our
narrator is careful to make the point that, since the master
has no hesitation about exploiting his apprentices, he bears
part of the responsibility for this degradation. Gradually,
however, the moral judgments multiply until it becomes
clear that Jobst invites—and indeed encourages—his master's exploitation. We are told that even on Sundays the
apprentice works through until the afternoon, and the
narrator is swift to control the reader's response to this
piece of information: "One must not imagine that he did
this with any good humor and pleasure" (262). We are later
told that Jobst's work reflects the joylessness of his whole
way of life: it is "sober and unimaginative" (263). When he
does take time off from work, it is only to stand around
"humbly and tediously" (263). Once again, the narrator intimates the strangeness of Jobst's behavior, gently imput-
ing certain normative responses to the reader by which the
apprentice is to be judged and found wanting: "So—for
him—time passed in the cheapest and most amusing way
possible" (263); or again, "This had, for him, been a
pleasurable Sunday" (264). The force of phrases such as
"for him"—*nach seiner Art*" or *"für ihn"*—is unmistakable.
Furthermore, this quirkiness of human response is, we are
told, not without its self-righteousness: there is about Jobst
"an implicit hint of inward irony . . . as though he were se-
cretly laughing at the frivolity and vanity of the world"
(264). The narrator then enters Jobst's mind, having up to
now been concerned principally with the observable facts
of his behavior. We are told of the apprentice's great
plan—to save up enough money to buy the business and
then to devote himself exclusively to the growth of his fortune. This explicit revelation of what goes on in Jobst's
mind leads to the first unequivocal condemnation from the
narrator:

> But the inhuman thing about this quiet, peaceable plan
> was the fact that Jobst had conceived it at all; for nothing

in his heart compelled him to stay specifically in Seldwyla, no fondness either for the area, or the people, or
the political constitution of this country, or its customs.
All this was as much a matter of indifference to him as
was his own home, for which he felt nothing; in a
hundred places in the world he, with his industriousness
and righteousness, could have taken hold as he had
here; but he had no free choice and in his empty mind
grasped the first strand of hope that by chance came his
way in order to hang on to it and suck it dry. My homeland is where I am doing well, it is often said, and this
proverb is absolutely valid for those who really can show
a better, more cogent explanation for why they are doing
well in their new fatherland, for those who went out into
the world of their own free will. . . . But all these people,
wherever they are, will at least have to be fond of this
new land of their prosperity and there, too, be a fair ap-
proximation of a human being (265f.).

The importance of this passage resides in its moral
scrupulousness. The narrator is explicit in his condemnation of Jobst for his inability to have any relationship either
to his country of origin or to his elected homeland. He argues that, if a man sets up a home in a country, this must
involve something more than an economic or pragmatic
calculation, that there must be some kind of deeper attachment to his new home. Yet Jobst "had no free choice."
He is subhuman; one notes the animal imagery of "to hang
on to it and suck it dry." He lacks all manner of responses
to what living entails. He is an automaton in every sense of
the word, and it is for this that the narrator condemns him.
The source of the narrator's judgment is the notion—
presumed as implicit in the reader—of what a human
being is and how he should be constituted. The narrator
appeals, then, to an inherent humane sense in his audience, to "the natural righteousness of the human conscience." By this criterion, a criterion the narration intimates at considerable length and by a kind of moral debate
with the reader, Jobst is found wanting. He is less a man,

we are told, than one of "those lower organisms" (267). Furthermore, one should note that the moral implications of such sternly discursive narrative comments are sustained throughout the story by the technique of characterization that is employed. When, for example, we see Jobst in action, we find ourselves watching a calculating machine rather than a human being. The humor with which the narrator portrays such behavior is an integral part of the moral judgment that he makes. The humor functions as the implicit underpinning of the passages of explicit evaluation.

Fridolin is the next apprentice to arrive. A tense few hours pass between him and Jobst, "and yet after the passage of a few hours, each knew that the other was more or less his complete double" (271). Their behavior is identical, as are their possessions. From this it follows that Fridolin subscribes to the same ethic as Jobst, an ethic that reduces man to a machine. Jobst and Fridolin's interchangeability, their lack of individual profile, is symptomatic of their total submission to the austere ethic that identifies functional impersonality as the highest good. This point is underscored by the arrival of Dietrich, the third Kammacher. Here the narrator spends hardly any time on introducing the new character—for the simple reason that Dietrich is not a new character. He is an exact replica of Jobst and Fridolin. All three share the same ethic, all three work with the single-mindedness of machines, all three reduce their every action and utterance to functional sameness. In the process, they reduce themselves to the same level as what they make, do, or say. Keller suggests this idea with superb economy by his use of images: we are told not only that Dietrich "lay like a match" (273) in bed, but that "the bed cover lay on them like a paper wrapping on three sardines" (273). When the three confront each other in the course of the day, they resemble "the corners of an equilateral triangle" (273). The images all suggest a comic perspective on the combmakers, a comedy that is used to make a point, to pass moral judgment. Both the comedy and the moral argument derive from the carefully intimated discrepancy between the combmakers' way of life and some implied norm of warm, flexible humanity.

Thus the scene is set for the three-cornered battle. The combmakers devote themselves with lunatic competitiveness to their work, each with the hope of making the others redundant. However, Dietrich, the youngest member of the trio, realizes that he is at a disadvantage because he has less savings than Jobst and Fridolin. He decides on a remedy—marriage. The narrator highlights the sheer moral perversion involved: "As his heart was free of every passion, as free as were his fellow apprentices, with the exception of the obsession to settle here and nowhere else, to realize the advantages of the situation, so he came up with the idea of falling in love and of asking for the hand of someone who owned approximately as much as the Saxon and Bavarian [Jobst and Fridolin] had hidden under the tiles" (274). The formulation here is particularly telling. Dietrich does more than simply arrange a mercenary marriage: he decides that he must also fall in love. The sense of a personality utterly out of joint is captured in the telling phrase: "He came up with the idea of falling in love." The extraordinary yoking of cerebral calculation with emotional attachment is both richly comic and very disturbing. Furthermore, the plan has an almost bureaucratic accuracy: Dietrich knows exactly how much of a dowry he needs to be thoroughly competitive. The narrator goes on to make the moral point explicit by drawing upon the Seldwyler as the contrasting agent: "It was one of the better characteristics of the Seldwyler that they did not take ugly or disagreeable wives simply because of their financial means" (274). Here the Seldwyler are identified with the implicit moral perceptions of the narrator, with that "natural righteousness of the human conscience" that is so much an evaluative touchstone throughout the story. Yet this is the only occasion on which such an overtly positive evaluation is made.

Dietrich decides upon an appropriate object for his designs, one Züs Bünzlin. In his characterization of Züs, the narrator (as he has done with the Kammacher) concentrates on those externals that express the personality, in this case, on her possessions:

> She kept the letter in a little lacquered drawer, where she also stored the statements of interest, her baptism certificate, her confirmation certificate, and a painted and gilded Easter egg; further, half a dozen silver teaspoons, the Lord's Prayer printed in gold on red, transparent material she called human skin, a cherrystone in which Christ's crucifixion was engraved, and a box of pierced ivory, lined with red taffeta, in which there was a little mirror and a silver thimble; further there was in the drawer another cherrystone in which a tiny set of skittles rattled, a nut in which the Blessed Virgin was enshrined behind glass, and when you opened it you found a silver heart containing a scented sponge, and a sweet box made of lemon peel on whose lid there was painted strawberry and in which a golden pin shaped like a forget-me-not lay embedded in cotton wool, and a medallion with a lock of hair . . . (275).

Züs, we must remember, is one of the Seldwyler. Hence, we would expect her to bring some kind of relief after the horrors of the combmakers' bare, impersonal world. Where they had virtually no trinkets, no personal possessions that have sentimental value, Züs is just the opposite. The narrator's listing of her possessions is richly comic, and the comedy is not so much conciliatory as disturbing. If one asks what makes the list have this impact, the answer lies not in any one factor, but in a combination of many.[3] First, there is the sheer length of the list, a length that reduces the syntax of the enormous sentence to a kind of desperate breathlessness. Second, there is the detail with which certain objects are described, a detail that becomes

---

[3] On the satirical import of the listing see Dietrich Pregel, "Das Kuriose, Komische und Groteske in Kellers Novelle *Die drei gerechten Kammacher*."

complicated and wearisome. One is left with an impression of labyrinthine confusion, which also informs the syntax: the cluttered relative clauses suggest the fussiness of the objects themselves. Furthermore, it is important to note that the list is divided into subgroupings, each of them opening with a phrase such as "further there was"—which in itself suggests a frantic concern for exhaustiveness. Also, the make-up of these subgroupings is important: "She kept the letter in a little lacquered drawer, where she also stored the statements of interest, her baptism certificate, her confirmation certificate, and a painted and gilded Easter egg." The grouping here consists of a series of objects that are of a kind (they are official documents, the notification of her inheritance, the statement of interest, birth and confirmation certificates), but the last item—the painted and gilded Easter egg—does not belong within this context. This discrepancy is a source of comedy, and, as elsewhere in the story, it is comedy that is used to make an important point. Here the suggestion is powerfully implanted that the various items of the list all have the same value for Züs, that they are *for her* all of a kind. Insofar as we instinctively notice differences to which Züs is blind, we both laugh at her and pass judgment on her. All the things in her possession become reduced to the same level: that of undifferentiated, interchangeable clutter. In this sense, Züs is guilty of the same diminution of her own humanity as are the Kammacher. The only difference is one of quantity—she has many possessions, they have few. Yet neither Züs nor the Kammacher make qualitative distinctions, neither is capable of perceiving that certain things are quite simply of a different order from others. That this involves something deeply disturbing in human terms is made clear in both cases. We note, for example, that Züs has "the Lord's Prayer printed in gold on red, transparent material she called human skin." The relative clause here suggests a degree of callousness, of sheer ghoulish delight, that makes of Züs something much more than a harmless figure of fun.[4] This becomes particularly clear when the narrator expands his depiction of Züs to take in the workings of her mind. We discover that her mind is like the drawer; she hoards information indiscriminately. We are told: "She still knew by heart the catechism, her declination tables, her arithmetic and geography book, her biblical history, and the worldly reading books" (279). Once again the listing effect of the sentence produces both humor and judgment. The narrator presides with this interpretative authority over the whole characterization of Züs, even to the point of offering us an explicit commentary on the significance of her most spectacular treasure—the Chinese temple made by a former suitor, a bookbinder. We are told: "It was also a symbol that it was she who had failed to understand the foolish, but sincere and well-intentioned nature of the bookbinder" (283). In the combmakers, however, Züs meets her worthy counterparts.

Dietrich has no sooner decided to court her than the others follow suit. Jobst particularly has to go through a considerable effort of reorientation at this point; up to now, he has resented Züs and her mother because he has to pay them for doing his laundry. Furthermore, marriage is an undreamed-of possibility: "He had never been in the habit of contemplating marriage, because he could only conceive of a woman as a being who wanted something from him that he did not owe her" (284). Here, as so often in the story, the narrator suggests the enormity of Jobst's attitudes. First, his mind is so debased that it cannot conceive of a wife as anything but a burden. Second, any notion of human interdependence, of moral relationship, is

[4] L. B. Jennings makes the telling point that Züs's trinkets for bloodletting give her a predatory, almost vampirelike quality ("Gottfried Keller and the Grotesque"). See also John M. Ellis's perceptive comment about the *Gewürzmörser*—that it is "suggestive of her treatment of the people with whom she comes into contact: they are crushed and ground up" (*Narration in the German Novelle*, p. 146). Ellis also rightly observes: "There is also in the many miniature things a suggestion of Züs, witch-like, reducing everything in size in order to lock it away in her cupboard" (p. 145).

for Jobst out of the question because it presupposes an interchange of giving and receiving that is not reducible to a quantifiable balance sheet. Once again, as in the introduction to the story, the notion of debt is important; Jobst can only owe someone something if he has formally signed an IOU.

However, the conquest of Züs becomes a necessary ingredient in his (and Fridolin's) plan. This second level of competition among them gradually puts pressure on their ability to live together. Before, they had been as peaceful in bed as ever—"quiet and seemly as three pencils" (286)—as the narrator so tellingly puts it. Now, the dream of possessing Züs proves so vivid to Jobst that, on one occasion, he knocks against Dietrich. The latter retaliates and a battle ensues. Gradually the three pairs of legs become so tangled up that all three fall screaming to the floor. In their half-sleeping state each imagines himself pursued by the Devil or by burglars, and all three end up standing over their treasure screaming at each other. Finally, they are separated and—"trembling with fear, anger, and shame" (287)—they crawl back into bed. At one level, this scene seems to be little more than a sequence of exuberant knockabout comedy. Yet there is more to it than this. The frenetic battle brings to the surface what has been an implicit undercurrent in their behavior up to now—panicky fear, rivalry, desperation. This scene in many ways prefigures the race that concludes the story: there as here one has the insane, mechanical fury of their struggle with one another, one has the impossible tangle of flailing limbs, one has the hideous fear, the somber manifestation of "fear, anger, and shame." The violence and grotesquerie of both scenes is an extension to radical proportions of what has been inherent in the behavior of the combmakers. The savagery is not, therefore, a break with the humor that has preceded it, but is, rather, the necessary and extreme enactment of the frantic, mechanical competitiveness of the Kammacher, of the ethic that has accounted for the comic monstrousness of their every action.

The final act of the drama follows immediately upon this scene. The owner of the shop has, we are told, done such a good business by exploiting the three apprentices that he has taken to living beyond his means. Hence, he decides on a policy of financial stringency that involves the dismissal of two of the Kammacher, and he proposes a race to decide who shall be allowed to stay. Züs associates her own desires with the proposed plan and agrees to give herself to the winner of the race. In a speech of sublime inconsequentiality—consisting principally of a list of towns and cities plus the relevant statistics she has learned about each—she urges them to be magnanimous to each other. This speech is one of the most richly comic moments in the whole story, and its comedy resides in the fact that the mind that produces such verbiage is a mind that hoards facts and information indiscriminately, obsessively, purely for the sake of possession. The words Züs speaks are the exact counterpart of the trinkets she collects in her drawer. The details of what she says are, like the objects she hoards, dead things, a meaningless and mindless jumble. The narrative attention paid to them—in the very full description of her drawer and in the extensive report of her speech—confronts us with a debased and reified universe. The objects and the facts are alien things, alien because they are not sustained by any act of human understanding or reverent cherishing. They all exist at an abstract level, they embody the *principle* of possession, they are not informed by any subtle accretions of human meaning. They are fetishist obsessions. Züs is as surely encapsulated in a dead and deadening world as are the Kammacher.

The point is made abundantly clear in the section that follows. The apprentices sleep uneasily that night and the following morning Jobst is the first to awake. He looks around the room and, under the present threat of expulsion from it, he suddenly sees it with immense affection. He studies every tiny detail with loving attention, noting the blue paint he had applied to the wall by his bed the previous autumn. Here it seems as though Jobst might experience some kind of change of heart, that his melancholy closeness to the things of his environment could allow him to see them anew as part of him, as extensions and realizations of his own existence. However, the promised epiphany does not come about; indeed, the mood changes drastically as the narrator reports a truly grotesque moment. Jobst notices that part of the blue painted wall is moving, and he discovers that, in his enthusiasm of the previous autumn, he had painted an insect that had been about to hibernate on the wall. The insect, revived by the warmer weather, begins to move slowly across the wall. The incident is a superbly handled piece of grotesquerie and works through a careful process of thematic argument. Jobst seems to be on the verge of some new perception of the world around him; he is about to see the things of his environment in a special way that allows them to come alive, to break out of their straitjacket. The blue dot does come alive—but in the most absurd (and reified) way possible.[5]

The combmakers then leave together with Züs to take up their positions outside the town in preparation for the race. Züs has, in honor of the occasion, dressed in all her finery, and once again, the narrator's description makes the details of her appearance congeal into a petrified clutter of ribbons, scarves, buckles, frills: "She wore a large hat with huge yellow ribbons, a pink calico dress with old-fashioned ruffles and decorations, a black velvet sash with a gilt buckle, and red saffron leather shoes, embellished with tassels. In addition she carried a green silk handbag, which she had filled with dried pears and plums, and an opened parasol, on the top of which stood a lyre made of ivory" (297).

Züs here emerges in the full panoply of her lifeless and life-denying possessions—and it is for this deadening display that she has become the eagerly sought goal of the Kammacher. They are, of course, moved by the imminent

---

[5] For a fuller discussion of the *Wanze* incident see Pregel's article (cf. note 3 above).

possibility of gaining all this treasure. Once again, under pressure, they almost enter into a recognizably human dimension of feeling and response. Almost, but, as the narrator makes abundantly clear, not quite: "The outward circumstances, the beautiful spring day that shone down on their exodus from the town, and Züs's finery injected into their tense emotional state almost something of what one really calls love" (298). There then follows the final scene between Züs and her three suitors, a scene that consists of specious declarations of love, of empty assertions of personal worth, and of Züs's hectoring dominance over her hapless victims. The competitive ethos of the combmakers here reaches grotesque proportions as they try to outdo each other in protestations of human excellence. Yet all their efforts pale beside the monumental verbosity of Züs. It is an immensely funny scene, but what vibrates behind it is something terrifying in its sheer moral falsity. This the narrator indicates in statements of savage denunciation: "The more Züs's nonsensical utterances became base, heartless, arrogant, the more the combmakers were in a wretched emotional state" (307).

Finally, the moment for the race arrives, and Jobst and Fridolin set off. Züs holds Dietrich back with protestations of love—in an attempt to make sure he has no chance of winning; but she is, in spite of herself, overcome by his passionate attentions, and the two agree to marry. Meanwhile, Jobst and Fridolin are about to enter the town. The Seldwyler are prepared to receive them; they have heard the news of the race and see in it the chance of some inexpensive entertainment. Hence, the whole town stops work and prepares to devote itself to the promised spectacle. They are not disappointed: "With one hand they dragged their knapsacks, which bounced madly over the stones, with the other they held on to their hats, which had slipped well down the back of their necks, and their long coats flew and waved in mad competition. Both were covered with sweat and dust, they had their mouths wide open and gasped for breath, they saw and heard nothing of what was happening all around them, and huge tears rolled down the poor men's faces, which they did not even have time to wipe away" (315). This register dominates throughout the description of the two Kammacher. The narrator stresses the horror, the terrible, manic intensity of what, to the two participants, is a life and death struggle: "The two ran like shying horses, their hearts full of pain and fear" (316). They end up locked in a grotesque embrace: "They wept, sobbed and cried like children, and screamed in unspeakable anxiety" (316). So anguished is their state that they do not even notice when they reach their goal, the shop. They go straight past it and emerge through the opposite gate of the town. Only when it is too late do they discover their mistake; at the end of the day they are left half-dead, ashamed, and humiliated, and it is Dietrich who wins the race and finally buys the business outright. However as the end of the story makes clear, this is a Pyrrhic victory.

The description of the Kammacher as they race through the town is of truly remarkable intensity. The source of the humor with which they have been viewed throughout the story is still there: their absurd competitiveness, their inter-changeability, their existence as automata rather than human beings. Yet in the closing scene, Keller pushes the ethos that dominates them to its most radical enactment, and the result is not so much comic as horrifying. The dis-crepancy between the combmakers' behavior and any norm of human conduct has grown so great that their actions on the day of the race become a jerky, degrading bal-let; the goal has been lost sight of, the competition becomes an end in itself. The sense of the sheer indecency of what is happening takes over from that mocking laughter that the narrator has hitherto brought to bear on his main charac-ters. The humor gives place to hurtful grotesquerie. Even so, the narrator does not withdraw his morally evaluative commentary. On several crucial occasions he expresses compassion for Jobst and Fridolin, the regret at the human debasement involved. One notes particularly the adjective "poor" ("*arm*") in the following phrases: "and fat tears rolled down the faces of the poor men," "the boys and the mob streamed along behind the two poor apprentices," "when the two poor devils saw. . . . " This response acquires particular importance in view of the reaction of the Seldwyler—which is one of unceasing, mindless merriment. The narrator's compassion highlights the callousness of the response of the townspeople: "The gentlemen in the gardens stood on tables and were almost sick with laughing. Their mirth thundered strong and clear over the ceaseless noise of the crowd, which had taken up a position along the street, and gave the signal for a day of unheard of jollity" (315). What the narrator captures about the scene is the unbearable noise of the laughter; just as the master was prepared to exploit the combmakers, so the whole town exploits them for its own entertainment. The Seldwyler become a "*tobender Haufen*," a "screaming mob": "Everybody leaped to their feet and pushed to get a good view, from all sides one heard: 'Well done, well done! Run, keep him off, Saxon! Keep at it, Bavarian. One has dropped out—there are only two left' " (315). Such glimpses as we get of individuals within the mass are without exception malignant figures, as when the narrator describes an urchin "kneeling like a goblin on Jobst's bouncing knapsack" (316). The image here carries an important interpretative load, for throughout the passage the narrator is at pains to stress the sinister callousness of the townspeople. This judgment—as is typical of the narrative mode—is both implicit and explicit. It is implicit in the way the narrator handles his descriptive task—as, for example, in the reference to the "assembled ranks of ladies who cast their silvery laughter into the surf that roared below them" (316). It can, however, become explicit as in the adjectives in the following phrases: "a terrible screaming and laughter," "a wild mass, kicking up a fearful cloud" (315). Such adjectives become the more weighty because they condemn that state of mind that prevents any of the Seldwyler from being even remotely aware that the spectacle they are wit-

nessing is a degrading one. The sense that Jobst and Fridolin are to be pitied never even occurs to them. Yet the narrator's position that pity is the only appropriate response to
what is taking place throws into relief the callousness of the
townspeople, a callousness that makes the festive day truly
unerhört—"unheard of."

On the whole, the Seldwyler have figured in a positive
light in the story. Certainly, beside the obsessiveness of the
Kammacher, their lightheartedness and gaiety seem immensely human and appealing. However, their *Leichtsinn* is
not, in itself, a humane value; the ethos of *Gemütlichkeit* is
no guarantee of moral rightness. The three combmakers
challenge this ethos in the most radical way imaginable. Yet
the challenge serves to bring into sharp illumination the
human basis on which this ethos rests—and it is a basis that
is squalid. In this story, Keller is anything but the apologist
of Seldwyler virtues. The presence of the combmakers in
the town, as it were, forces Seldwyla to show its hand—
with deeply disquieting results.

It is this radicalism in the story that accounts for its
humor, for its imaginative and stylistic intensity, for its
critical energy. The story is, in the spirit of Keller's remarks
in the preface to the Seldwyla tales, both exceptional and
typical, both unique and utterly characteristic. In this sense
the story manifestly belongs within the loosely defined
framework that is the social *donnée* of the tales. The combmakers are the figures from outside, who bring a foreign
ethos into the community. The friction between the two
ways of life, between *Gerechtigkeit* and *Leichtsinn* shows us
exactly what the Seldwyla community is made of. The
familiar is, as it were, made to show its hand, and in the
process it becomes the exceptional. For all its appealing
easygoingness, Seldwyla produces a Züs, it produces the
communal nastiness of the ending. The Kammacher, in
their utter alienation from Seldwyla, in their manifest and
uncompromising marginality, force an exceptional enactment of what the Seldwyla ethos stands for. By means of
this constellation—one that is characteristic of the

novelle—Keller is able to give a suggestive examination not only of a small Swiss community in the nineteenth century, but also of some important issues in nineteenth-century bourgeois society. In effect, he polarizes the social situation into two extreme possibilities: on the one hand, *Leichtsinn*, the irresponsibility of speculative existence, of monetary lightheartedness involving the incurring of debts and the scorn for practical work, for a properly acquired trade; and, on the other hand, *Gerechtigkeit*, the obsessive concern for hard work, for accumulation of savings, for the relentless production of goods, for self-defeating competitiveness. Moreover, he suggests that both extremes harbor an inherent moral falseness, a reduction and degradation of man. The radicalism of the challenge to the familiar world of Seldwyla is the measure of Keller's artistic success. With that artistic success goes a thematic energy that transcends the provincialism of his setting.

IX. Meyer: *Das Leiden eines Knaben**

Conrad Ferdinand Meyer came from a cultivated, patrician Swiss family. He was a refined, unstable person whose pathological timidity issued in a series of nervous crises and breakdowns. His art, mostly produced during the years from 1870 to 1890, was the result of great effort, a hardwon, stable achievement in answer to the increasing lability of his emotional life. It has often been argued that Meyer's stories are the expression of a certain aesthetic fastidiousness, of an aristocratic individualism that sought refuge in the carefully wrought artifact and in the historical settings that could house great individual personages. The formal complexity of several of Meyer's stories has been seen as deliberate virtuosity, a tour de force that is self-validating by virtue of its manifest difficulty. Moreover, his fondness for the historical past has commonly been interpreted as a mode of escapism, as the quest for a refuge from present insecurity and inadequacy—but one that inevitably betrays its questionable provenance in that it exudes the special pleading of the wish-dream.

There is, of course, much truth in such generalizations about C. F. Meyer. Equally, there are misleading elements. There is, for example, the all-too-seductive temptation to operate with a kind of biographical reductionism, whereby Meyer's stories are viewed as "merely" the products of one pathological individual. Rather, his uncertainties, his unremitting sense of the loss of personal and social stability are recognizably a part of the spiritual precariousness of bourgeois society in late nineteenth-century Germany. Moreover, the sense of strain, of difficulty that pervades Meyer's novellen is the measure of his artistic honesty in dealing with the uncertainties he so cruelly felt—and not of

* This chapter is a revised version of my paper "Fagon's Defeat: Some Remarks on C. F. Meyer's *Das Leiden eines Knaben*," due to appear in a forthcoming issue of *Germanic Review*. I am most grateful to the editors for allowing me to draw on this material here.

easy escapism in which fragility becomes transmuted into facility.

Das Leiden eines Knaben (*The Sufferings of a Boy*, 1883) is, like so many of his stories, a "frame narration," and much time and space is devoted to the specific *Rahmensituation* — "frame situation." King Louis XIV of France goes, as is his wont, to the rooms of Madame de Maintenon in the early evening. He complains to her of the impolite treatment that Fagon, his personal physician, has accorded to Père Tellier, the King's newly appointed father confessor. Fagon appears, and renews the attack on Tellier in terms of extraordinary virulence: "It was something quite repulsive and devilish that I avenged, unfortunately only with words: an evil deed, a crime, which the unexpected sight of this spiteful wolf brought again so vividly before my eyes that the feeble dregs of my blood began to boil. For, Sire, this villain murdered a noble boy" (105).[1] The King, not surprisingly in view of the fact that the object of this onslaught has just received a royal appointment, resists Fagon's accusations: "I ask you, Fagon . . . what a fairy tale!" (105). However, the King is intrigued and asks who the boy in question was. Yet on being told that it was one Julian Boufflers, he is disappointed; he has already heard the outline of the story from the boy's father. He knows that Julian was totally ungifted intellectually, that he ruined his health in desperate attempts to make himself learn his schoolwork. The King therefore concludes that, as Père Tellier was in charge of the college where the boy was a pupil, the Jesuit is, in Fagon's eyes, responsible for Julian's sorry end. We read: "Louis shrugged his shoulders. Nothing more. He had expected something more interesting" (105). However, the matter is not left there; the King recalls his one and only meeting with Julian, a meeting that Madame de Maintenon, who was very close to the boy's mother, also witnessed. She reminds the King of the nickname—"*le bel idiot*"—that Saint-Simon bestowed upon the boy. Fagon asserts that even Saint-Simon would have

[1] References throughout are to C. F. Meyer, *Sämtliche Werke*, vol. 12, ed. Hans Zeller and Alfred Zäch, Bern, 1961.

pitied the boy if he had known the full facts, and above all, if he could have witnessed how Julian died: "If he had been, as I was, present at the boy's end, as he in his feverish delirium, with the name of his King upon his lips, imagined that he was rushing into the enemy fire" (107). At this—and perhaps particularly because of the gratifying reference to himself—the King's interest is aroused, and he invites Fagon to tell him the story.

All this may seem at first sight an overleisurely—and largely unnecessary—prelude to the events of Julian Boufflers's life that constitute the substance of Meyer's story. Yet, on closer examination, one finds that the frame situation plays a role of particular significance in the overall import of Meyer's tale. We are rarely, if ever, allowed to forget that the story of Julian Boufflers is told within a specific context—and with a particular aim in view. Indeed, the frame is the setting for a full-blooded battle of wills, and the story is a vital ingredient in that battle. Hence, the lead-in, which I have summarized above, is a necessary part in the all-important process of defining the frame situation, of defining Fagon's position as narrator.

One notes in these opening pages the King's irritation with Fagon's behavior, his insistence that Fagon has overstepped the bounds of decency by hissing insults at Père Tellier: "He takes too many liberties" (103). Strangely enough, when Fagon appears, he makes no attempt to be less provocative. In fact, he adopts the opposite approach and seems to be attempting to capture the attention of the King by the very fury and outrageousness of his onslaught on Père Tellier. Fagon's promise of narrative fireworks is effective. While Louis XIV immediately repudiates the accusations against Tellier, he is obviously intrigued in spite of himself. Hence, he is disappointed when he discovers that the story Fagon has to tell is one he already knows. Fagon has, then, managed to capture the King's attention and has, in fact, persuaded him that at the very least the details of Julian's story will make a gripping tale. Yet the crucial issue is, of course, still left open. Fagon is telling the story not simply to lament the sad fate of a helpless, innocent boy, but in order to justify his dislike of Père Tellier and thereby to enlighten the King as to the kind of man he has raised to the influential position of royal confessor. For this reason, the suspense and tension generated by *Das Leiden eines Knaben* derive less from the plot sequence of the inset story than from the possible effect that the telling of that story may have on the frame situation. Fagon has promised the King high drama, a story full of mischief and crime, with a cast that includes a *"tückischer Wolf,"* a "spiteful wolf," and an *"edler Knabe,"* a "noble boy." Louis has already described Fagon's outline of events as a *Märchen*—but he is prepared to listen to this fairy tale for its colorful events, for its sharply delineated characters, for its simple narrative appeal. However, Fagon's aim is to persuade the King that the outrageous tale he is about to recount is not a fairy tale: it happened in the real world of the Sun King's Paris, and it is relevant to the present constellations of power and influence around the person of the King. The frame situation is, then, fraught with considerable political tension; for this reason the *act* of narrating is as important as what is narrated.

As if aware of the risks involved, Fagon begins by capitalizing on the King's evident eagerness to hear the story of Julian Boufflers and covers himself against possible offense that the story might give. He asks for three "freedoms," for three "lives" as narrator; and the King grants them. This exchange between Fagon and his master has several important implications for the former's position as narrator. The King knows—and Fagon knows—that there are certain limits of decency and decorum that must be observed. In a sense, Fagon's very undertaking is an offense against these limits—because it involves virulent criticism of a decision that the King has made. However, the device of storytelling does give Fagon certain advantages: it can, as it were, allow him to have his cake and eat it—to both offend the King and please him, to tell a story whose import is offensive, but whose sheer narrative energy makes it a thoroughly engrossing tale. Fagon is, in many respects, in the situation of the fool or court jester; because of the aesthetic pleasure he can give, he is allowed a certain amount of license. He can exploit this license in order to formulate cogent criticisms of his master, but at all times the pill has to be coated with sugar. Of course, there is always the danger that the monarch will take the sugar without swallowing the pill. It is this tension between the narrative (artistic) success and the polemical import that gives especial fascination to Fagon's performance within the frame situation.

Having obtained his three "freedoms," Fagon begins his tale. He opens at a leisurely pace with a disarmingly chatty introduction. He recalls to Louis XIV the time when Molière was at the height of his purpose. He refers to *Le Malade Imaginaire* and reminds the King of a passage in the play where a father praises the limitations of his utterly stupid son in such a way that the whole speech becomes an implicit mockery of the character speaking. Here Fagon breaks off and says: "But Your Majesty knows the passage," to which Louis replies: "It would give me pleasure, Fagon, if you recited it to me" (109). Fagon proceeds to do this at some length. The point of this introduction is only reached when Fagon explains how, on the occasion of a specific performance, he noticed a woman in the audience whose laughter gradually turned to tears. Her reactions told him that she had a stupid son, and that her anxieties were being cruelly parodied on the stage. The woman was none other than Julian's mother. Only now does Fagon's narration proper get under way as he goes on to describe how Madame Boufflers, shortly before her death, asked him to keep a careful eye on Julian.

This seemingly digressive start to Fagon's narration is, in fact, a calculated piece of salesmanship. The mention of Molière is pleasing to Louis; it recalls happy memories of a much more secure and brilliant period of his reign. Furthermore, it reminds him of something that used to give him intense pleasure. We read that his "mouth . . . involuntarily broke into a smile as he recalled the good companion, whom he had enjoyed having around him and whose masks had given him great pleasure" (109). Furthermore, one should note how carefully Fagon controls the response of the King; his remark "But Your Majesty knows the passage" implants in the King the wish to hear the passage. Fagon is promptly invited to recite it, and we read: " 'It is not because,' Fagon performed the role of Doctor Diaforius, whose lines he, oddly enough, knew by heart, 'I am the boy's father . . .' "(109). One notices the authorial comment "oddly enough"—*"seltsamerweise"*—a comment in which Meyer draws specific attention to Fagon's remarkable feat of memory. The implications of this are obvious. Fagon is able to recite by heart a lengthy passage from the Molière play for the simple reason that he has learned it for the occasion; he has carefully prepared the story he is going to tell the King and has deliberately made the opening engaging, unpolemical, lighthearted. Thereby Fagon establishes his capabilities as entertainer, his skill as performing artist. The opening register of theatricality is sustained throughout. Over and over again Fagon does not simply report the gist of a conversation he has had with somebody, but he renders it in direct speech, thus extracting the greatest possible dramatic immediacy from it. It is a technique that reaches its climax at the end of the story in the interview with Père Tellier and in Julian's death. Moreover, it is clear from one revealing comment Fagon makes that he knows full well the potentially critical and polemical power of art, a power on which he is trying to capitalize. He says that he made a point of seeing *Le Malade Imaginaire* because he knew that his profession—and perhaps he himself—would be Molière's targets. Here he suggests to the King something that the latter presumably recalls very precisely: the experience of confronting a work of art that had an unmistakably direct—and critical— relationship to the reality of its audience, even to specific persons or classes. It is for this kind of relevance that Fagon himself strives in telling the story of Julian Boufflers.

Hence, Fagon's set piece from Molière has a quite specific purpose. Indeed, when he goes on to report his interview with Madame Boufflers, he also recites her speech (in which she commends Julian to his care) at great length. One notes how he controls the rhythm of the scene changes. He introduces the account of his interview with the following words: "A few days before her end she called me to her . . ." (111). He then plays the role of Madame Boufflers, ending with her last words: " 'So you promise me that you will take my place in the boy's life. You will keep your word and, what is more . . . ' I promised the Marschallin, and she died easily. In front of the bed on which she lay, I observed the boy who had been entrusted to my care. He was dissolved in tears . . ." (112). Yet, on Fagon's own admission, there was a gap of several days between these words spoken by Madame Boufflers and her actual death. What Fagon has done in his narration is to telescope the two scenes into one: to make the mother's plea, which is "acted out," even more poignant by the suggestion that these are her last words, a testament made on her death bed.

Fagon then describes the decision to entrust the boy to a Jesuit college and his own careful precautions to make sure that Julian is treated well by the fathers. (Only later do we discover the precise nature of these precautions—and it will cost Fagon one of his "freedoms.") We then hear of Marshall Boufflers's successful unmasking of an attempted financial swindle by certain Jesuits, and how this action of his father makes Julian the object of consistent and vengeful persecution at school. At this point in the story Fagon begins to introduce a polemical note. Having praised the Jesuits for their pedagogic skill (which led him to recommend that Julian be entrusted to their care), he now paints them in the blackest possible colors, referring to their "obsessive hatred," "repressed fury," "thwarted covetousness," to the "delicately poisoned atmosphere of stealthy revenge" (118), which destroys Julian. Here the King raises objections and accuses Fagon of willful distortion: "You are

186

seeing ghosts, Fagon. You are very partisan here, and you have perhaps, beside your inherited prejudice, some personal grudge against the worthy order" (119). For the first time, open and violent conflict flares in the *Rahmensituation*. For all Fagon's narrative success so far—the King has raised no objections and has clearly listened intently—we now come to the crucial issue. Quite clearly, the King repudiates all the tendentious aspects of his physician's story as fantasies, as *Gespenster* ("ghosts"). *Märchen*—fairy tale— was the word Louis had used initially to Fagon. However much he has enjoyed the story up to this point, the King has neither been convinced by Fagon's onslaught on the Jesuits, nor has he been lulled by the sheer drama of Fagon's narration into a suspension of disbelief. Fagon is furious, and in stammering, incoherent anger, he turns on the King. Here Meyer reminds us of the desperate seriousness that underlies Fagon's act of storytelling—and of the sheer precariousness of his position. As the King's personal physician he enjoys a certain freedom in that he can allow himself a degree of direct criticism of his master that is quite exceptional—but there is a limit to how far he may go. Similarly, as a narrator he is allowed only a certain license. There is a weakness inherent in Fagon's privileged position—the King may not take him quite seriously in that anything offensive the old man says can be explained away as an example of his irascibility. Fagon turns on the King and accuses him of simply refusing to believe unwelcome truths. The attack is savage, and encompasses both scathing sarcasm ("Tell me, O King, you who know reality so well") and the reference to a highly loaded political issue: "Can you also not believe that within your realm force is being used in the conversion of Protestants?" (120). In reply, the King warns Fagon that he has now used up the first of his three "freedoms," but he answers the charge. Louis's answer is a reply not simply to Fagon's question but also to his whole behavior. The King quite simply asserts his power as absolute monarch, as someone whose every command is followed to the letter: "With a few, increas-

ingly rare, exceptions, no force is used in these conver-
sions, because I have explicitly forbidden it once and for all
and because my orders are carried out" (120). At this point
Fagon has to lose. Once the argument between them comes
into the open, Fagon has no weapons left. However, he
makes one last attempt to prove his point—significantly, by
telling a story. He recounts how pressure was put on his
father to convert to Catholicism. He was a chemist who
found that the community simply refused to buy from a
Calvinist. So, the father abjured his Calvinism, but only to
find that his conscience gave him no peace. In despair he
hanged himself. Obviously, Fagon's little inset story here
has the force of personal experience and conviction. In this
sense, it is unanswerable. The King replies by reproaching
Fagon with tactlessness and crudity. As he puts it, *"unselige
Dinge verlangen einen Schleier"*—"unfortunate matters need
to be veiled" (121). At this level, too, Fagon is beaten. With
as much grace as he can muster, he accepts the reproach
and buys forgiveness by surrendering his second "freedom." Hence, Fagon is driven back to the one weapon he
has—his story. His only chance of confronting the King
with certain unpalatable truths is by veiling the "unfortunate matters"—veiling them in his performance as narrator. The image of the veil raises what is the central issue
in the *Rahmensituation* namely the relationship between the
"Schleier" ("veil") and the *"unselige Dinge"* ("unfortunate
matters"). One is tempted to reflect that much depends on
the thickness of the veil. If it is too thin, then the King will
simply know how fiercely he is being buttonholed; if it is
too thick, then there is the danger that the *"unselige Dinge"*
will disappear from sight altogether.

Understandably, when Fagon resumes his narration, he
does so with the kind of leisurely lead-in with which he
began his story: " 'Sire,' Fagon asked almost casually, 'did
you ever know your subject, Mouton, the artist who
painted animals?' " (121). We have a lengthy digression on
the character and talents of Mouton, liberally laced with
flattery: "Did Mouton know the Sun of our times? Did he

know of your existence, Your Majesty? Unbelievable as it sounds—perhaps he did not even know your name, that name that fills the world and human history . . ." (122). This harmless prelude leads to another of Fagon's theatrical performances as he reports in direct speech a dialogue between Julian and Mirabelle. He then goes on to refer to the growing love between Julian and Mirabelle and to his affection for the boy. On the whole, the material is, from the King's point of view, uncontentious. Yet Fagon wrings as much special pleading as he can out of his direct quotation of the words the boy speaks. At one point he quotes his own advice to Julian, that the boy should join the army, should be a simple servant of the King. This advice, as reported in the present context, represents an attempt to involve the King in a kind of vicarious assent to Julian— which can then be channeled into disgust at the cruelty of the boy's tormentor.

Fagon then comes to the climactic scene of his story: the beating of Julian and the interview with Père Tellier. At this stage, he has to admit something that he has already hinted at: that, in order to protect Julian, he had circulated the rumor that the boy was perhaps the illegitimate son of the King. Louis is deeply offended and makes it clear to Fagon that the latter has now used up his third and last "freedom":

"If you did play so thoughtlessly with my name and the reputation of a woman whom you worshiped, you should at least have kept silent about this enormity— even if your story thereby became less comprehensible. And tell me, Fagon: have you not here acted according to the much criticized principle that the end justifies the means? Have you joined the Jesuit order?"

"We all have a little, Your Majesty," smiled Fagon (146f.).

This is a revealing exchange. Fagon has given offense not only by what he did—but also by the act of recounting it to the King. Yet Fagon is caught either way: either he conceals his behavior and renders the story less comprehensible, or he reveals it and the story gives offense. His only comment is the wry recognition that, in so many spheres of human activity, man finds himself having to compromise over the means for the sake of the end, a comment that also contains a dig at the complex political maneuvering within court circles—and perhaps also at the ever-increasing influence of the Jesuits. Whether Fagon's undertaking will be successful, at this stage of the story, is still undecided. However, the decision follows almost immediately. In his account of the argument with Tellier, Fagon makes no attempt to play down the tendentiousness of his narrative, and at one point he breaks out of the dramatic mode and addresses the King directly, describing "how arrogance and ambition battled with each other in the dark features of your father confessor, Sire" (151). One notes the phrase "your father confessor" (*"Eures Beichtvaters"*). Here Fagon forces home the polemic by explicitly linking the past events of the story with the present world to which he is narrating; he stresses that this dangerous priest has now been raised to a position where he wields great political and spiritual influence over the King. This section is the climax of Fagon's onslaught on Tellier and the decisive point of the battle enacted in the frame has now arrived:

> Fagon observed the King from behind his bushy gray eyebrows—watching for the impression that the proffered mask of his father confessor had made on the King. Not that he flattered himself that Louis would revoke his appointment. But he had wanted to warn the King about this enemy of mankind who, with his daemonic wings, was to cast his dark shadow over the end of a brilliant reign.
>
> But Fagon read in the features of the Most Christian of Men nothing but natural pity for the fate of a boy whose mother had fleetingly pleased the monarch and pleasure in a story whose paths—like those of a garden—led to one and the same center: the King, again and again the King!

"Go on, Fagon," his Majesty commanded, and the former obeyed, irritated, his mood soured (152f.). The outcome of the struggle is clear: Fagon has, quite simply, lost. Louis, we are told, is impressed by the story; he is moved by what he has heard. Yet his response does not go beyond pity for Julian; the social and political implications of the story do not strike home. Furthermore, the King's pleasure in the tale is not without its selfish features; it is even implied that such pity as he feels for Julian is to a certain extent dependent on the fact that he found the boy's mother particularly attractive. In E.T.A. Hoffmann's story *Das Fräulein von Scudéry*, Louis XIV is so moved by the resemblance between a young girl and a previous mistress of his that he exercises his prerogative of royal pardon. In Hoffmann's story there is a resolution, a "happy ending," although the process by which this is brought about means that the conclusion is particularly precarious and tentative. Yet in Meyer's story, not even a tentative "happy ending" is possible. Moreover, it is made clear that one of the chief sources of the King's involvement in the story is the fact that it appeals to his vanity; he finds himself to be the unspoken center of all the events that are reported.

The King has, then, been moved by the pathos of Fagon's narration, by its nostalgic appeal, by its flattery—but there is no more to it than this. He has, as it were, swallowed the sugar coating, but rejected the unpalatable pill. He forces Fagon into the uncontentious role of royal entertainer. He orders him to continue with the story, and Fagon has no option but to obey. A few minutes later, Dubois, a servant, comes in to announce that dinner is served. The King chides him—"You are intruding, Dubois"—and the latter leaves "with a restrained expression of astonishment on his impeccable features—for the King was the embodiment of punctuality" (153). In this little incident we sense that something remarkable has happened: King Louis XIV is so caught up in the story of Julian Boufflers that he breaks with his deeply engrained habit of dining punctually. As a storyteller, Fagon could hardly ask for a higher tribute to his narrative powers; but it is an achievement that succeeds brilliantly on all levels except the one that matters most.[2] It is significant that, at this crucial stage in the story, Meyer should add a particularly telling authorial comment: Fagon knew that nothing would induce the King to revoke his nomination of Tellier, but simply wanted to warn his master "about this enemy of mankind who, with his daemonic wings, was to cast his dark shadow over the end of a brilliant reign " (153). What Meyer adds here is the uniquely authorial perspective of historical hindsight; the modal verb "was to" ("*sollte*") gives authoritative assent to the rightness of Fagon's understanding of the political situation, and underlines the desperate seriousness of what he attempts in his narration. Until this point in the story, we the readers cannot be sure how right Fagon is. We are made consistently aware of his dislike of the Jesuits, of his especial hatred for Père Tellier, but we have no means of knowing how far this is personal prejudice, and how far it is genuine insight into an objective danger in the real social world. When it finally comes, Meyer's all-important endorsement of Fagon's aim coincides with the clear statement of Fagon's failure to achieve that aim. This gives bitterness and poignancy to the end of the story.

Fagon now concludes his narration swiftly. He recounts the gradual deterioration of the boy's condition, his delirium and death. The polemic is as strong as ever, but it is, as we now know, a polemic to no avail. Even the reference to Julian's agony as his "Golgotha at the hands of the Jesuits" (156) is presumably reduced, in the King's mind, to a vivid figure of speech that adds color and urgency to the narrative, but that is bereft of any capacity to shock. The story closes as follows:

Fagon had finished and got up. The Marquise was moved.

[2] I take a much darker view of Fagon's defeat than does W. D. Williams (*The Stories of C. F. Meyer*, pp. 84ff.).

"Poor child," sighed the King, and he, too, got up. "Why poor," Fagon asked cheerfully, "as he died a hero's death?" (157).

The King sighs and expresses his pity for Julian—and in so doing, shows once again his refusal to draw any conclusion from the events he has heard. There is no blame to be apportioned, no action to be taken, no lesson to be learned. Fagon has been kept firmly in the role of entertainer, and he has no option at the end of the story but to accept that role. His last words, we are told, are "cheerful" (*"heiter"*) in tone. He can only conclude on a register of harmlessness, a register that removes all the sting from his narration. The tone may be cheerful, but the import of his last words is anything but conciliatory. He asserts that Julian died like a hero, that his was, in effect, a martyr's death. Julian is martyred by political intrigue, by the corrupt manipulations of the world of the Sun King's court.

While in specific terms Fagon's narration is a denunciation of the Jesuits, in a more general sense it offers a devastating picture of life at court. The court has no place for a Julian or for those like him. Of Mirabelle we are told: "The air that she breathes out is purer than that which she breathes in" (133), and her innocence is the measure of her unacceptability to the world in which she finds herself. Fagon's passionate involvement with Julian leads him to a total devaluation of all that Louis XIV's court stands for. When he goes to Versailles on the day of Julian's death, Fagon finds a number of courtiers together. His description of them is pure vitriol:

In Versailles . . . I found the Marshall at table with some of his peers. Villars was there, every inch a braggart—a hero, it is commonly said and who am I to contradict?— and the most shameless beggar as you know, Your Majesty; Villeroy was there, the great loser of battles, the most worthless of mortals, who lives from the crumbs of your charity, with his unshakable arrogance and his grand manners; Grammont with his distinguished head, who yesterday cheated me in your hall, at your gambling tables, Your Majesty, with his marked cards, and Lauzun, behind his gentle expression utterly cynical and mean. Forgive me, but I saw your courtiers distorted in the glaring light of my heartfelt anguish (153f.).

Fagon apologizes for this description, and attributes it to his fear for Julian's life. Yet the disclaimer is clearly only a tactful maneuver, because there is a sense in which the distortion is not willful, but is profoundly revelatory. It is this disillusioned—and disillusioning—perspective that obtains throughout Fagon's passionate narration, and it accounts for its overt theatricality and special pleading. It is also, we remember, the perspective of Molière's art as Fagon describes it, an art that works with "garish lamps and the distorted faces of the present brought on the stage" (108). For Fagon—and for any who are prepared to share his "anguish" (*"Herzensangst"*) at the fate of Julian—society is a jungle made up of, at best, indifference, and, at worst, unadulterated malice. Fagon's story offers the King not simply "the profferred mask of his father confessor" (152f.), but the distorted yet revealing mask of the world over which he presides. The harsh illumination of Molière's art becomes the savage narrative viewpoint of Fagon; but the only response this elicits from the King is pity for the individual who is destroyed by the social machinery. There is no critical awareness of this machinery as such—nor, of course, of the position of its lynchpin, "the King, again and again the King" (153).

At one point in *Das Leiden eines Knaben*, Fagon comes across a sketch done by Mouton the painter: "I studied the page, which contained the remarkable parody of a scene from Ovid: Pentheus, hounded by the Maenads, is running away and Bacchus, the cruel god, in order to destroy the fugitive, causes a sheer mountain to grow out of the ground before him. . . . A young boy, unmistakably Julian in all his physical attributes . . . a slender runner fled, looking back over his shoulder, with an expression of deadly fear on his face, at a number of ghostly creatures who were chasing him. . . . One of these horrors wore a long Jesuit hat on its shaven head" (135). The painting can, in my view, be seen as a kind of cipher for C. F. Meyer's art. All his novellen have a historical setting, and this fact has given rise to certain commonplaces about his work. Most obviously, there is the frequently made generalization that Meyer was a desperately nervous and insecure person who sought refuge in the past and turned, for this reason, to the historical novelle. Meyer himself commented on his relationship as creative writer to the past in the following terms: "I use the historical novelle purely and simply as a vehicle for my personal feelings and experiences; I prefer it to the novel of contemporary life because it is a better mask and because it distances the reader more. Hence, under the cloak of a most objective and eminently artistic form, I am completely individual and subjective. In all the figures of *Pescara*, even in the repulsive Moroni, there is something of C.F.M."[3] Here, Meyer talks of the historical novelle as something that conceals his own persona, that distances the reader. However, he goes on to lay particular stress on the *artistic* gain of this distance; he says that his work is intensely personal, but that the historical novelle allows him a reworking of these experiences that is "eminently artistic." The distance Meyer gains by his use of history, then, is aesthetic distance; it is not the distance of escapism. Similarly, the distance Mouton gains by basing his picture of Julian on a scene from Ovid is the distance of controlled artistic illumination and statement.

Meyer often makes particularly elaborate use of the frame technique. This, too, it has often been suggested, is symptomatic of his attempt to escape his problematic self, to keep even the act of narrating separate from his own persona. However, this argument does not account for the use of the fully developed *Rahmensituation*. Why should he bother to create not only a fictitious narrator, but also a fic-

[3] *Briefe*, vol. 1, ed. A. Frey, Leipzig, 1908, pp. 138f.

titious audience? The answer, in my view, lies in the fact that the nature of art itself is a central thematic preoccupation within his finest *Rahmenerzählungen* (stories with a narrative frame). Over and over again he shows himself to be acutely aware of the nature of his own artistic creations. In a letter he speaks of "the strong stylization of my work."[4] Also, the influence of the plastic arts on his technique—his fondness for the denotative tableau—has often been commented upon. Elsewhere Meyer writes that the past allows him to treat eternally human problems with greater artistry: "I much prefer to immerse myself in past ages, which allow me to give a more artistic treatment of eternal human problems than would be possible with the brutal immediacy of contemporary material."[5] Art, then, implies interpretative control, implies a degree of distance from the material to be treated. In history Meyer finds the artistically manageable correlative for his own problems and anxieties; and the presence of a developed frame situation makes the nature of artistic achievement a manifest thematic presence in the work as whole. In one of his finest stories, *Die Hochzeit des Mönchs* (*The Marriage of the Monk*), Meyer uses the narrative frame in order to ask what impact the fictional interpretation of a specific world can have on an audience that inhabits that world. Both Fagon's and Dante's narrations have a formal and interpretative control that derives from the careful artistic shaping of material. (The same is true of the stylization of Mouton's painting.) In both stories, the *Rahmensituation* shows what the audience makes of this kind of art. Both Fagon's and Dante's stories are, by implication, savage indictments of the society to which they are told; their artistic sharpness is the measure of their interpretative energy. Yet in both cases, the society does not heed the image of itself that the narrators give. It ignores the voice of Dante, the "wanderer

---

[4] Ibid., p. 411.

[5] *Louise von François und C. F. Meyer: Ein Briefwechsel*, ed. Anton Bettelheim, 2d ed., Berlin, 1920, p. 12.

196

through Hell"[6] (and the Hell referred to is not only the *Inferno*, but also the world that Dante re-creates before the eyes of Cangrande and his courtiers); it ignores the voice of Fagon, the physician who diagnoses the sickness of Louis XIV's court. It is not that the social world refuses to listen to what Fagon and Dante recount. The audience follows with rapt attention, but with an attention that degrades both narrators to entertainers. At the end of *Die Hochzeit des Mönchs* Dante takes leave of Cangrande's court with words that, in essence, could have come from Fagon: "I have paid for my seat by the fire."[7] The court audience enjoys the entertainment afforded by a narrative tour de force; but there is no more to it than this. Both rulers—Cangrande and Louis XIV—are flattered by what they hear, but the implications are lost on them. In these two stories Meyer uses the frame to express devastating doubts about the value of art, about its ability to have any decisive effect on the real world to which it is directed. As Meyer himself put it, art can order and control experience, and can, thereby, interpret the world of man; but, in a strange way, art can neither answer, nor help toward the solution of the problems that it so precisely uncovers. The clarity it attains remains a function of its specifically fictional existence: "Where art purifies passion, i.e. where man is portrayed as finding peace and contentment, the notion can arise of a deceptive unity, whereas we (and this is how realistic art photographs us) are so fundamentally divided and can only be healed by a force other than ourselves, by God."[8] Meyer's historical fiction allowed him to impose artistic control and interpretative insight on the threatening flux of his experience. Yet he was bitterly aware that he had not thereby brought a solution any nearer. He knew that art could reveal profound truths, but that there was no guaranteed mediation between the artistic vision and the

[6] Meyer, *Sämtliche Werke*, vol. 12, p. 57.
[7] Ibid., p. 98.
[8] *Briefe*, vol. 1, p. 60.

real world on which it commented so powerfully. In *Das Leiden eines Knaben* and *Die Hochzeit des Mönchs* he faces the possibility that an audience can listen carefully to a story and can, quite simply, evade the issue with which it is being so cogently confronted.

The implications of this argument are, in my view, important for an understanding of Meyer's place within certain literary-historical developments. It is interesting to note that many commentators have suggested that the novelle is born in the Renaissance, at a time when individualism becomes a governing principle in human affairs. It is particularly noteworthy that C. F. Meyer, who is in many ways the writer who pens the epitaph to the great line of nineteenth-century novellen, should turn his attention so frequently to the Renaissance, should go back to the starting point of the genre in order, as it were, to proclaim its demise. Obviously, any such argument, while suggestive in itself, savors of a suspect schematism. Yet clearly Meyer was a writer who stood in a thoroughly critical relationship to the narrative tradition within which he worked. This relationship becomes strikingly apparent in his handling of the narrative frame. The situation of the threatened narrator is one of the oldest ingredients of the frame situation. In the *Arabian Nights* the threat is execution, in Boccaccio the threat is the plague and the moral and social chaos it entails, in Goethe's *Unterhaltungen deutscher Ausgewanderten* it is the social and political turmoil of the French Revolution. In all these cases, the act of narration is an attempt to answer a danger, to overcome a threat by the—in both the aesthetic and the social sense—*formal* art of storytelling. C. F. Meyer clearly draws on this tradition in *Das Leiden eines Knaben*, but only to reach a conclusion of disturbing implications for his situation as an artist. Fagon's story does not work. It is powerless before the corruption, nastiness, and bigotry of the social world; it is unable to change the consciousness of its hearers.

At the deepest level, a story such as *Das Leiden eines Knaben* questions the value of the achieved work of art. Formal control is the source of the narrative energy in Fagon's story, and yet it seems to achieve so little; form is not allowed to acquire the status of an unequivocal value. Here Meyer is both part of the late nineteenth century—and a precursor of the moderns. In a suggestive essay entitled *"Bürgerlichkeit und l'art pour l'art,"* Georg Lukács argues that many of the great writers of the second half of the nineteenth century in Germany were obsessed by the notion of art as a carefully wrought construct that demanded from its maker the sheer hard work and regular working hours of any other craftsman.[9] Lukács argues that for Mörike, Keller, and Storm, art involved solid workmanship rather than inspiration; for them the carefully achieved form was proof of the solidity—in both moral and aesthetic terms—of the artist's endeavor. Meyer, too, was part of this ambience, but at the same time he saw its problematic aspects.[10] For this reason his art looks forward to the work that offers the most radical exploration—and critique—of this ethos: Thomas Mann's *Der Tod in Venedig* (*Death in Venice*). Mann's story is about an artist for whom order and orderliness is a way of life, for whom hard work, the ceaseless striving for formal control at all times, is an unequivocal answer to the relentless ambiguities of his life. In the course of the story, Mann shows how this worship of form does not represent security, but is, rather, the very source of Aschenbach's blindness and vulnerability. The story itself—Mann's story—as a superbly controlled and sustained novelle, becomes the embodiment of the problem that it is principally concerned to explore. Hence, the import of *Der Tod in Venedig* is the ultimate critique of its own existence as an aesthetic object.

In Mann's story, the novelle, as developed in the German

[9] Georg Lukács, *Die Seele und die Formen*, in *Werke*, vol. 1, Neuwied and Berlin, 1963.

[10] In his study *Die Rahmenerzählungen C. F. Meyers*, Sjaak Onderdelinden comments very cogently on Fagon's personal implication in Julian's story (pp. 117–118). I feel, however, that he tends to overlook the public (and theatrical) aspects of Fagon's narration.

nineteenth century, stands poised on the verge of its own impossibility.[11] The nineteenth-century novelle is sustained by an interpretative tension between the claims of unique, unprecedented experience on the one hand, and the generality of the common human universe on the other. Conciliations are always possible; but the lifeblood of the genre is a vital friction, a friction that is enacted centrally in the persona of the narrator and in the function of the narrative voice. In Meyer's two great stories the exceptional event is announced early on: the King's father confessor has murdered a boy, a monk lies buried beside his wife. The telling of these two stories involves a reaching out for an understanding of these remarkable, unique events, and the process of interpreting such occurrences becomes a critique of the experiential modes of the commonly accepted social universe. The crucial issue—as so often in the stories here discussed—is one of relationship between the two interpreted worlds, between the marginal and the everyday. In *Das Leiden eines Knaben* and *Die Hochzeit des Mönchs* Meyer polarizes the situation by means of a carefully constructed frame situation within which and to which the narrator figure tells of the unprecedented. In both cases, the story told is vivid and persuasive, as well as formally and interpretatively disciplined. Yet, the relationship between the story and the world, between the narrative act on the one hand and the social reality of the frame on the other is strained to the breaking point. We, the readers, know of the relationship, but the audience in the *Rahmensituation* does not. Where Goethe in the *Unterhaltungen deutscher Ausgewanderten* could believe in the humanizing, educative force of storytelling, Meyer can only

[11] Not only in the structural sense does Mann's story recall the nineteenth-century novelle. There are, I would suggest, thematic links, as when we are told of the social and moral chaos produced by the cholera (plague) in Venice, a chaos of which Aschenbach is part: "Thus the monstrous seemed full of promise to him, and the moral law a feeble irrelevancy" (Thomas Mann, *Sämtliche Erzählungen*, Frankfurt am Main, 1963, p. 411).

record a hardening of fronts, the ˇfinal impossibility of mediation.

The sheer challenge of the narrative act and of the hermeneutic problem it poses is central to the meaning of the stories I have discussed in this study. Yet with Meyer the challenge has ceased to be comprehended as such. His skepticism about the act of narration allows only one last-ditch vindication: that the narrative act sustains the narrator in his isolation, that it represents *his* value, a value to which we as privileged hearers assent. With Mann's *Der Tod in Venedig* even this much validation is withdrawn. What seems to sustain Aschenbach and his art in fact drives him to perdition; and in the process the work of art we are reading and the possibility of our assenting to it as an artistic and human achievement are cruelly called into question. Fagon's and Dante's narrations do stand on their own terms, and these terms are shown to be utterly their own in the sense that they are denied recognition from their hearers. However, in *Der Tod in Venedig* the act of narration is shown to stand on precisely those terms that the story itself systematically erodes. Thus a narrative tradition argues the case against its own viability.

X. Conclusion

Many of the deepest intellectual issues explored in the novelle genre recur throughout the German nineteenth century. In one way or another, the literature of the period is an imaginative probing of conflicts inherent in the social experience of the time, conflicts within the whole complex ethos of bourgeois individualism. In this sense, the novelle is not unique, and there would seem to be considerable overlap between its thematic concerns and those of the novel, for example. Yet there are certain important differences. It is worth recalling Hegel's famous dictum about the novel: "As regards its subject matter, the true novel demands—like the epic—the totality of an overall view of life and the world, whose manifold presence and import come to the surface within the individual event, which constitutes the center of the whole."[1] The totality that sustains the novel is, for Hegel, modern, prosaic, bourgeois reality. In the novel the interpretative weight is placed on this totality that will inform the specific events. By contrast, the novelle places its emphasis on the individual event that stands in some hermeneutically strained relationship to the totality of man's general social assumptions. If anything, the novelle is the more radical of the two in that the tension between the unmistakably individual and the manifestly general becomes the cardinal principle behind its aesthetic structuring. This has led critics to speak of the implicit individualism of the novelle genre—one remembers, for example, Friedrich Schlegel's aphoristic assertion that "individuality is the essence of the novelle."[2]

The most striking example of this individualism is Paul Heyse. Most of his novellen, in one way or another, tend

---

[1] *Ästhetik*, ed. Friedrich Bassenge, Berlin, 1955, p. 983.

[2] *Fragmente zur Poesie und Literatur*, vol. 2, Notebook 1799–1801. An unpublished note, quoted by Karl Konrad Polheim in *Theorie und Kritik der deutschen Novelle von Wieland bis Musil*, p. 8.

to be straightforward glorifications of individualism. Moreover, precisely because of their unproblematic nature, precisely because they are so strident and total in the assertions they make, so unaware of the hermeneutic problem of trying to mediate between the individual and the general, they tend to be inferior and crude narrative productions (for all their stylistic and technical skill). In a very revealing theoretical passage Heyse makes his credo explicit: "From the simple recounting of a remarkable event or of a wittily conceived adventure story, the novelle has gradually developed into the form in which precisely the deepest and most important moral questions are discussed—because in this modest literary genre even the exceptional case, even those individual and most intensely personal rights are given their due within the scheme of competing moral values."[3]

Here it becomes clear that, by definition, the deepest moral questions are those that vindicate the exceptional, the unusual, and that, in Heyse's view, the novelle genre is the perfect artistic medium for this vindication. Hence, the novelle will offer "a by no means generally valid solution"[4] to the problems it raises—quite simply because, for Heyse, it is a form that by definition excludes any general evaluative perspective beyond that which recognizes the particular in all its specific quirks and oddities. The one-sidedness of Heyse's theory is sustained in his actual novelle production. Time and time again we are concerned with an unusual figure, an eccentric, somebody who manifestly stands apart from the generality of the human community. There is a story to be told about this strange, recluselike figure, a story that reveals the fascinating and uniquely intense experiences that have made of the person what he now is, that have driven him into a kind of self-imposed isolation. There is no interpretative problem here: the protagonist simply is what he is, and we are required to accept this fact. A comparison with a story such as *Der arme Spielmann*

---

[3] *WB*, p. 66.
[4] Ibid.

makes clear what Heyse's art lacks: any sense of evaluative difficulty. Because his stories operate in terms of simple, unequivocal narrative assent, they do not generate that interpretative tension that is so characteristic of the novelle genre. A contemporary critic, Georg Brandes, wrote of Heyse that his stories are case histories in which the common laws of society are broken or flaunted "in such a way ... that the exception seems to be vindicated over the rule, and even the most hardened philistine will pause to think before passing judgment here."[5]

This relationship between problematic individualism and the narrative constellation of the novelle does, in my view, help to answer the crucial question of why the novelle should become particularly dominant in both the theory and the practice of prose writing in Germany. Several critics have concerned themselves with the sociological implications of the novelle genre, and two outstanding contributions have been made by Georg Lukács and Fritz Martini. It is pertinent to summarize their findings here. Both have maintained the general thesis that the increasing specialization—and individualization—of nineteenth-century social life finds both expression and critique in the literature of the time. Lukács argues: "The individualizing of man, produced by the development of bourgeois society, by the impact of capitalist division of labor that means that less and less of the human personality is channeled into the job, that growing separation of private and public life, ... all this means that the truly typical quality of the characters can only be convincingly portrayed as the result of great artistic endeavor, as the final conclusion to a story, as the narrative overcoming of the mere individuality that was initially given."[6] Lukács, from an overtly Marxist position, argues here that it is in the very nature of bourgeois capitalism that any participant in that socio-economic system sees himself supremely as a private individual; his links

[5] *Moderne Geister: Literarische Bildnisse aus dem 19. Jahrhundert*, Frankfurt am Main, 1887, p. 25.

[6] *Deutsche Realisten des 19. Jahrhunderts*, in *Werke*, vol. 7, pp. 374f.

with the social generality outside himself are at best purely pragmatic (he spends a certain number of hours per day devoting himself to some alien task in order to earn money) and, hence, are partial and tentative. If an artist, then, chooses to explore such a person, he finds that he is confronted by an embattled individual, and the relationship between the individual and the general can only be established by an intense and sustained process of artistic interpretation. The general is in no sense inherent; it has to be interpreted out of the specific, and this is a process that involves considerable hermeneutic difficulty. Implicit in Lukács's argument, of course, is the paradox that extreme individuality is in fact typical of the society as a whole; fragmented, isolated pockets of experience constitute the general law of this particular society. If the artist wishes to illuminate some kind of generality that presupposes such values as a community of men, as a humane collective, then he will have little concrete evidence at his disposal in the society around him. He will have to face the fact that any notion of an ordered, cohesive human universe has taken refuge in the inwardness of the characters, where it can only exist as some abstract ideal, some wish or dream. The more any character is dominated by this inward intuition of value that is denied any substantial existence, the more he will be unable to fit in with the demands of the society in which he finds himself, the more he will become an oddity (*Der arme Spielmann*). It follows, then, that the deepest conflicts of bourgeois society are enacted in their clearest and most radical form not in the center of that society, but on its periphery. Marginality becomes the sharpest focus point for the whole malaise of bourgeois capitalism, the marginal figure of the eccentric becomes both its victim and truest representative. If one takes Lukács's overall framework, one could argue that the novelle stems from a confrontation with a world where the fronts have hardened, where the paradoxical ethos of capitalism yields a livid polarization of the exceptional on the one hand and the commonly interpreted social generality on the other. The interpretative problem is acute—not simply artistically, but also ontologically: because the social universe can only be retained in its intactness if the odd, quirky experience is kept at bay, is dismissed as a kind of pathological exception.

The above represents a tendentious reading of the social experience of the nineteenth century—and of the novelle as its imaginative reworking. Yet, in spite of the fact that some of the issues are more complex than Lukács is prepared to allow, the basic force of his argument is pertinent because it suggests that the hermeneutic gamble at the heart of the the novelle derives from certain conceptual tensions inherent in the social experience of nineteenth-century Germany.

Many of Lukács's points are taken up and differentiated by Fritz Martini in his excellent article *"Die deutsche Novelle im 'bürgerlichen Realismus.'"*[7] Martini acknowledges Lukács's insights into the problematic nature of nineteenth-century German realism, and he highlights the specific contribution made by the novelle genre. He insists, for example, that the novelle was, by its very nature, supremely able to sustain the dialectic of the prevailing world view: "the paradox occurs that the illusion of objective, actually experienced reality increases, the more the narrative concentrates on the limited, becoming personal or 'subjective.' "[8] Moreover, Martini insists that the novelle, because of the interpretative tension that informs it, is one of the central expressions of nineteenth-century German realism: "The uneasy balance between the specific, which tends to subjectify—and reify—itself into the isolated, and the overall 'order of things,' which for its part withdraws further and further into the intangible, vaguely perceivable, into that which can only be intimated through the concealment of the symbol, is the central formal concern of German literary realism. In the novelle it found the form that gave it its purest artistic expression."[9]

Obviously, the point must be made that this "German"

[7] *WB*, pp. 346ff.
[8] Ibid., p. 362.
[9] Ibid., p. 372.

version of realism does not automatically qualify as realism in the accepted sense of the term. Rather, the novelle embodies, to borrow a recent critic's phrase, an act of "realistic brinkmanship."[10] As Lukács puts it in his discussion of Solzhenitsyn, the novelle has its being "either in the 'not yet' phase of the artist's attempt at the universal rendering of the specific social world—or in the 'no longer' phase."[11] Clearly, a great gulf separates the German novelle from the classics of nineteenth-century European realism. Because of its very brevity, the novelle is not able to offer extensive documentation of the palpable facts of a given social reality. Society is only present as a *perspective*, as a set of narratively intimated assumptions. Moreover, what in my view particularly distinguishes the German novelle from the major achievements of literary realism is the hermeneutic unease that pervades the genre, an unease that casts doubt on the validity of the social universe as traditionally defined and inhabited. This in many ways accounts for the remarkable modernity of the nineteenth-century novelle, for it raises issues that challenge many accepted "realistic" certainties. For Balzac, society, however unpleasant it may be, is ultimately binding in a philosophical sense. It constitutes the framework within which man must endeavor to fulfill himself. This philosophical attitude inherent in European realism is only tentatively present in the German novelle (if at all). The challenge to social assumptions is relentless, and its urgency (and the friction it sets up by coming into contact with the established presuppositions of ordered, practical reality) tends to push the genre beyond what would normally be accounted realism.[12] This

---

[10] T. J. Reed's comment on Kleist in *Thomas Mann: The Uses of Tradition*, Oxford, 1974, p. 31.

[11] *Solschenizyn*, p. 5.

[12] It is, for example, significant that Richard Brinkmann's study *Wirklichkeit und Illusion*, which stresses the growing subjectivity and inwardness of German fiction in the nineteenth century, should refer exclusively to novellen. Similarly, much of the illustrative material for J. P. Stern's magnificent book *Re-Interpretations* is very largely novellen— perhaps because the genre tends inherently to suggest a reinterpretation of the accepted social universe.

is, of course, an observation rather than a value judgment. Where Martini's assertion is important, however, is that it reminds us that the novelle was, in some respects at least, the most telling expression of certain intellectual, moral, and spiritual issues that were very much at the heart of nineteenth-century German society. The concern with exceptional events is not, then, an evasion of social reality, a flight into some fairy-tale world where magic can replace mundane reality. Rather, it expresses a readiness to have common denominators of social certainty challenged, a readiness to assert the importance of marginal experience. Arguably, this takes us much deeper into the conflicts at work in nineteenth-century German society than does any painstaking attempt at social documentation.

In sociological terms, the central issue that finds its imaginative reworking and exploration in the novelle has, I believe, been suggested again by Martini when he describes the novelle as the form "that gave especially pointed and acute expression to the societal and personality problems of liberal individualism."[13] This is a very general assertion, and one needs a more precise definition of the way in which the imaginative universe of the novelle partakes of the (individualist) social experience of the world within which it is created. This has been attempted recently (although in a study pertaining not to the nineteenth-century novelle but to earlier examples of the genre) by Peter Brockmeier in his *Lust und Herrschaft: Studien uber gesellschaftliche Aspekte der Novellistik*.[14] Brockmeier suggests that the birth of the genre is linked with the rise of individualism, with the particular situation of the emerging bourgeoisie: "News is the medium of trade, and good news has always meant both profit and pleasure to the bourgeois. Luxurious collections of a hundred—or even of three hundred—novellen accompany the birth of the urban

[13] *WB*, p. 261.

[14] See also Brockmeier's articles "Das Privileg der Lust: Bemerkungen zur Darstellung der irdischen Liebe im *Heptameron*," *GRM*, n.f. 17 (1967): 337ff., and "Aristokratische Händler und käufliche Adlige."

middle class from the end of the Middle Ages. The genre name 'Novella' means news, novelty. The short tale is the amusing or uplifting reflection of the commercial news item."[15] Many aspects of plot, therefore,—such as "the pleasure in trickery, the quick exploitation of the chance to make profit"[16]—are symptomatic of the ethos of the quick-witted entrepreneur in a market economy where everything depends on swift obtainment of and reaction to news, on the speed with which one responds to the capricious movements of the market situation (hence the all-important theme of chance). However, Brockmeier goes on to make the point that, while such economic developments were gradually loosening the fabric of Boccaccio's Italy, the norms of that society had not caught up with the economic changes. The values remained those of a feudal order. This tension becomes, in Boccaccio's art, the conflict between events on the one hand and values on the other. Similarly, Brockmeier sees Marguerite de Navarre's novellen as shot through with a moral tension, one that derives from certain ambiguous movements within the structure of the social order and its preferments. In sixteenth-century France the monarchy openly derived funds from the selling of certain offices to the highest bidder, while at the same time insisting that certain spheres of influence (particularly the judiciary and the military) must remain the exclusive preserve of the nobility. In Marguerite's fiction, this tension between the hierarchical principles of feudal privilege and the social mobility allowed to certain energetic individuals issues in a contradiction between absolute power on the one hand and a kind of privileged self-assertiveness on the other.[17] In other words, Brockmeier demonstrates that the most profound connections between the novelle as an art form and the society that produces it are those that operate at a conceptual level. Furthermore, it is the uneasy relationship between individual capacities

[15] *Lust und Herrschaft*, p. viii.
[16] "Aristokratische Händler," p. 52.
[17] See especially "Aristokratische Händler," p. 75.

and the norms of the societal generality that yields the central interpretative issues of the stories produced.

The nineteenth-century version of this ambiguity has been analyzed in general terms by a variety of sociologists, economists, political scientists, and historians. To take one obvious example, Karl Polanyi in *The Great Transformation* argues that the central focus of nineteenth-century economic liberalism is the notion of the self-regulating market. Inherent in this premise is the assumption that man is dominated by a ruthlessly competitive individualism, the mainspring of which is the desire for maximum monetary gain. When this attitude is attributed to all members of a society, then that society is a jungle with which one should tamper as little as possible. For the jungle has its own laws—the survival of the fittest—and is self-regulating in that the weak are eliminated and the capable find their appropriate level. Yet there are other forces at work. Liberal laissez-faire economics are driven to advocate—almost in spite of themselves—a certain degree of intervention to prevent the worst effects of the man-made jungle. Moreover, Christian moral teaching also demands compassion, a concern for others. Polanyi argues that from this ambiguous situation certain unresolved issues, certain conflicting norms emerge as dominant problems: the relationship between individual and community, between the social and the natural.

Comparable arguments are advanced by Heinz Rieder in his *Liberalismus als Lebensform in der deutsche Prosaepik des 19. Jahrhunderts*. He too stresses the individualist focus of bourgeois capitalism, and the fact that the ethos of "every man for himself" produces an overall social design that is inherently rational because it embodies the economic good sense of supply and demand. Ultimately, therefore, one does not need to concern oneself with the social totality; according to a kind of Darwinian law, the survival of a tough and capable species will be ensured. Hence, society as a whole is something that looks after itself. There are, then, two basic beliefs at the heart of this social ethic. First,

"harmony in economic and social life is based on the principle of free competition," and, second, "with the greatest
possible independence of the individual, the whole will
regulate itself."[18] The uneasy attempt to reconcile individual and community is, Rieder argues, part of the overall
uncertainty of the ambitious middle class in nineteenth-
century Germany. Furthermore, precariousness is built
into the economic foundation of the bourgeois way of life.
The job is only as secure as it is competitive; investment is
dependent on the vagaries of the stock exchange that in an
inscrutable way can simply make or break lives. All these
uncertainties, Rieder argues, issue in a fear of oddities, a
fear of those who do not belong within the system or have
been destroyed by it, a fear of strange forces (whether they
be attributed to chance or to the workings of certain un-
canny agencies), a fear of the nakedly exceptional, *einmalig*
character or event that can challenge the whole founda-
tions of the seemingly ordered and understood world.
Hence, the narrative and structural constellation of the
novelle derives its persistent relevance from the degree to
which it partakes of deep-seated spiritual issues in the society within which it comes to prominence. The notion of the
interpretative unease, the hermeneutic gamble, of the
genre—the whole question of how far the narrative voice
can or dare relate to the unprecedented—emerges as the
expression in aesthetic terms of one of the most problematic aspects of social philosophy that dominates the nineteenth century.

Such arguments in my view help us to understand the
importance of the novelle form for nineteenth-century
German society, in that they place its central concern
within the context of the social experience of the time. For
a variety of reasons, the whole ambiguity of nineteenth-
century European society is enacted with a peculiar
radicalism in Germany. Some of the reasons for this have
been listed by Jürgen Habermas: "The defeat of the peas-
ants . . . the territorial division of the Empire and the late

[18] *Liberalismus als Lebensform*, pp. 11f.

attainment of national unity, the slow inroads of new methods of production, the delayed—but then explosive—development of industrial capitalism, the class-compromise between a politically unsure middle class and a nobility whose social bases and whose entrenchment in the bureaucratic-military hierarchy were for many years unshaken, the quasi-religious redemptive promise of bourgeois-humanist *Bildung*, radicalized—but unpolitical—inwardness, the cult of intellectual elitism and the ideology of the state, the rigidly authoritarian structures of the bourgeois family unit, the delay in urbanization. . . ."[19]

A list of comparable factors is also put forward by Ralf Dahrendorf in his *Gesellschaft und Demokratie in Deutschland*. He suggests that the development of industrial capitalism never quite filters through the—resolutely unpolitical—consciousness of German society. Power is very much concentrated in the hands of a few large banks, and the middle class lacks the enlightened, liberal, energetically mercantile spirit of their English or American counterparts. State ownership comes to play an extensive part in the industrialization process, and there is a great deal of social planning and state interventionism. In a curious way, then, Germany is a particularly radical—and institutionalized—example of the economic paradoxes to which Polanyi draws our attention. This is the Germany that Dahrendorf defines as a "society of industrial feudalism," as an "authoritarian welfare state."[20] It is a society that, because of its ambiguities, evolves that tentative relationship to accepted definitions of the social universe that in many ways distinguishes nineteenth-century German literature from its European counterparts. It helps, for example, to account for the lack of realism that has so frequently been noted by scholars and critics—and nowhere more cogently and more sympathetically than by Roy Pascal in his study *The German Novel*. At the risk of indulging in excessive generalizations, it could be said that German prose narrative of the

[19] *Philosophisch-politische Profile*, Frankfurt am Main, 1971, pp. 18f.
[20] *Gesellschaft und Demokratie in Deutschland*, pp. 67f.

nineteenth century falls into two basic categories: on the one hand, the novel (which tends to be very much dominated by the *Bildungsroman*), and on the other, the novelle. Common to both is an awareness of the growing fragmentation—and devaluation—of man's practical social existence, a conviction that the individual stands in an increasingly marginal relationship to any totality—whether it be a notion of societal community or of human wholeness.[21] Broadly speaking, the *Bildungsroman* represents an attempt at conciliation, at mediation between the two. Yet, so intense is the problem that the form becomes increasingly problematic and yields either irony and evaluative uncertainty (as in Goethe's *Wilhelm Meister* or Keller's *Der grüne Heinrich*) or massive and overtly sacramental facticity (as in Stifter's *Der Nachsommer*.)[22] On the other hand, the novelle makes less attempt to mediate. By its brevity and its concentration on the exceptional (*Einmaliges*) it confronts experience at the point where it is at its most intractable, where the marginality is manifest from the outset. What results is almost a shock confrontation between the presuppositions of an ordered social totality and the uncompromising uniqueness of the event or character with which the story is centrally concerned. The interpretative problem is, then, double-edged. On the one hand, there is the question of how far the social universe can and dare relate to the exceptional experience (*Einmaligkeit*). On the other, there is the question whether the social universe, if it is unable to come to terms with the *Einmaliges*, does not thereby reveal its partialness and fragility. Quite clearly, the possibility of mediation does exist in the novelle and can be realized. Yet the tension is there, the gulf that has to be bridged is broad. For this reason, the mediation is often at best tentative. This is the inherent risk of the novelle, its

[21] See Roy Pascal, " 'Bildung' and the Division of Labour," in *Studies presented to W. H. Bruford*, London, 1962, pp. 14ff. Revised version in Pascal, *Culture and the Division of Labour*, pp. 5ff.

[22] See especially Georg Lukács, *Goethe und seine Zeit*, in *Werke*, vol. 7, and most recently, Jürgen Jacobs, *Wilhelm Meister und seine Brüder*, Munich, 1972.

Select Bibliography

Because of the admirable bibliography of novelle theory
contained in Josef Kunz's anthology *Novelle (Wege der
Forschung)*, Wissenschaftliche Buchgesellschaft, Darmstadt,
1968, revised 1973, I have only included in my bibliography works that are particularly relevant to my argument—or those that have appeared since Kunz's compilation. The bibliography of general works and of criticism on
individual authors is also selective: I have endeavored to
list those studies that helped me, both through assent and
through disagreement, to clarify my own position.

I. GENERAL WORKS

Adorno, T. W. *Noten zur Literatur*. 4 vols. Frankfurt am
Main, 1958–74. (See especially the essay "Balzac-
Lektüre" in vol. 2, pp. 19ff.)
Adorno, T. W. *Ästhetische Theorie*. Frankfurt am Main,
1973.
Auerbach, Erich. *Mimesis: Dargestellte Wirklichkeit in der
abendländischen Literatur*. 2d ed. Bern, 1959.
Booth, Wayne C. *The Rhetoric of Fiction*. Chicago, 1961.
Brinkmann, Richard. *Wirklichkeit und Illusion*. Tubingen,
1957.
Brinkmann, Richard, ed. *Begriffsbestimmung des literarischen
Realismus*. Darmstadt, 1969.
Dahrendorf, Ralf. *Gesellschaft und Demokratie in Deutschland*.
2d ed. Munich, 1972.
Friedemann, Käte. *Die Rolle des Erzählers in der Epik*. Bonn,
1910.
Fügen, Hans Norbert. *Dichtung in der bürgerlichen
Gesellschaft*. Bonn, 1972.
Gadamer, Hans-Georg. *Wahrheit und Methode*. 2d ed.
Tubingen, 1965.

Goldmann, Lucien. *Pour une Sociologie du Roman*. Paris, 1964.

Grimm, Reinhold, ed. *Deutsche Romantheorien*. Frankfurt and Bonn, 1968.

Heller, Erich. "Imaginative Literature." In *The Zenith of European Power 1830–1870*, edited by J.P.T. Bury. *The New Cambridge Modern History*, vol. 10. Cambridge, England, 1960, pp. 156ff.

Heller, Erich. *The Disinherited Mind*. Harmondsworth, 1961.

Hempfer, Klaus W. *Gattungstheorie*. Munich, 1973.

Hernadi, Paul. *Beyond Genre: New Directions in Literary Classification*. Ithaca and London, 1972.

Hirsch, E. D. *Validity in Interpretation*. New Haven and London, 1967.

Jauss, Hans Robert. *Literaturgeschichte als Provokation*. Frankfurt am Main, 1970.

Kahrmann, B. "Bürgerlicher Realismus: Ein Forschungsbericht." *WW* 23 (1973): 53ff.

Kaiser, G. "Realismusforschung ohne Realismusbegriff." *DVjS* 43 (1969): 147ff.

Killy, Walther. *Wirklichkeit und Kunstcharakter*. Munich, 1963.

Kinder, Hermann. *Poesie als Synthese: Ausbreitung eines deutschen Realismus-Verständnisses in der Mitte des 19. Jahrhunderts*. Frankfurt am Main, 1973.

Kohn, Hans. *The Mind of Germany*. London, 1965.

Löwenthal, Leo. *Erzählkunst und Gesellschaft*. Neuwied and Berlin, 1971.

Lukács, Georg. *Die Theorie des Romans, Die Seele und die Formen, Deutsche Realisten des 19. Jahrhunderts*. In *Werke*. Neuwied and Berlin, 1963–1974.

Martini, Fritz. *Deutsche Literatur im bürgerlichen Realismus*. Stuttgart, 1962.

Ohl, Hubert. *Bild und Wirklichkeit: Studien zur Romankunst Raabes und Fontanes*. Heidelberg, 1968.

Pascal, Roy. *The German Novel*. Manchester, 1956.

Pascal, Roy. " 'Bildung' and the Division of Labour." In

Culture and the Division of Labour. University of Warwick Occasional Papers, no 5. Warwick, England, 1974.

Polanyi, Karl. *The Great Transformation.* Boston, 1957.

Preisendanz, Wolfgang. *Humor als dichterische Einbildungskraft.* Munich, 1963.

Rieder, Heinz. *Liberalismus als Lebensform in der deutschen Prosaepik des 19. Jahrhunderts. Germanische Studien*, vol. 212. Berlin, 1939.

Sell, F. C. *Die Tragödie des deutschen Liberalismus.* Stuttgart, 1953.

Sengle, Friedrich. *Biedermeierzeit.* (See especially vol. 2, *Die Formenwelt*, Stuttgart, 1972.)

Stern, J. P. *Re-Interpretations: Seven Studies in Nineteenth-Century German Literature.* London, 1964.

Stern, J. P. *Idylls and Realities: Studies in Nineteenth-Century German Literature.* London, 1971.

Stern, J. P. *On Realism.* London, 1973.

Todorov, T. *The Fantastic: A Structural Approach to a Literary Genre.* Cleveland and London, 1973.

II. STUDIES OF THE NOVELLE

Arx, Bernhard von. *Novellistisches Dasein.* Zurich, 1953.

Auerbach, Erich. *Zur Technik der Frührenaissancenovelle in Italien und Frankreich.* Heidelberg, 1921.

Benjamin, Walter. "The Storyteller." In *Illuminations,* edited by Hannah Arendt. London, 1970.

Bennett, E. K., and Waidson, H. M. *A History of the German "Novelle."* Cambridge, England, 1961.

Blunden, Allan. "Notes on Georg Heym's Novelle *Der Irre.*" *GLL* 28 (1975); 107ff.

Brockmeier, Peter. "Aristokratische Händler und kaufliche Adlige: Gesellschaftliche Spiegelungen in den Novellen Giovanni Boccaccios und Margaretes von Navarra." In *Gestaltungsgeschichte und Gesellschaftsgeschichte*, edited by H. Kreuzer. Stuttgart, 1969, pp. 51ff.

Brockmeier, Peter. *Lust und Herrschaft: Studien über gesellschaftliche Aspekte der Novellistik.* Stuttgart, 1972.

Castex, P.-G. *Le Conte fantastique en France*. Paris, 1951.

Cohn, Dorrit. "Kleist's *Die Marquise von O*: The Problem of Knowledge." *Monatshefte* 67 (1975): 129ff.

Deloffre, F. *La Nouvelle en France à l'Age classique*. Paris, 1967.

Eckert, Hartwig. "Towards a Definition of the 'Novelle.' " *New German Studies* 1 (1973): 163ff.

Eisenbeiss, Ulrich. *Das Idyllische in der Novelle der Biedermeierzeit*. Stuttgart, 1973.

Ellis, John M. *Narration in the German Novelle*. Cambridge, England, 1974.

Hirsch, A. *Der Gattungsbegriff "Novelle."* Berlin, 1928.

Jolles, André. *Einfache Formen*. 2d ed. Tubingen, 1958.

Kern, Edith. "The Romance of Novel/Novella." In *The Disciplines of Criticism*, edited by P. Demetz et al. New Haven and London, 1968, pp. 511ff.

Klein, Johannes. *Geschichte der deutschen Novelle*. 4th ed. Wiesbaden, 1960.

Kuipers, J. *Zeitlose Zeit: Die Geschichte der deutschen Kurzgeschichtsforschung*. Groningen, 1970.

Kunz, Josef. *Die deutsche Novelle zwischen Klassik und Romantik*. Berlin, 1966.

Kunz, Josef. *Die deutsche Novelle im 19. Jahrhundert*. Berlin, 1970.

Leibowitz, Judith. *Narrative Purpose in the Novella*. The Hague, 1974.

LoCicero, Donald. *Novellentheorie: The Practicability of the Theoretical*. The Hague, 1970.

Lockemann, Fritz. *Gestalt und Wandlung der deutschen Novelle*. Munich, 1957.

Lukács, Georg. *Solschenizyn*. Neuwied and Berlin, 1970.

Malmede, H. H. *Wege zur Novelle*. Stuttgart, 1966. (See also Karl Konrad Polheim's review in *ZfdP* 85 [1966]: 615ff.)

Martini, Fritz. "Die deutsche Novelle im 'bürgerlichen Realismus.' " *WW* 10 (1960): 257ff.

Müller, Joachim. "Zur Entstehung der deutschen Novelle: Die Rahmenhandlung in Goethes *Unterhaltungen deutscher Ausgewanderten* und die Thematik der Französischen Revolution." In *Gestaltungsgeschichte und Gesellschaftsgeschichte*, edited by H. Kreuzer. Stuttgart, 1969, pp. 152ff.

Musil, Robert. "Die Novelle als Problem." In *Tagebücher, Aphorismen, Essays und Reden*, edited by A. Frisé. Hamburg, 1955, pp. 684ff.

Negus, Kenneth. "Paul Heyse's 'Novellentheorie': A Reevaluation." *GR* 40 (1965): 173ff.

Neuschäfer, Hans-Jörg. *Boccaccio und der Beginn der Novelle.* Munich, 1969.

Pabst, Walter. "Die Theorie der Novelle in Deutschland." *Romanistisches Jahrbuch* 2 (1949): 81ff.

Pabst, Walter. *Novellentheorie und Novellendichtung: Zur Geschichte ihrer Antinomie in den romanischen Literaturen.* 2d ed. Heidelberg, 1967.

Polheim, Karl Konrad. *Novellentheorie und Novellenforschung (1945–1963).* Stuttgart, 1965.

Polheim, Karl Konrad. *Theorie und Kritik der deutschen Novelle von Wieland bis Musil.* Tübingen, 1970.

Pongs, Hermann. *Das Bild in der Dichtung.* Vol. 2. 2d ed. Marburg, 1963.

Rohner, Ludwig. *Theorie der Kurzgeschichte.* Frankfurt am Main, 1973.

Rowley, Brian. "The Novelle." In *The Romantic Period in Germany*, edited by S. S. Prawer. London, 1970, pp. 121ff.

Schönhaar, Rainer. *Novelle und Kriminalschema: Ein Strukturmodell deutscher Erzählkunst um 1800.* Bad Homburg v. d. Höhe, 1969.

Schröder, Rolf. *Novelle und Novellentheorie in der frühen Biedermeierzeit.* Tubingen, 1970.

Schunicht, Manfred. "Der 'Falke' am 'Wendepunkt:' Zu den Novellentheorien Tiecks und Heyses." *GRM*, n.f. 10 (1960): 44ff.

Silz, Walter. *Realism and Reality: Studies in the German Novelle of Poetic Realism.* 2d ed. Chapel Hill, N. C., 1962.

Stamm, Ralf. *Ludwig Tiecks späte Novellen*. Stuttgart, 1973.
Steinhauer, Harry. "Towards a Definition of the Novelle." *Seminar* 6 (1970): 154ff.
Todorov, T. *Grammaire du Décameron*. The Hague, 1969.
Voerster, Erika. *Märchen und Novellen im klassisch-romantischen Roman*. Bonn, 1966.
Weinrich, Harald. *Tempus: Besprochene und erzählte Welt*. Stuttgart, 1964.
Wiese, Benno von. *Die deutsche Novelle von Goethe bis Kafka*. 2 vols. Dusseldorf, 1956 and 1962.
Wiese, Benno von. *Novelle*. 4th ed. Stuttgart, 1969.

III. INDIVIDUAL STORIES ANALYZED

Goethe

Beutler, E. "Ursprung und Gehalt von Goethes *Novelle*." *DVjS* 16 (1938): 324ff.
Edel, Edmund. "Johann Wolfgang Goethes *Novelle*." *WW* 16 (1966): 256ff.
Fink, G.-L. "*Das Märchen*: Goethes Auseinandersetzung mit seiner Zeit." *Goethe* 33 (1971): 96ff.
Fricke, Gerhard. "Zu Sinn und Form von Goethes *Unterhaltungen deutscher Ausgewanderten*." In *Formenwandel*, edited by W. Müller-Seidel et al. Hamburg, 1964, pp. 273ff.
Grolman, Adolf von. "Goethes *Novelle*." *GRM* 9 (1921): 181ff.
Jessen, M. R. "Spannungsgefüge und Stilisierung in den Goetheschen Novellen." *PMLA* 55 (1940): 445ff.
Jürgens, Ilse. "Die Stufen der sittlichen Entwicklung in Goethes *Unterhaltungen deutscher Ausgewanderten*." *WW* 6 (1966): 336ff.
May, Kurt. "Goethes *Novelle*." In *Form und Bedeutung*. Stuttgart, 1957, pp. 116ff.
Popper, H. "Goethes *Unterhaltungen deutscher Ausgewanderten*." In *Affinities*, edited by R. W. Last. London, 1971, pp. 206ff.
Russ, C.A.H., ed. *Goethe: Three Tales*. Oxford, 1964.

Schönberger, O., ed. *Goethe: Novelle*. Munich, 1965.

Seuffert, B. "Goethes *Novelle*." *Jahrbuch der Goethe-Gesellschaft* 19 (1898): 133ff.

Staroste, W. "Die Darstellung der Realität in Goethes *Novelle*." *Neophilologus* 44 (1960): 322ff.

Staiger, Emil. *Goethe*. Vol. 3. Zurich, 1959.

Stöcklein, Paul. *Wege zum späten Goethe*. 2d ed. Hamburg, 1960.

Wäsche, Erwin. *Honorio und der Löwe*. Sackingen, 1947.

Ziolkowski, Theodore. "Goethe's *Unterhaltungen deutscher Ausgewanderten*: A Re-Appraisal." *Monatshefte* 50 (1958): 57ff.

Chamisso

Atkins, Stuart. "*Peter Schlemihl* in Relation to the Popular Novel of the Romantic Period." *GR* 21 (1946): 191ff.

Baumgartner, U. *Adalbert von Chamissos Peter Schlemihl*. Frauenfeld and Leipzig, 1944.

Flores, Ralph. "The Lost Shadow of Peter Schlemihl." *GQ* 47 (1974): 567ff.

Loeb, Ernst. "Symbol und Wirklichkeit des Schattens in Chamissos *Peter Schlemihl*." *GRM*, n.f. 15 (1965): 398ff.

Mann, Thomas. "Chamisso." In *Das essayistische Werk*, edited by H. Bürgin, vol. 1. Frankfurt am Main, 1968.

Schulz, Franz. "Die erzählerische Funktion des Motivs vom verlorenen Schatten in Chamissos *Peter Schlemihl*." *GQ* 45 (1972): 429ff.

Weigand, Hermann J. "*Peter Schlemihl*." In *Surveys and Soundings in European Literature*, edited by A. Leslie Willson. Princeton, 1966, pp. 208ff.

Wiese, Benno von. *Die deutsche Novelle von Goethe bis Kafka*. Vol. 1. Dusseldorf, 1956.

Büchner

Baumann, Gerhart. "Georg Büchner, *Lenz*: Seine Struktur und der Reflex des Dramatischen." *Euphorion* 52 (1958): 153ff.

Benn, M. B. "Anti-Pygmalion: An Apology for Georg Büchner's Aesthetics." *MLR* 64 (1969): 597ff.

Büchner, Georg. *Leonce und Lena and Lenz.* Edited by M. B. Benn. London, 1963.

Fischer, Heinz. *Georg Büchner: Untersuchungen und Marginalien.* Bonn, 1972.

Hasubek, Peter. " 'Ruhe' und 'Bewegung': Versuch einer Stilanalyse von Georg Büchners *Lenz.*" *GRM*, n.f. 19 (1969): 33ff.

Hauser, Ronald. *Georg Büchner.* New York, 1974.

Jansen, Peter K. "The Structural Function of the 'Kunstgespräch' in Büchner's *Lenz.*" *Monatshefte* 67 (1975): 129ff.

King, Janet K. "Lenz Viewed Sane." *GR* 49 (1974): 146ff.

Lindenberger, Herbert. *Georg Büchner.* Carbondale, Ill., 1964.

Mayer, H. *Georg Büchner und seine Zeit.* 2d ed. Wiesbaden, 1960.

Neuse, Erna K. "Büchners *Lenz:* Zur Struktur der Novelle." *GQ* 43 (1970): 199ff.

Parker, J. J. "Büchner's *Lenz* and the Oberlin Record." *GLL* 21 (1968): 103ff.

Pütz, H. P. "Büchners *Lenz* und seine Quelle." *ZfdP* 84 (1965): 1ff.

Stern, J. P. *Re-Interpretations.* London 1964.

Wiese, Benno von. *Die deutsche Novelle von Goethe bis Kafka.* Vol. 2. Dusseldorf, 1962.

Grillparzer

Alker, E. "Komposition und Stil von Grillparzers Novelle *Der arme Spielmann.*" *Neophilologus* 11 (1925): 15ff.

Baumann, G. *Franz Grillparzer: Dichtung und österreichische Geistesverfassung.* Frankfurt am Main, 1966.

Brinkmann, Richard. *Wirklichkeit und Illusion.* Tubingen, 1957.

Ellis, John M. *Narration in the German Novelle.* Cambridge, England, 1974.

Heine, Roland. "Ästhetische oder existentielle Integration? Ein hermeneutisches Problem des 19. Jahrhunderts in Grillparzers *Der arme Spielmann.*" *DVjS* 46 (1972): 650ff.

Hodge, J. "Symmetry and Tension in *Der arme Spielmann*." *GQ* 47 (1974): 262ff.

Jungbluth, Günther. "Franz Grillparzers *Der arme Spielmann*: Ein Beitrag zu ihrem Verstehen." *Orbis Litterarum* 24 (1969): 35ff.

Krotkoff, Hertha. "Über den Rahmen in Franz Grillparzers Novelle *Der arme Spielmann*." *MLN* 85 (1970): 345ff.

Papst, E. E. *Grillparzer's Der arme Spielmann and Prose Selections*. London and Edinburgh, 1960.

Paulsen, Wolfgang. "Der gute Bürger Jakob: Zur Satire in Grillparzers *armem Spielmann*." *Colloquia Germanica* 2 (1968): 272ff.

Politzer, Heinz. *Franz Grillparzers Der arme Spielmann*. Stuttgart, 1967.

Schäublin, Peter. "Das Musizieren des armen Spielmanns." *Sprachkunst* 3 (1972): 31ff.

Silz, W. *Realism and Reality*. Chapel Hill, N. C., 1954.

Stern, J. P. *Re-Interpretations*. London, 1964.

Straubinger, O. P. *"Der arme Spielmann."* *Grillparzer Forum Forchtenstein* (1966): 97ff.

Wiese, Benno von. *Die deutsche Novelle von Goethe bis Kafka*. Vol. 1. Dusseldorf, 1956.

Stifter

For an admirable survey of recent Stifter scholarship see Herbert Seidler, "Adalbert-Stifter-Forschung 1945-1970," *ZfdP* 91 (1972): 113ff. and 252ff. On some of the problems raised by Stifter criticism see J. P. Stern's excursus in *Re-Interpretations*, London, 1964, pp. 358ff.

Blackall, E. A. *Adalbert Stifter: A Critical Study*. Cambridge, England, 1948.

Bleckwenn, Helga. "Adalbert Stifters *Bunte Steine*." *VASILO* 21 (1972): 105ff.

Dehn, W. *Ding und Vernunft: Zur Interpretation von Stifters Dichtung*. Bonn, 1969.

Ehrentreich, A. "Zur Gestalt der Novelle bei Adalbert Stifter." *GRM* 23 (1935): 192ff.

Gelley, A. "Stifter's *Der Hagestolz*: An Interpretation." *Monatshefte* 53 (1961): 59ff.

George, E. F. "The Place of *Abdias* in Stifter's Thought and Work." *FMLS* 3 (1967): 148ff.

Gump, Margaret. *Adalbert Stifter*. New York, 1974.

Hahn, Walther L. "Zeitgerüst und Zeiterlebnis bei Stifter: *Granit.*" *VASILO* 22 (1973): 9ff.

Hunter, Rosemarie. "Wald, Haus und Wasser, Moos und Schmetterling: Zu den Zentralsymbolen in Stifters Erzählung *Der Waldgänger.*" *VASILO* 24 (1975): 23ff.

Ketelsen, Uwe. "Geschichtliches Bewusstsein als literarische Struktur: Zu Stifters Erzählung aus der Revolutionszeit *Granit.*" *Euphorion* 64 (1970): 306ff.

Ludwig, Marianne. *Stifter als Realist*. Basel, 1948.

Lunding, Erik. *Adalbert Stifter*. Copenhagen, 1946.

Mühlher, R. "Natur und Mensch in Stifters *Bunten Steinen.*" *Dichtung und Volkstum* 40 (1939): 295ff.

Müller, Joachim. "Adalbert Stifter: Weltbild und Erzählkunst." In *Neue Beiträge zum Grillparzer- und Stifterbild*. Graz and Vienna, 1965, pp. 83ff.

Preisendanz, W. "Die Erzählfunktion der Naturdarstellung bei Adalbert Stifter." *WW* 16 (1966): 407ff.

Rossbacher, Karlheinz. "Erzählstandpunkt und Personendarstellung bei Adalbert Stifter." *VASILO* 17 (1968): 47ff.

Seidler, Herbert. *Studien zu Grillparzer und Stifter*. Vienna, 1970. (See especially pp. 241ff., "Die Kunst des Aufbaus in Stifters *Der Waldgänger*," and pp. 257ff., "Adalbert Stifters Novelle *Der Hagestolz*.")

Smeed, J. W. "The First Versions of the Stories Later Appearing in Stifter's *Bunte Steine.*" *GLL* 12 (1959): 259ff.

Steffen, K. *Adalbert Stifter: Deutungen*. Basel, 1955.

Stern, J. P. *Re-Interpretations*. London, 1964.

Stern, J. P. *Idylls and Realities*. London, 1971.

Stiehm, L., ed. *Adalbert Stifter: Studien und Interpretationen*. Heidelberg, 1968.

Stillmark, A. "Stifter contra Hebbel: An Examination of the Sources of their Disagreement." *GLL* 21 (1967): 93ff.

Stopp, F. J. "Die Symbolik in Stifters *Bunten Steinen*." *DVjS* 28 (1954): 165ff.

Thurnher, Eugen. "Stifters 'sanftes Gesetz.' " In *Unterscheidung und Bewahrung*, edited by K. Lazarowicz and W. Kern. Berlin, 1961, pp. 381ff.

Weiss, Walter. "Adalbert Stifter, *Der Waldgänger*." In *Sprachkunst als Weltgestaltung*, edited by A. Haslinger. Salzburg, 1966, pp. 349ff.

Wiese, Benno von. "Adalbert Stifter, *Abdias*." In *Die deutsche Novelle von Goethe bis Kafka*. Vol. 2. Dusseldorf, 1962.

Keller

Allemann, Beda. "Gottfried Keller und das Skurrile: Eine Grenzbestimmung seines Humors." *Jahresbericht der Gottfried-Keller-Gesellschaft* 28 (1959): 1ff.

Ellis, John M. *Narration in the German Novelle*. Cambridge, England, 1974.

Fischer, Christine. "Roman, Novelle und künstlerische Subjektivität bei Gottfried Keller." *WB* 18 (1972), 117ff.

Hoverland, Lilian. "Gottfried Kellers Novelle *Die drei gerechten Kammacher*." *ZfdP* 90 (1971): 499ff.

Irmscher, Hans Dieter. "Konfiguration und Spiegelung in Gottfried Kellers Erzählungen." *Euphorion* 65 (1971): 319ff.

Jennings, L. B. "Gottfried Keller and the Grotesque." *Monatshefte* 50 (1958): 9ff.

Kaiser, M. *Literatursoziologische Studien zu Gottfried Kellers Dichtung*. Bonn, 1965.

Kayser, Wolfgang. *Das Groteske in Malerei und Dichtung*. Hamburg, 1960.

Mews, Siegfried. "Zur Funktion der Literatur in Kellers *Die Leute von Seldwyla*." *GQ* 43 (1970): 394ff.

Ohl, Hubert. "Das zyklische Prinzip von Gottfried Kellers Novellensammlung *Die Leute von Seldwyla*." *Euphorion* 63 (1969): 216ff.

Pregel, Dietrich. "Das Kuriose, Komische und Groteske in

Kellers Novelle *Die drei gerechten Kammacher*." *WW* 13 (1963): 331ff.

Preisendanz, W. "Gottfried Kellers *Sinngedicht*." *ZfdP* 82 (1963): 129ff.

Preisendanz, W. *Humor als dichterische Einbildungskraft.* Munich, 1963.

Richter, Hans. *Gottfried Kellers frühe Novellen.* Berlin, 1960.

Stern, J. P. *Re-Interpretations.* London, 1964.

Meyer

Brunet, Georges. *C. F. Meyer et la Nouvelle.* Paris, 1967.

Hohenstein, L. *Conrad Ferdinand Meyer.* Bonn, 1957.

Jackson, D. "Recent Meyer Criticism: New Avenues or Cul-de-Sac?" *RLV* 34 (1968): 620ff.

Jeziorkowski, Klaus. "Die Kunst der Perspektive: Zur Epik C. F. Meyers." *GRM*, n.f. 17 (1967): 398ff.

Löwenthal, Leo. *Erzählkunst und Gesellschaft.* Neuwied and Berlin, 1971.

Øhrgaard, Per. *C. F. Meyer: Zur Entwicklung seiner Thematik.* Copenhagen, 1969.

Onderdelinden, Sjaak. *Die Rahmenerzählungen C. F. Meyers.* Leiden, 1974.

Wiesmann, L. *C. F. Meyer: Der Dichter des Todes und der Maske.* Bern, 1958.

Williams, W. D. *The Stories of C. F. Meyer.* Oxford, 1962.

Index

Library of Congress Cataloging in Publication Data

Swales, Martin.
   The German Novelle.

   Bibliography: p.
   Includes index.
      1.   German fiction—19th century—History and
criticism.   2.   Short stories, German—History and
criticism.   I.   Title.
PT763.S86   833'.02   76-45913
ISBN 0-691-06331-1